The Politics of Lists

The Politics of Lists

—

Bureaucracy and Genocide under the Khmer Rouge

James A. Tyner

West Virginia University Press
Morgantown 2018

ISBN:
cloth   978-1-946684-40-0
paper   978-1-946684-41-7
ebook   978-1-946684-42-4

Library of Congress Cataloging-in-Publication Data
Names: Tyner, James A., 1966- author.
Title: The politics of lists : bureaucracy and genocide under the Khmer Rouge /
    James A. Tyner.
Description: Morgantown : West Virginia University Press, 2018. | Includes
    bibliographical references and index.
Identifiers: LCCN 2018010573| ISBN 9781946684400 (cloth) | ISBN
    9781946684417 (pb) | ISBN 9781946684424 (ebook)
Subjects: LCSH: Cambodia--Politics and government--1975-1979. |
    Government information--Cambodia--History--20th century. |
    Bureaucracy--Cambodia--History--20th century. | Genocide--
    Cambodia--History--20th century. | National security--Cambodia--
    History--20th century.
Classification: LCC DS554.8 .T965 2018 | DDC 959.604/2--dc23
LC record available at https://lccn.loc.gov/2018010573

Cover design by Than Saffel / WVU Press

Contents

—

Preface

On November 14, 1976, a young woman named Kim Ham Bin was arrested and detained at a secretive prison designated S-21. Located in Phnom Penh, the security center was established as one of approximately two hundred detainment sites located throughout Democratic Kampuchea, as Cambodia was renamed. During its formal existence, between October 1975 and January 1979, more than twelve thousand men, women, and children were warehoused under inhumane conditions. Many were tortured and forced to confess to various crimes; all but a handful were eventually executed, either within the greater S-21 compound or at the nearby killing fields known as Choeung Ek. These deaths were but a subset of countless other people who were purged by members of the Khmer Rouge security apparatus.

Little is known of Kim Ham Bin. Archives from S-21 indicate that she was twenty-five years old. Her position is recorded simply as "wife of Chhim Sak." No documents have survived that might indicate why she was arrested, other than the fact that she was the wife of Chhim Sak. As to Chhim Sak, he was arrested on January 16, 1976, and executed on July 22, 1976, four months prior to his wife's arrest. On the day of Kim Ham Bin's detainment, forty-five other people were arrested. Of these, at least forty were women, all of whom were classified as "wife," "mother," or "sister" of other detainees. And with few exceptions, all of these women, including Kim Ham Bin, were executed within twenty-four hours. In Democratic Kampuchea, to be accused was to be guilty; to be guilty was to be sentenced to death. Indeed, the Khmer Rouge term for those imprisoned was *neak tos*, meaning, literally, those who are already convicted.

The Politics of Lists provides a theoretically informed, empiri-
cally grounded study of the Khmer Rouge security apparatus. More
precisely, it engages with the intersection of material documents
and bureaucratic power. "The material culture of bureaucracy and
empire," Geoffrey Bowker and Susan Star write, "is not found in
pomp and circumstance, nor even in the first instance at the point
of a gun, but rather at the point of a list."[1] Their observation is fitting
for any analysis of S-21 or Democratic Kampuchea writ large, for
prior to their execution, the names of thousands of victims, such as
Kim Ham Bin and Chhim Sak, appeared on lists. Indeed, throughout Democratic Kampuchea bureaucratic *lists* were pervasive. As
Michelle Caswell explains, Khmer Rouge cadres were meticulous
record-keepers.[2] Officials of all ranks were continuously sending,
by messenger or telegram, lists of people to be arrested, interrogated, released, or executed; lists also were compiled of names
mentioned in forced confessions, to be used for the generation of
ever more lists of arrests, interrogations, and executions.
Collectively, lists were used to generate lists of alleged strings of
traitors: networks of conspirators that, for high-ranking officials of
the Communist Party of Kampuchea (CPK), established the proof
of traitorous activities. These documents therefore served as actionable evidence to engage in a crude form of preemptive punishment,
that is, a legal order predicated on the arrest, detainment, and execution of suspected people before treasonous plans could be put
into operation.

The impetus of this project, but also its premise, is intimately
tied to current events, namely the legal proceedings of the
Extraordinary Chambers in the Courts of Cambodia (ECCC),
better known as the Khmer Rouge tribunal. The ECCC's first trial,
Case 001, convened four years after the establishment of the
tribunal. On July 31, 2007, Kaing Guek Eav (alias Duch), commandant of the S-21 security center, was formally charged with crimes
against humanity and grave breaches of the Geneva Conventions of
August 12, 1949.[3] Duch's initial hearing was held on February 17,
2009, with the substantive part of the trial beginning on March 30,
2009. The trial lasted seventy-seven days, culminating on November

27, 2009, with a final verdict delivered on July 26, 2010. Duch was found guilty of crimes against humanity, including extermination, enslavement, imprisonment, torture, rape, and other inhumane acts. He was also found guilty of grave breaches of the 1949 Convention, including the willful causing of great suffering or serious injury to body or health, willfully depriving a prisoner of war or civilian of fair trial rights, and of unlawful confinement of civilians.[4] Following an appeals proceeding, in 2012 Duch was sentenced to life imprisonment for his crimes.

On September 15, 2010, Nuon Chea (former deputy secretary of the CPK), Khieu Samphan (former president of Democratic Kampuchea), Ieng Sary (former minister of foreign affairs), and Ieng Thirith (former minister of social affairs) were indicted on charges of crimes against humanity, genocide, and grave breaches of the Geneva Conventions of 1949. The following year the Trial Chamber decided to sever the charges in Case 002 into a series of smaller trials; the first trial, Case 002/01, commenced on November 21, 2011. For many observers, the advanced age of the defendants was of great concern. Both Nuon Chea and Ieng Sary were eighty-five years old, Khieu Samphan was eighty, and Ieng Thirith was seventy-nine. It was also noted that because of their advanced age, even if convicted, they were unlikely to serve a significant portion of any prison sentence handed down.[5] These fears only added to a more pervasive sense that the tribunal was, ultimately, too little and too late. Indeed, prior to the commencement of the trial, in August 2011, Ieng Thirith was diagnosed with dementia and subsequently declared incompetent to stand trial.[6] Ieng Sary died prior to the completion of the trial.

On August 7, 2014, a verdict was rendered in Case 002/01 against Nuon Chea and Khieu Samphan. Both were found guilty of crimes against humanity and both were sentenced to life imprisonment. In reaching its verdict, the Trial Chamber determined that both men were guilty of participation in a "joint criminal enterprise," the purpose of which "was to implement rapid socialist revolution." The Trial Chamber concluded also that "certain policies formulated by the Khmer Rouge involved the commission of crimes as the means to bring the common plan to fruition" and that these included "a policy to forcibly remove people from urban to rural areas" and "a policy to target officials of the former Khmer Republic."[7] Case 002/02, in which Nuon Chea and Khieu Samphan were charged with a series of crimes, including genocide, commenced on October 17, 2014, and the presentation of evidence began on January 8, 2015.[8]

Notably, in September 2012 the Supreme Court Chamber of the ECCC ordered that 1,749 documents of the tribunal be made public. In addition, a total of 13,383 documents related solely to S-21 have been declassified; these include S-21 daily entry logs, monthly entry logs, yearly entry logs, periodical entry logs, sectional entry logs, prisoner biographies, interrogation lists, and execution lists.[9] Most of these documents have not widely been incorporated into the scholarly account of the Cambodian genocide. Indeed, it is not uncommon still for some scholars to lament the "lack of materials" available, or—incredulously—to conclude that documentation and administrative protocol were anathema to CPK officials. Many of these records were initially archived by the staff at the Documentation Center of Cambodia (DC-CAM).[10] DC-CAM is the principle archive of documentary materials related to the Cambodian genocide and includes two main types of documents: primary documents (i.e., those produced during the genocidal years) and secondary documents (i.e., those produced after 1979, including interviews with both Khmer Rouge members and survivors of the genocide). Overall, the archives at DC-CAM include approximately one million pages of documents from the Khmer Rouge period, including meeting minutes, telegrams, reports, party periodicals, and files from the Khmer Rouge secret police. In addition, the archives include documentation of over 20,000 mass grave sites, 196 prisons, 6,000 photographs from the Khmer Rouge period, 260 documentary films shot during and directly after the Khmer Rouge regime, and approximately 50,000 interviews conducted by DC-CAM staff with perpetrators and survivors.

In my assessment of the Khmer Rouge bureaucracy I follow Kirsten Weld, who details how documents, at different historical moments, may represent distinct archival logics.[11] Writing in the context of Guatemala's violent past, Weld identifies two organizing principles surrounding the voluminous materials archived by Guatemala's secret police. The first logic, Weld explains, "was one of surveillance, social control, and ideological management," while the second, "emerging from the records' rescue, is one of democratic opening, historical memory, and the pursuit of justice."[12] In Cambodia, before the many Khmer Rouge documents were archived at DC-CAM or the ECCC, they were stored by the Khmer Rouge in countless file cabinets, binders, or desks throughout Democratic Kampuchea. Lawyers and scholars have given these documents a second life.[13] Less attention has been focused on the first life of these documents: their original production, circulation, and usage.[14] Thus, I want to "document the process, not to process the documents."[15] My overriding purpose is to redirect attention toward the processes of documentation and to interpret the documents as they were produced by the CPK toward particular purposes. In other words, my intent is not to document so much what the Khmer Rouge did as it is to understand why the Khmer Rouge documented the way they did.

The politics of how archives are compiled, created, and opened are intimately tied to the politics and practices of government.[16] Consequently, a focus on the documentary processes of the CPK will shed insight into the broader coordinates of governance both as envisioned and practiced by the Khmer Rouge, for as Ann Stoler relates, "Filing systems and disciplined writing produce assemblages of control and specific methods of domination."[17] Such a journey, therefore, requires that we step into the mundane world of the bureaucrat, a passage that seems incongruous with more conventional understandings of the Cambodian genocide. To speak of the Khmer Rouge is to bring to mind black-clad youth wielding AK-47s; bureaucrats, conversely, are mild-mannered administrators toiling behind desks, all but forgotten in their tiny cubicles. And yet as the voluminous materials compiled by both DC-CAM and the ECCC demonstrate, Democratic Kampuchea was flush with documents. These documents did not materialize in a vacuum but instead were the products of innumerable men and women, who may have wielded weapons, but also were armed with pens, paper, and typewriters.

The term *bureaucracy* originated as a protest against incompetence, inefficiency, and excessive governmental regulations.[18] In the late seventeenth century the French king designated Jean-Baptiste Colbert comptroller general of finance. Subsequently, Colbert initiated a series of rules that were to be applied uniformly throughout the realm. He believed that the uniform application of rules would demonstrate fairness and equality of the government. Nearly a century later, however, France's administrator of commerce, Jean-Claude Marie Vincent de Gournay, derided the ever-increasing rules and regulations as harming business activity. Thus, to "symbolize the idea that rule-makers and rule-enforcers who did not understand or care about the consequences of their actions were ruining the French government, he coined the sarcastic term *bureaucratie*—government by desk."[19]

The prominence of bureaucrats and bureaucracies within the practice of statecraft has received considerable, if uneven, attention in recent years.[20] Merje Kuus, for example, finds that the "effects of bureaucratic processes are well documented in their convoluted, contested, and indeterminate character as well as their far-reaching impacts on human lives, but the production of bureaucratic knowledge inside policy-making institutions has received less attention."[21] Following Ben Kafka, therefore, we should concentrate on putting the "bureau" back into "bureaucracy" and to "investigate the pens, papers, and other raw materials of power."[22] Required is an explicit focus on the tasks of bureaucrats in the course of their everyday activities, not least of which is the preparation, circulation, and filing of documents.

Documents are essential for bureaucratic rule. Indeed, recent scholarship has shown how bureaucratic documents are produced, used, and experienced through procedures, techniques, aesthetics, ideologies, cooperation, negotiation, and contestation.[23] In short, recent scholarship has effectively detailed the importance of understanding "the materiality of information."[24] Two functions are particularly notable. First, "documents promote control within organizations and beyond not only through their links to the entities they document but through the coordination of perspectives and activities."[25] This implies that we take seriously the "objects" of politics, including "both the militarized and the mundane."[26] Second, bureaucratic documents entail a "generative capacity" in that they bring *things* into existence.[27] Marie-Andrée Jacobs, for example, details how documents, but especially consent forms, generate "form-made persons." Jacobs elaborates that while documents "answer the bureaucratic needs for efficiency and for comparability of documents," they also "make political subjects visible." In turn, these subjects may more readily be "archived, classified, measured, compared, and controlled on a mass scale."[28] In short, documents "are central to how bureaucratic objects are enacted in practice."[29]

In his pioneering work *Economy and Society*, Max Weber argues that "bureaucratic administration means fundamentally domination through knowledge."[30] Relatedly, in the writings of Michel Foucault, knowledge, but more precisely the truth function of knowledge, assumes a central place. Indeed, a dominant motif of Foucault's work was to provide a critique of the way modern societies control and discipline their populations by sanctioning the knowledge claims and practices of the human sciences.[31] For Foucault, therefore, knowledge is inseparable from power. Foucault explains that power and knowledge directly imply one another; that there is no power relation without the correlative constitution of a field of knowledge, nor any knowledge that does not presuppose and constitute at the same time power relations.[32]

Power is often equated with brute force: jackbooted thugs wielding truncheons or armed police in riot gear suppressing a protest. We readily understand the muscle of massed troops, fleets of naval vessels, and squadrons of fighter jets. However, power is not synonymous with violence, although power does enable violence to flourish. For Foucault, power is exercised rather than possessed. He elaborates that "Power must be analyzed as something which circulates, or rather as something which only functions in the form of a chain. It is never localized here or there, never in anybody's hands, never appropriated as a commodity or piece of wealth."[33] This conception overlaps with that of Hannah Arendt, who writes, "Power is indeed the essence of all government, but violence is not. Violence is by nature instrumental: like all means, it always stands in need of guidance and justification through the end it pursues. And what needs justification by something else cannot be the essence of anything."[34] Arendt elaborates that "Where commands are no longer obeyed, the means of violence are of no use. . . . Everything depends on the power behind the violence."[35] Significantly, both Foucault—but especially Arendt—locate this form of power within the bureaucracy, a "rule by Nobody," [36] a form of governance where those who wield power do so not with guns, knives, or explosives but with pen, ink, and paper; where the main actors are not readily visible kings or generals, soldiers or police, but instead anonymous clerks and typists. In so doing, both Foucault and Arendt readily understand that "the entry of life into politics" is occasioned by the emergence of the bureaucracy as a form of power.[37]

A focus on bureaucratic documents calls to question the materiality of power as it is administered behind the scenes, for here we see how seemingly mundane technologies—files, charts, and records—become the means that enable a few to know about or to rule over many.[38] Indeed, as Kenneth Dauber describes, "record keeping makes it possible to characterize and administer large populations with a (relatively) small staff."[39] This observation holds considerable purchase when understanding, for example, the rule of the Khmer Rouge throughout Democratic Kampuchea. As detailed in subsequent chapters, the Communist Party of Kampuchea never enjoyed mass popular support; in fact, even those cadres who fought and died in the civil war leading up to the CPK's revolutionary victory did so not for ideological reasons. Consequently, it was incumbent upon the CPK to effectively wield power over an increasingly discontented population. Direct force was used; and this violence has been well documented by scholars of Democratic Kampuchea. But so too was control facilitated through mundane exercises of power.

Recent scholarly accounts have detailed how bureaucracies are essential for the production of knowledge and how knowledge is critical to the exercise of power. To this end, the "rule of experts" has figured prominently.[40] What, though, constitutes an expert? Dominic Boyer provides an initial definition whereby "an expert [is] an actor who has developed skills in, semiotic-epistemic competence for, and attentional concern with, some sphere of practical activity."[41] Boyer quickly acknowledges that such a definition may lead to the conclusion that "there is no human being who is not 'expert' in some fashion," but this openness, however, "highlights the tension between the experiential-performative and social-institutional poles of skilled knowing and doing."[42] In other words, it is necessary to consider not simply the symbolic and practical qualifications that underscore a claim to expertise; it is also necessary to engage with the intangible dimensions by which anyone is fashioned as an expert. Senior leaders of the Khmer Rouge, for example, branded themselves experts on any number of subjects. Such self-positionality conformed to their understanding of the CPK as a vanguard, but it also highlighted a profound belief in their own infallibility. It was this presumption of technical expertise in all fields of politics and economics that provided for the senior leadership a rationalization for purges directed against people who were unable to meet CPK expectations but also the elimination of perceived "strings of traitors" and enemy infiltrators.

Widespread purges throughout Democratic Kampuchea were the result of bureaucratic procedures: a complex interplay of surveillance techniques, biopolitical documentation, and preemptive policing strategies. Underscoring the administration of violence was a pervasive paranoia. This paranoia, however, should not be conceived simply as a "pathological and unwarranted phobia" but instead a particular form of governance.[43] As Nicholas Holm explains, "notions of 'paranoia,' and the commingled sense of conspiracy that accompanies them can be considered more than just inevitable impediments to be overcome when addressing surveil-lance; they can also be productive."[44] This statement admittedly appears somewhat incredulous at first blush. And yet, as detailed in the chapters that follow, a pervasive mistrust among Khmer Rouge cadres conditioned their attempt to establish a socialist state. For the Khmer Rouge, paranoia and an attendant conspiratorial con-sciousness provided the context for subsequent disciplinary action and policing functions, both informed materially by the compila-tion, evaluation, and archiving of documents.

A guiding thesis I develop is that the power of the Communist Party of Kampuchea was derived in no small part from the material production of information by a small cohort of self-styled experts. This challenges more conventional accounts of the Khmer Rouge in that I place equal weight on the administration of power as well as the ruthless imposition of direct violence of killings and the struc-tural violence of famine.[45] Democratic Kampuchea, in other words, is not reducible to the moniker of terror state. Rather, Democratic Kampuchea exemplifies the calculative power of bureaucratic rule. As Foucault explains, "It is only if we grasp these techniques of power and demonstrate the economic advantages or political utility that derive from them in a given context for specific reasons, that we can understand how these mechanisms come to be effectively incorporated into the social whole."[46] Consequently, it is necessary to interpret S-21 not in isolation but as a key node in a larger bureaucratic rule of governance. Rather than merely a place of bru-tality and horror, S-21 must be understood, following Bruno Latour, as a "center of calculation," where truth and knowledge became manifest, materially, in the form of documents.[47]

In so doing, my work is couched within a larger historiography of bureaucratic power, for it is my contention that the power and violence that demarcated Democratic Kampuchea was not unique.[48] Rather, my reading of the Khmer Rouge security apparatus resitu-ates the Cambodian genocide squarely within the study of the necropolitics of bureaucracy and a longer history of state knowl-edge production and the practices of killing. My overriding purpose therefore extends beyond the particulars of Cambodia. For it is my intention to speak directly to the theoretical understanding of security discourses and apparatuses, networks within a security context, and the politics of lists associated with security practices. In short, my work aims to contribute to the rapidly developing scholarship that has critiqued the politics of calculation and the materiality of information that underpin contemporary practices of surveillance and violence. Important parallels are thus made between the techniques of security as enacted by the Khmer Rouge with similar practices forwarded within the global war on terror. The current debates centered on surveillance and subterfuge, of torture and interrogation, of targeted killings, find resonance in numerous antecedents, including that of the Khmer Rouge. It is necessary therefore to draw parallels with other accounts in that they point us toward a much longer history of the ways modern bureaucracies make mass murder possible.[49]

Acknowledgments

Rosa Luxemburg, while imprisoned in 1918, wrote an essay entitled *The Russian Revolution*. This work was later published after her execution. In the essay Luxemburg provides a critique of Bolshevik policies enacted following the October Revolution. Notably, she cautions that the whole mass of people must take part in the socialist revolution, otherwise socialism will be decreed from behind a few official desks by a dozen intellectuals. The words of Luxemburg would prove prophetic for much of what went wrong with twentieth-century communism. Exemplary in this regard is the brutal bureaucracy imposed throughout Stalinist Russia, but also the secretive machinations of the Communist Party of Kampuchea. *The Politics of Lists* provides an account of this latter episode of rule by bureaucrats.

The writing of this book was a collective effort, the culmination of years of conversations and consultations, discussions and debates. Primary thanks are due to Derek Krissoff and the entire staff at West Virginia University Press, who shepherded the manuscript from initial proposal submission through final production. Special thanks are extended also to the editorial board at West Virginia University Press and the anonymous reviewers who provided critical feedback. At Kent State University I express my appreciation to Jim Blank, Todd Diacon, Marcello Fantoni, Mandy Munro-Stasiuk, and Scott Sheridan for their continued support of my research. Kent State University is a remarkable institution and I am deeply grateful for the productive working environment provided by these individuals. In Cambodia I am indebted to the support and assistance of Youk Chhang and the staff at the Documentation Center of Cambodia, and also Visoth

Chhay and the staff at the Tuol Sleng Genocide Museum. The center has been exceptionally generous in the provision of documents and photographs for this project and others over the years. Likewise, the museum has been equally generous in their provision of materials. I humbly offer my thanks to both institutions. More specifically, however, I thank Dara Vanthan and Phirun Suon for their assistance in obtaining permissions for the photographs used in this book. Special thanks are also extended to Sokvisal Kimsroy and Kok-Chhay Ly for their input and insight and for their translation of documents. Lastly, I thank Chenjian Fu, Kok-Chhay Ly, and Zheye Wang for their help with the empirical analyses in Chapter 4.

Over the years I have benefited immensely from critical feedback and comments of my students: Gabriela Brindis Alvarez, Alex Colucci, Gordon Cromley, Christabel Devadoss, Kathryn Hannum, Sam Henkin, Josh Inwood, Sokvisal Kimsroy, Robert Kruse, Kok-Chhay Ly, Mark Rhodes, Stian Rice, Savina Sirik, Dave Stasiuk, Rachel Will, and Chris Willer. I have also drawn inspiration from and been challenged in my thinking through conversations with innumerable scholars over the years, including Derek Alderman, Caroline Bennet, Stéphanie Banzaquen-Gautier, Noel Castree, Youk Chhang, Visoth Chhay, Randle DeFalco, Khamboly Dy, Craig Etcheson, Julie Fleischman, Jim Glassman, Michelle Hamers, Rachel Hughes, Helen Jarvis, Ben Kiernan, Caroline Laurent, Dany Long, Andrew Mertha, Don Mitchell, Anne-Laure Porée, Vicente Sánchez-Biosca, Ian Shaw, Simon Springer, Sarah Williams, and Melissa Wright. During the development of this book I have been fortunate to provide preliminary results and interpretations at the Department of Geography, Pennsylvania State University, the Department of Geography, West Virginia University, and the seminar on "Traces and Memories of the Cambodian Genocide: Tuol Sleng in Testimony, Literature and Media Representations" held in conjunction with the American Comparative Literature Association. I thank the audiences for their comments and suggestions and for pushing me to reinterpret preliminary ideas and concepts.

I thank my parents, Dr. Gerald Tyner and Dr. Judith Tyner, for their unwavering support and encouragement. Three decades ago my parents made a considerable sacrifice so that I could attend the University of Bradford as an exchange student. My year in England was transformative and set the stage for my eventual career in academia. It sounds clichéd, but I honestly would not be where I am today without their support, both emotionally and materially. To this end, I would also like to thank my mother specifically. An accomplished author and scholar in her own right, I have enjoyed thoroughly our long conversations about the ups and downs of writing and I hope to have many more conversations in the years ahead. For my mom, I dedicate this book.

Since the publication of my first book over ten years ago I have been accompanied in my writing by two late-night friends: my cat Jamaica and my dog Bond. Sadly, Jamaica passed away during the completion of this book. Bond and I will continue to read and write late into the night, but our friend and companion will be deeply missed. My daughters, Jessica and Anica, continue to make me laugh and keep things in perspective. They are a welcome reprieve from hours spent reading and writing about genocide, mass violence, torture, and execution and from my incessant following of U.S. politics. And lastly, I thank my wife, Belinda, and not just for the usual reasons. Belinda is the beacon in our household, a shining light that illuminates all that is good and all that needs attention. And I promise, now that this project is complete, to do something about that stack of books and papers that has been sitting on the dining room table for the past several months.

CHAPTER 1

———

Emerging from the Shadows

On September 27, 1977, Pol Pot delivered a long, rambling speech that was subsequently broadcast throughout Democratic Kampuchea.[1] This particular speech is remarkable, in part, because it was the first public announcement of the CPK's existence and Pol Pot's leadership.[2] It is also meaningful insofar as it expresses the official objectives of the Khmer Rouge. A recurrent theme throughout the 1977 speech, but prevalent also in scores of other public pronouncements and propaganda materials disseminated by the CPK, is that of defending the country. More than a simple call to arms, however, the CPK's security discourse is connected to the wider political economy of Democratic Kampuchea. Pol Pot exhorted his audience that the duty ahead was "to contribute to the national defense, the building up of the country, and the raising of the people's living standard, all toward carrying out, with a high sense of revolution responsibility, the glorious task which the Party has entrusted to them."[3]

By this point, the postrevolutionary period was well under way. The CPK had been in power for nearly thirty months, communes had been initiated throughout the country, and an assortment of bureaucratic ministries and departments had been established. For nearly thirty months, people had been reclassified as Party members, cadres, base people, or new people. They had been subjected to near-starvation food rations, denied adequate health care, separated from their families, and forced to labor on massive infrastructure projects. And to maintain internal order, an extensive security apparatus composed of approximately two hundred prisons was installed.

1

It is not known how those who heard Pol Pot's speech responded to his hyperbolic platitudes. No doubt they were sensitive to the disconnect between Pol Pot's geographic imaginary of Democratic Kampuchea as a bountiful land and the reality of privation. But by September 1977, most people had learned to remain quiet, for the eyes and ears of Angkar were ever present, ever watching, ever listening. Linguistically, Angkar is derived from the Pali word *anga*, meaning a part of the body; it is also related to the Khmer word *angk*, which also denotes a structure, or a limb of a body. The term speaks of mana-filled objects, or orderly institutions. And for most people of Democratic Kampuchea, it was unclear as to whether Angkar was a person, a group, or an organization. As John Marston explains, "There was always an ambiguity in its usage" and that "this was not incidental to its usage but very much of the essence of what the word signified in practice."[4] What was clear was that Angkar represented power, an absent authority other than the person who was immediately speaking.[5] All orders and slogans, for example, were issued in the name of the Angkar Padevoat, or Revolutionary Organization.

Historically, the use of Angkar among Cambodian revolutionaries preceded the Khmer Rouge. Stephen Heder explains that Angkar was used as early as the 1940s as a catchall term for "organization."[6] It was not a term purposively adopted by the CPK to sow confusion among the populace. During the 1960s, however, it was increasingly used by a cohort of revolutionaries, including but not limited to Pol Pot, Ieng Sary, Nuon Chea, and Khieu Samphan, who adhered loosely to a Marxist-Leninist doctrine. Prior to this time, the Cambodian revolution was an ad hoc assortment of individuals and groups, all operating with different objectives and methods. Throughout the 1940s, for example, many Cambodians sought to liberate their country from French colonialism; following independence, most of these revolutionaries laid down their arms and returned to farming. Others were disillusioned with the existent monarchy and desired to overthrow the long-standing prince, Norodom Sihanouk. Since being placed on the throne by French authorities during the Second World War, Sihanouk had dominated

Cambodian politics. And a minority of revolutionaries pursued a more radical form of politics; these men and women wanted not to simply replace the existing system of governance with their own politicians but instead desired to effect sweeping changes throughout the whole of society. This was the Pol Pot faction; this was the cohort of revolutionary cadre who, in the 1960s, formed the Workers' Party of Kampuchea (WPK) which, in time, would transform into the Communist Party of Kampuchea.

The Workers' Party of Kampuchea was itself a reconfiguration of an earlier party, the Khmer People's Revolutionary Party (KPRP), which was heavily influenced, if not outright dominated, by Vietnamese Communists. It was this history that haunted Pol Pot and served as backdrop for his 1977 speech. Throughout the course of Cambodia's two thousand–year history, Pol Pot explained, the country had experienced a series of class-based revolutions. In previous slave societies, for example, Pol Pot stated that the "exploited class struggled against the exploiting class," but, he clarified, "this struggle was not guided by a correct line." He identified also a revolutionary struggle against feudalism. Victory, again, "was temporary, because those who were the victors did not possess a correct line to really liberate the country and really liberate the people, the exploited masses who comprise the peasant class." Past failures, Pol Pot reasoned, stemmed from the fact that those who overthrew the previous class, the revolutionaries, "made themselves warlords and ruled like kings and viceroys, and they became the new exploiters of the peasant class."[7] Nothing short of a complete and total revolution would ensure victory; nothing less would safeguard a communal utopia devoid of class conflict, poverty, and malaise.

Real revolution, Pol Pot explained, necessitated "self-mastery" and "self-reliance," two phrases that peppered both official and operational objectives forwarded by the CPK. Combined, these concepts signified an exceedingly cautious approach to the international community and an overall approach to foreign policy based on fear of betrayal and deceit. For Pol Pot, such an approach was warranted, for the years of revolution were marked by a series of betrayals and traitorous activities. Secrecy was necessary because enemies were thought to be everywhere. The revolution, Pol Pot explained, required sacrifice and hardship, but these were small prices to pay by "the Kampuchean people, who [had] suffered enslavement, deceit, oppression and exploitation for centuries."[8]

Victory on April 17, 1975, for Pol Pot, marked a momentous period in Cambodia's history, for this was the first time the country "was totally and definitively liberated."[9] And while this was a time to rejoice and exhort the revolutionary sacrifices made, it was also a time to remain ever vigilant against enemies, both external and internal. He explains that "Our revolutionary task . . . is no longer the same; no longer is it the revolution for national liberation and independence. Our revolutionary task now is to defend our country, to defend Democratic Kampuchea; defend our independence, our sovereignty and our territorial integrity within our present borders, defend the worker and peasant power of our Party, and safeguard the sacred victories of the revolution."[10] To achieve these ends, however, Pol Pot cautions against contradictions that threatens the security of the Party, the revolution, and the country. Here, his speech takes on a darker, more ominous tone. He warns against contradictions among the people, of men and women who retain vestiges of their old class character; of reactionary elements; and of enemy agents, who belong to various spy networks and who secretly implant themselves to carry out subversive activities.[11] Pol Pot's summation is foreboding:

> We do not consider these traitors, these counterrevolutionary elements, to be part of the people. They are enemies of Democratic Kampuchea, of the Kampuchean revolution and of the Kampuchean people. Contradictions within these elements must be solved by the measures proper for enemies: separate, educate and win over the elements which can be won over; neutralize the elements which are wavering, preventing them from doing any damage to the revolution; and, finally, isolate and eradicate only the smallest possible number of those elements who are cruel and persist in acting

4

against the revolution and the people, and collaborate with foreign enemies to destroy their own people and their own revolution.[12]

In September 1977 the CPK emerged from the shadows, only to reveal that other, more deceitful creatures remained hidden in the darkness. Pol Pot's speech is illuminating, therefore, in that it highlights not only a pervasive sense of mistrust but also the justification of a ruthless approach to dealing with betrayal. Such was the context for the establishment of S-21 and other security centers throughout Democratic Kampuchea.

The Politics of Lists constitutes an exegesis of S-21 as a center of calculation. Although variously described as an extermination center or death camp, such comparisons with Nazi-organized institutions provide little in the way of analytical insight. With an emphasis on the production and documentation of information in material form by Khmer Rouge bureaucracies, I provide a critical account of the administrative context of mass violence during the Khmer Rouge regime. More precisely, I consider the overarching security discourses forwarded by high-ranking officials of the Communist Party of Kampuchea; how these discourses materialized in the form of prisoner biographies, confessions, and myriad other lists; how these documents provided the fodder to construct elaborate conspiracy theories of networks of traitors; and how the presumed existence of these networks necessitated (from the perspective of these officials) a security apparatus that operated on the basis of precrime and preemptive punishment. In short, my thesis is that the paranoia-induced purges of the Khmer Rouge are best explained within a framework of bureaucratic necropolitics. Before explicating the resultant conspiracy of culture that would come to dominate Democratic Kampuchea, however, it is necessary to first situate the security concerns of the CPK within a historical context of perceived treacheries.

5

The Unexpected Revolution

By the mid-1950s the future of Cambodia appeared promising, with independence having been achieved in 1953. A foreign observer captured some of this optimism, writing in 1955 that "Cambodia seems to stand at the extended new road to life among the many nations. She has passed several tollgates and is entering the main highway. . . . In certain places in the world, there are unspoiled places awaiting training and education for the new era; Cambodia is one of those places."[13] Over time, this optimism dissipated, replaced by unattained aspirations, increased disillusionment, political factions, and war.[14]

The long-standing Franco-Viet Minh War (1946–54), culminating with the defeat of the French at Dien Bien Phu, and the subsequent Geneva Accords, left the future of Indochina in doubt. Most pressing was the decision to temporarily divide Vietnam into two political entities, the Communist-dominated Democratic Republic of Vietnam (DRV) in the north, and a United States–supported Republic of Vietnam in the south, with nationwide elections to be held in two years. For many observers, the cessation of hostilities was but a respite as the region assumed greater importance in the rapidly expanding Cold War between the United States and the Soviet Union. Cambodia's future was very much in doubt.

Politics in Cambodia were characterized by Sihanouk's monopoly of political power and his positioning of Cambodia on the international stage.[15] Sihanouk was widely popular, and the young prince capitalized on his approval to deepen his role in governance. By constitution, the monarchy in Cambodia was largely ceremonial and so in 1955 Sihanouk abdicated the throne in favor of his father in order to take full executive control of the government. Furthermore, he consolidated a number of contending political parties under the banner of the Sangkum Reastr Niyum (People's Socialist Community) to more fully dictate the future of Cambodia. Foremost among his concerns was to retain Cambodia's neutrality in the brewing conflict in Vietnam. However, as David

Chandler concludes, Cambodia would remain neutral and at peace only as long as its neutrality served the interests of other states.[16]

Difficulties in maintaining neutrality stemmed from France's colonial neglect of Cambodia. As Margaret Slocomb writes, following independence the "production of electrical energy, the supply of petroleum products and the water supply were controlled by foreigners, as were the few major industrial establishments."[17] Consequently, Sihanouk was forced to enter into economic alliances with foreign powers, thereby placing in jeopardy his proclamations of neutrality. Depending on the political winds, Sihanouk allied with members of both the Soviet-dominated Eastern bloc and the American-dominated Western bloc. Over time, these economic arrangements placed Sihanouk and Cambodia on a collision course with opposition from across the political spectrum.

Throughout the 1950s decisions forwarded by the DRV were greatly tinged by the prospect of war with the United States. Thus, while Communist insurgents throughout southern Vietnam pressed for permission to wage armed rebellion, DRV leaders refused. Patience was required, they argued, lest the United States be drawn into open warfare. So intense was this concern that revolutionary activities in the south were limited to political agitation.[18] It was not until 1959 that the Vietnamese leadership agreed to armed resistance in the south. In the following year, the National Front for the Liberation of South Vietnam, better known as the National Liberation Front (NLF, derisively known as the Viet Cong), was established.

That a successful insurgency in the south was dependent upon the ability to provision the NLF was widely understood by the DRV's military leaders. Indeed, even before the formal constitution of the NLF, North Vietnamese military planners had begun the arduous task of establishing a series of supply lines through eastern Laos, the Central Highlands of Vietnam, and eventually eastern Cambodia. Known as the Ho Chi Minh Trail, this was a vast network of roads and footpaths whereby food, weapons, medicines, and other supplies were transported by groups of men and women. In time, even North Vietnamese Army (NVA) troops would utilize the Ho Chi Minh Trail. North Vietnamese access through Cambodia, however, was conditional upon Sihanouk's assurance or, at the minimum, his acceptance, of neutrality.

In June 1965 Pol Pot and a handful of associates traveled to Hanoi, where they stayed for nine months. Their purpose was, on the one hand, to undertake political studies and to learn from Vietnamese military theoreticians and, on the other hand, to discuss the role of the Khmer Communist movement within the context of the escalating war in Vietnam.[19] By this point the United States was actively engaged in armed conflict against the DRV and the NLF. Following a perceived attack by North Vietnamese forces against an American naval vessel, on August 7, 1964, the U.S. Congress hurriedly passed the Gulf of Tonkin Resolution, authorizing President Lyndon Johnson to use armed force in Indochina. Sustained aerial bombing campaigns against the DRV had commenced in mid-February 1965.

It is probable that Pol Pot expected support from his Vietnamese counterparts to at least make contingency preparations for armed struggle in Cambodia; more optimistically, Pol Pot probably hoped to acquire weapons needed for the revolution.[20] However, for the Vietnamese, the foremost priority remained the defeat of the United States. This necessitated continued access to sanctuaries within Cambodia, as well as the ability to transport weapons and other war materiel into southern Vietnam. Indeed, the Vietnamese Communists had recently reached an agreement with Sihanouk that allowed the NLF and other Vietnamese insurgents access to Cambodian territory.[21] In exchange, the Vietnamese pledged to honor Cambodia's territorial borders at war's end.

Pol Pot was rebuffed in his request to expand the revolution in Cambodia. Indeed, the Vietnamese leadership berated the Khmer Communist for pursuing a nationalist agenda and for wanting to put the Cambodian revolution ahead of the greater regional conflict. In no uncertain terms, Le Duan, secretary-general of the Vietnamese Communists, stressed that the Khmer's strategy of "self-reliant struggle" was inappropriate, and that the Khmer Rouge were to subordinate their objectives to that of the DRV.[22] More precisely, Le Duan "recommended that the Cambodians combine building revolutionary bases in the countryside through unarmed mass mobilization with continued infiltration of parliament and government, in order to position the Party to make a bid for power, perhaps through violence, once the Vietnamese had won the war."[23]

Having failed to secure a go-ahead to launch an armed revolution, Pol Pot next traveled to Beijing. There, he met with several high-ranking officials of the Chinese Communist Party (CPP), including Deng Xiaoping and Liu Shaoqi.[24] Pol Pot's visit, from February to May 1966, happened during the early months of Mao Zedong's Cultural Revolution—a movement that many scholars surmise to have influenced Pol Pot's later policies. Chandler, for example, suggests that Pol Pot was drawn to Mao's emphasis on "continuous class warfare, individual revolutionary will, and the importance of poor peasants—ideological areas in which China differed from Vietnam and which were later emphasized in Democratic Kampuchea." Furthermore, Chandler contends that Pol Pot must have been impressed by the scale, autonomy, and momentum of China's social mobilization. It was, Chandler concludes, China's triumphant revolution rather than Vietnam's arduous, unfinished struggle that Pol Pot desired to bring back to Cambodia.[25]

Aside from any insights Pol Pot may have gleaned regarding the ideology of class struggle, he failed to receive the material support required to wage armed conflict. Chinese officials, similar to their Vietnamese counterparts, urged restraint. They cautioned that it was necessary to maintain a wider perspective on events in Indochina; that liberation required solidarity between the Vietnamese and the Khmer. This meant, once again, to support Sihanouk despite the monarchs' ongoing purges of Khmer revolutionaries.

Meanwhile, conditions within Cambodia continued to deteriorate. Mass protests erupted in Phnom Penh and other provincial towns, often led by students and civil servants who objected to widespread corruption and an overall lack of political and economic opportunities. Even within the countryside, support for Sihanouk was waning as the gap between urban wealth and rural poverty became more pronounced. Rice farmers, in particular, were hard-pressed. In 1963 Sihanouk had refused U.S. aid, nationalized the import-export sector of the economy, and closed Cambodia's privately owned banks. He hoped, through these steps, to encourage stronger relations with China and the Soviet Union and, in the process, curtail the escalating war in Vietnam from expanding further into Cambodia. However, by severing relations with the United States, Sihanouk further crippled Cambodia's faltering economy. Neither China nor the Soviet Union was willing to invest substantial funds in Cambodia; consequently, Sihanouk was forced to make drastic reductions in defense spending, thereby incurring the ire of the minister of national defense, Gen. Lon Nol, and the broader military establishment. Moreover, the nationalization of foreign trade encouraged the commercial elite to trade clandestinely with Communist insurgents in Vietnam.

As the United States intensified its military actions in Vietnam—over 536,000 U.S. military personnel were stationed in Vietnam by 1968—both the NLF and the military forces of the DRV increased their use of Cambodian territory as sanctuary and for resupply. In turn, U.S. officials steadily, secretively, expanded the war into Cambodia. In 1967 American military advisers initiated Operation Salem House. Whereas U.S. personnel had been operating in Cambodia since at least the early 1960s, Salem House systematized these operations. Teams of six to eight Americans and South Vietnamese would enter Cambodia seeking tactical intelligence. At first, missions were restricted to the northeastern tip of Cambodia; over time, as the operation was renamed Daniel Boone, the base of operation included the entirety of the Cambodian-Vietnamese border. Limitations on the number of American personnel were also lifted, as were restrictions on the conduct of operations. The use of antipersonnel land mines, for example, was allowed—a tactic that would take a devastating toll on Cambodian peasants. By 1969, U.S. forces had conducted 454 covert missions into Cambodia; this figure increased to 558 the following year. The number of

Cambodian civilians killed between 1969 and 1973 is placed as high as 150,000.[26]

Cambodian officials condemned these missions. In just one month, October 1969, representatives protested eighty-three separate incidents of American intervention. Aerial and artillery attacks, supposedly targeting NLF strongholds, were more likely to destroy Cambodian villages—houses, schools, bridges—killing more Cambodian civilians than enemy personnel.[27] Pointedly, Sihanouk did not give his permission for the U.S. military violation of Cambodian territory. Certainly, he tolerated limited actions, and he did acquiesce to some demands of both the DRV and the United States to operate within Cambodia's borders. However, as Kenton Clymer explains, these were specific and limited arrangements, agreed to in a desperate bid to preserve Cambodia from the excesses of all-out war.[28]

More devastating than these limited incursions, however, was the United States and its South Vietnamese ally's escalating aerial bombardment of Cambodia. On February 9, 1969, Gen. Creighton Abrams recommended a single, intensive attack on a site within Cambodia that was suspected to be the headquarters of NLF forces, identified as the Central Office for South Vietnam (COSVN). The previous administration of President Johnson had repeatedly refused such a strike; for the incoming president, Richard Nixon, the operation aligned strongly with his desire to expand the armed conflict in a futile attempt to extradite the United States from the quagmire of Vietnam. Thus, on March 18, 1969, Nixon ordered a series of secret and illegal B-52 bombing raids to be conducted inside Cambodia. Known as Operation Menu, the campaign would last for fifteen months, during which time more than 3,800 B-52 sorties were flown, disgorging more than 100,000 tons of bombs.[29]

While traveling to France, Sihanouk had entrusted his government to Lon Nol and his pro-Western deputy prime minister, Prince Sisowath Sirik Matak. In Sihanouk's absence, Lon Nol and Sirik Matak launched attacks on the Vietnamese Communist positions, organized anti-Vietnamese demonstrations, and reestablished ties with various non-Communist groups. Sihanouk, upon learning of these actions, condemned both Lon Nol and Sirik Matak. In response, Sirik Matak pressured Lon Nol to depose Sihanouk and, in turn, the National Assembly voted eighty-nine to three to remove Sihanouk from power.[30]

The coup d'état was a turning point in the geopolitical chess match. Initially, Chinese leaders sought to align themselves with the government of Lon Nol and Sirik Matak. Crucial to this strategy was the necessity of retaining DRV access to bases in Cambodia. In essence, the Chinese were willing to postpone the Khmer Communist revolution in order to help the Vietnamese defeat the United States. This too was the immediate intention of the DRV. Refusing, however, to work with the Chinese, Lon Nol adopted a hard-line anti-Vietnamese and anti-Communist position. In part this reflected Lon Nol's own political leanings, but it also reflected his misreading of the wider geopolitical climate. Lon Nol believed, naively perhaps, Nixon's rhetoric. The Cambodian general supported the expanded U.S. military presence on Cambodian soil, the ongoing bombing campaigns, and the presence of thousands of troops of the Army of the Republic of Vietnam. Lon Nol believed also in Nixon's promise that military and economic aid would be forthcoming.

Sihanouk similarly made a fateful decision. The leadership in China, having been rebuffed in their overture to Lon Nol, encouraged Sihanouk to form a military alliance with the Vietnamese and Cambodian Communists and to lead a government in exile.[31] Sihanouk, as Arnold Isaacs explains, was far too clear-eyed not to have realized, even in these early weeks, that he was tying himself to interests that were mortally dangerous to Cambodia's survival.[32] Cold War calculus, however, forced the prince into a Faustian bargain. Having received no support from the United States, Sihanouk had few options.

In response to the coup, Sihanouk issued an appeal to the Cambodian people, whereupon Royalist supporters would join the Khmer Rouge in a unified effort to defeat the Lon Nol government. More formally, on March 23, 1970, Sihanouk announced the formation of the National United Front of Kampuchea (Front Uni

National du Kampuchea, or FUNK), a political and military coalition of Royalists and the Khmer Rouge, committed to destroying Lon Nol's republican forces. Two months later, the Royal Government of National Union of Kampuchea (Gouvernement Royal d'Union Nationale du Kampuchea, or GRUNK) was announced. Sihanouk assumed the post of GRUNK head of state, while Penn Nouth was designated as prime minister. Other high-ranking positions were occupied by Khmer Rouge cadre: Khieu Samphan was designated deputy prime minister, minister of defense, and commander-in-chief of the GRUNK armed forces; Hu Nim served as minister of information; and Hou Yuon assumed the position of minister of interior, communal reforms, and cooperatives.[33]

Both Sihanouk and the Khmer Rouge leadership recognized the tenuous basis of their alliance. The Khmer Rouge continued to hold Sihanouk responsible for the war in Cambodia, but well understood his mass appeal. Pol Pot, in particular, used Sihanouk's popularity for propaganda and recruitment purposes. Sihanouk likewise understood that his role in the alliance was little more than as titular figurehead. He gambled, however, that he might use the arrangement as a means of deposing Lon Nol and eventually returning to power.

The geopolitical machinations of China and the United States would reverberate across the fields and forests of Cambodia. With Sihanouk removed, and the more pliable and pro-American Lon Nol in power, Nixon expanded even more the American military presence in Cambodia. On April 30, 1970, Nixon announced to the American public that U.S. ground forces, accompanied by the Army of the Republic of Vietnam (ARVN) had made a strategic advancement into Cambodia. Nixon explained that "North Vietnam [had] increased its military aggression," especially in Cambodia, and that "to protect [Americans] who are in Vietnam and to guarantee the continued success" of U.S. operations, the time had come for action. Nixon was disingenuous when he explained that "American policy [had] been to scrupulously respect the neutrality of the Cambodian people." No mention was made, for example, of the ongoing covert operations dating back to the mid-1960s or of the bombings associated with Operation Menu. Rather, Nixon avowed that the United States had "maintained a skeleton diplomatic mission of fewer than 14 in Cambodia's capital," and that "for the past five years [the United States had] provided no military assistance whatsoever and no economic assistance to Cambodia." North Vietnam, Nixon asserted, was guilty of interference in the sovereignty of Cambodia; North Vietnam had established military sanctuaries along the Cambodian border with South Vietnam; and that these sanctuaries contained "major base camps, training sites logistics facilities, weapons and ammunition factories, airstrips, and prisoner-of-war compounds." Nixon further explained that Cambodia "sent out a call to the United States" for assistance, and that without American support, Cambodia would become a vast enemy staging ground and springboard for attacks on South Vietnam.[34]

Employing the euphemistic term *incursion*, Nixon stressed that ongoing military operations did not constitute an invasion. The purpose, Nixon stated, was not to occupy Cambodian territory but to drive the Vietnamese Communists out of the country. And wary of Soviet or Chinese responses, Nixon avowed that the actions were "in no way directed to the security interests of any nation," and that any government that chose to use the incursion as "a pretext for harming relations with the United States" would be doing so on its own responsibility, and on its own initiative. Nixon then repeated that the United States undertook the incursion "not for the purpose of expanding the war into Cambodia, but for the purpose of ending the war in Vietnam and winning the peace."[35]

On July 27, 1970, Nixon subsequently announced the resumption of B-52 carpet-bombing raids over Cambodia; these would continue until the American Congress called a halt to all American military operations in Cambodia in 1973. Estimates of Cambodian casualties range from 150,000 to nearly 750,000.[36] Moreover, the bombing campaign further devastated an already deteriorating infrastructure. William Shawcross details the lingering effects of the bombing campaign: "Eighty percent of the country's prewar paddy fields had been abandoned, and the government's own figures showed that in 1974 rice production was only 65,000 metric tons—as opposed to 3.8 million tons in the last year before the war."[37] Henry Kamm concludes that "With the callous disregard of the interests of the Cambodian people that marked all of America's wartime involvement in that country, and in full knowledge that Cambodia's demented and corrupt regime could only prolong their people's suffering, America did all that it could to drag out senselessly the life of a hated government and a war that Washington knew was lost."[38]

The air war did not bring victory to either Lon Nol's republic or the United States. It did, however, create a ground swell of support for the Khmer Rouge.[39] The carpet bombing "gave the Khmer Rouges a propaganda windfall which they exploited to the hilt—taking peasants for political education lessons among the bomb craters and shrapnel, explaining to them that Lon Nol had sold Cambodia to the Americans in order to stay in power and that the US, like Vietnam and Thailand, was bent on the country's annihilation so that, when the war was over, Cambodia would cease to exist."[40] As explained by one survivor, who experienced the bombings in Svay Rieng Province, "Then in 1972 B-52s bombed three times per day, fifteen minutes apart, three planes at a time. They hit houses in Samrong and thirty people were killed. There were no troops in these villages. At that time there were some Vietnamese [Communist] troops on the border [nearby], but they didn't bomb the border: they bombed inside it, people's houses."[41] As Anthony Barnett concludes, "the Pol Pot regime would not have emerged in the form it took without the war from 1970–1975, when US intervention in Vietnam spread across the whole of Indochina."[42] Indeed, in 1970 Khmer Rouge forces were described as "marginal." Consequently, when the Khmer Rouge achieved victory in April 1975, they constituted neither a unified party nor an organization that enjoyed popular support.

The Khmer Rouge Culture of Conspiracy

In a speech delivered before an assembly of cadres in June 1976, the speaker, most likely Pol Pot, described the role of the vanguard in its liberation of Cambodia from its oppressors. In 1970, the speaker questioned, "Our armed forces were small. . . . The [outside] world said we were weak, small, few; how could we win?" He explained, however, that "We had to have our own Party, our own army, our own people, and be our own leaders regardless of the difficulties." There were two paths: "We could win quickly, in three to four or five years" or "The war could extend for ten to fifteen or twenty years." Opting for the first path, "We organized forces, attacked, and won in a period of five years. This was because of the Party. If the Party had not been absolute, with no correct line on strategy or tactics, we would not have won like that."[43] Throughout this speech, and in many other public and private statements, numerous themes are developed and repeated: that the CPK vanguard achieved victory through their sheer determination, tenacity, and pursuit of a correct line; that the Khmer Communist revolution was accomplished without any assistance, including that of their Vietnamese counterparts; and that their revolution was unprecedented, both in scale and scope.

Were the senior leaders who professed such beliefs sincere in their interpretations? Certainly there was a disconnect between reality and rhetoric. We know also that several key leaders understood very well that certain public and private statements were false. Indeed, by 1979 many men and women would be purged because they challenged the official Party line.[44] It is necessary, however, to contextualize these statements not solely or even exclusively as evidence of delusion, but instead as a contributing factor in the emergence of a conspiracy culture.

Academics are often reluctant to take seriously conspiracy theories. The promotion of conspiracy theories, for example, is taken to be an irrational response rooted in a pathological condition—whether of a psychological or sociological nature—in a word, paranoia.[45] In colloquial language, conspiracy theory is not a neutral label but rather a pejorative expression, an evaluative term used to dismiss a particular explanation as untrue.[46] As corollary, any competing explanation derives legitimacy, in that the "category *conspiracy theory* polices the borders of legitimate versus risible statements, and intellectually competent actors versus paranoiacs."[47]

It is widely held among scholars of the Khmer Rouge that the top echelon of leadership subscribed to conspiracy theories of networks of traitors, and that Pol Pot (especially) was prone to paranoia. The widespread labeling of senior leaders of the Khmer Rouge as conspiracy theorists has, I maintain, contributed to an exceptionally myopic view of CPK policy and practice. Too often Khmer Rouge governance has been dismissed as irrational, unfounded, or simply absurd, and that the CPK eschewed bureaucracy to the point of chaos. These platitudes, however, fail to square with the documentary evidence. What is needed is a scholarly interpretation of Khmer Rouge paranoia and how this intersects with CPK bureaucracy. Indeed, to simply identify senior Khmer Rouge cadre as paranoid is not particularly helpful. A more fruitful path is to take seriously the claims of the Khmer Rouge that their government was infiltrated with networks of traitors burrowing from within. Let me be clear: this is not an argument that conspiratorial networks of traitors were in fact ubiquitous throughout Democratic Kampuchea. Rather, it is to interpret specific actions of the Khmer Rouge, from their own perspective, based on the material record documented and archived during their time in power. It is imperative, in other words, to parse out the materiality of bureaucratic violence through an understanding of their own security discourses. Following Laura Jones, it is necessary to "critically interrogate the discourses— representations and practices—of conspiracy which circulate across and between actors, networks, scales and territories and which have the capacity to shape how people understand the world around them."[48]

Much like the term *conspiracy theory* the term *paranoia* marginalizes or discredits certain individuals. And yet, following Anne McClintock, it is possible to salvage this term as it intersects with the power/knowledge relationship.[49] Recall that survival is perhaps the most fundamental objective of any government. It is for this reason that discourses of security are so important. As Jonathan Bach explains, to better understand the imbrication of power/ knowledge and paranoia, it is necessary to begin with the proposition that "there is no political system without a system of rule, and central to any form of rule is the urge to survive."[50] However, Bach elaborates that "survival necessitates anticipation, and anticipation requires the employment of secrecy."[51] Here we begin to see the work performed by lists, in that the bureaucratic compilation of personal information, interpreted through data analytics of network logics, is essential to the survival of the government. Secrecy is paramount and only trusted bureaucrats are informed of the operations.

Taken together, the conspiratorial beliefs of pervasive networks of traitors imagined by the Khmer Rouge and a tendency among academics to discount these beliefs has led to a stunted critique of CPK policy and practice. This is not to argue that key leaders of the CPK were justified in their pronouncement of traitors infusing government and society. It is to argue that we must understand how Khmer Rouge conspiracy theories materialized and intersected with the broader political economy of Democratic Kampuchea. We need to document and interpret how a burgeoning conspiracy culture was articulated within the Khmer Rouge security apparatus. This requires a deeper engagement with paranoia as a form of power.

In a perverse way, bureaucratic processes contribute to a particular form of paranoid politics. According to Bach, "the structure of rule comes to imitate the symptoms of paranoia, which include a slowly developing mistrust, suspicion of others, delusions of grandeur, feeling of being persecuted, theories of a highly organized system that appears as a conspiracy, fear of loss of autonomy, projective thinking, and hostility."[52] This statement effectively captures the waning years of the Khmer Rouge regime, but it also highlights the contradictions of governance—contradictions that will likewise become apparent in later chapters. On this point,

McClintock defines paranoia as "an inherent contradiction with respect to power: a double-sided phantasm that oscillates precariously between deliriums of grandeur and nightmares of perpetual threat, a deep and dangerous doubleness with respect to power that is held in unstable tension, but which, if suddenly destabilized, can produce pyrotechnic displays of violence."[53] The term *paranoia*, therefore, becomes analytically useful not as pathology but instead as an "analytically strategic concept, a way of seeing and being attentive to contradictions within power, a way of making visible . . . the contradictory flashpoints of violence that the state tries to conceal."[54] Together, the concepts of paranoia and conspiracy recast as political practices provide a more robust approach to understanding Khmer Rouge governance and, more pointedly, to the initiation and conduct of a series of bloody purges that would ultimately destroy the regime in a spasmodic fit of violence.

In this book I appraise the conspiracy theories of the Khmer Rouge as "a tradition of explanation, characterized by a particular rhetorical style."[55] More precisely, I understand the CPK's claims of prevalent strings of traitors as a particular security discourse, a discourse derived from the compilation of lists interpreted as proof of traitorous networks. In security practice, the network constitutes a particular technology of risk. For example, in recent years the deployment of network logics has been routinely and repeatedly applied to so-called dark networks: social organizations of criminals and terrorists. Growing numbers of criminologists and counterterrorism experts are now routinely analyzing large data sets and using computer simulations to identify and anticipate national security threats.[56] To this end, within the war on terror, organized terrorist groups are widely interpreted as comprising intricate, transnational social networks.[57] Indeed, within terrorism research, social network analyses promise the ability to map whole networks and to prioritize security action for maximum disruptive effect.[58] By conceptualizing criminal and militant or terrorist groups as networks, the use of the network as metaphor subjects men and women to a functional analysis in which they are seen as comprising a series of connections or layers of relationships.[59] In this way, previously compiled lists of thousands upon thousands of names produce the object of which they speak: networks of suspected criminal elements.

Long considered the rudimentary raw material of scholarly analyses, lists have now attracted critical attention as objects in their own right.[60] As Cornelia Vismann explains, "individual items are not put down in writing for the sake of memorizing spoken words, but in order to regulate goods, things, or people. Lists sort and engender circulation."[61] It is necessary, in other words, to account for the particular operations that the format of the list enables. List-making, whether derived through the assemblage of digitally acquired information or through biographies written with pen and ink, is not only a problem of selection, but rather is a "transformative and performative practice that produces the items which the list will comprise."[62] Urs Stäheli maintains that we have to understand the "mediality" of a list—in other words, that we recognize that the list must come into existence before someone may be rightly or wrongly included on the list.[63] As a case in point, it becomes possible to list a person as a traitor or terrorist only if we have already determined the existence and presence of traitors or terrorists. In this way, lists produce their own reality and, by extension, the actuality of listable men and women becomes a self-evident fact. Approaching lists in this way invites us to think differently about how diffuse security powers are created, expanded, and sustained.[64] To this end, and departing from an instrumentalist perspective that understands lists as simply the compilation or representation of preexisting information, lists are more robustly understood as "inscription devices" that produce specific material, political, and legal effects.[65] It is necessary, therefore, to consider more precisely the work that lists perform as a specific technique of government.[66] Security lists, for example, may be viewed as knowledge practices and modes of legal ordering.[67] Consequently, following de Goede and Sullivan, "situating the materiality of the listing process at the center of analysis helps to bring the specific legal ordering capabilities of lists—that is, the ways they work to constitute law and establish new modes of legal transmission—into clearer view."[68]

The use of a network as metaphor is highly problematic and has received considerable criticism, especially within the context of list-making. Of particular concern is that the use of data-mining techniques on contrived lists of suspected men and women, when interpreted through the metaphor of the network, becomes also a self-fulfilling procedure. The interpretation of kill lists, for example, is based principally on a "quantitative link analysis methodology." This works, Weber explains, on the basis of a two (or three)–hop query through data collections to find connections to other suspected terrorists or members of terrorist organizations.[69] As Mac Ginty elaborates, "The nature of technology means that analysts may be tempted to identify connection after connection, potentially criminalizing an entire community."[70] This process will become patently obvious when we later explore the day-to-day mechanisms of the purges initiated by the CPK, as entire units of men and women were arrested en masse. On the other hand, the network has the ability to endlessly generate investigative leads. The practice of engineering networks is never-ending, as analysts are always expanding the net wider and wider. In so doing, these bureaucratic procedures deepen the political ontology of the threat and seemingly affirm the existence of conspiratorial networks. To this point, Anna Leander explains that because lists work by disconnection and by tying contexts together, they follow an open-ended logic—additions can *always* be made. Moreover, this openness and future orientation make lists appear full of potential. Attention is thus directed away from an inscrutable present/past and toward an open future.[71]

Crucially, the calculations involved in developing a list of networked people as a security risk affords a veneer of empirical rigor and objectivity to policing practices. The network as metaphor as it relates to the production of lists therefore highlights the importance of data gathering, of organizing masses of disparate data sources, and of anticipating future actions. Weber affirms, noting that "It is not only senior leaders of a 'terrorist' group who are regarded as valid objects for targeted assassination but also anybody who is identified (by an algorithm or an analyst) as being vital to the group—according to their strategic position in the network."[72] The clear and present danger, analytically, is that the number of names that may possibly be added to any given kill list is infinite. In other words, networks derived from lists may be understood as auto-referential statements. This is not to deny that networks do not necessarily exist. It is to emphasize that there is a danger in creating false positives—that is, to assert the existence of criminal networks that have no material reality. Such simulated networks provide the foundation for the concept of guilt by association.

Network logics do not just visualize fields of intervention. They also calculate, order, and classify objects—whether people, ideas, or material things—and the relations between these objects.[73] In this manner, the use of social network analyses does not simply uncover or display preexisting networks but instead establishes the existence of networks even, potentially, when no such networks actually exist. Innocent men and women are thus subject to prosecution through guilt by association. Viewed in this light, bureaucratic invocations of criminal or terrorist networks are not simply metaphorical representations of danger or objective threats but materialize as security devices that render the world actionable and amenable to intervention.[74] The dividing line between perceived networks and conspiracy theories becomes very fine indeed.

Security discourses do not so much respond to objectively existing threats, but instead these discourses themselves constitute and actualize dangers, select risks, and prioritize threats.[75] In other words, following Marieke de Goede and Samuel Randalls, "threats do not exist prior to practices of articulation and identity" but rather "it is through modes of representation and imagination that threats are brought into being, and are perceived as endangering particular communities and as demanding particular forms of social action."[76] More to the point, security discourses often assume a future-oriented, speculative act of preemption, which takes as its target potential rather than actual risks.[77] Here, security is less about reacting to, controlling, or even prosecuting crime than it is addressing the preconditions of a security breach. The presumption is that an assemblage of relations may identify criminals who are planning to commit a crime before any such crime has actually happened.[78]

Once the realm of science fiction, as exemplified notably by Philip Dick's short story "The Minority Report" and the subsequent film of the same name, the calculative potential of big data situated within state-sanctioned security apparatuses is "intimately tied to the contemporary turn to pre-emptive security techniques."[79] It now becomes a matter of preventing crimes before they happen. Indeed, Lucia Zedner details that "we are on the cusp of a shift from a post- to a pre-crime society, a society in which the possibility of forestalling risks competes with and even takes precedence over responding to wrongs done."[80]

Precrime policing is predicated on presumed intentions, and the algorithmic calculations of big data, of the massive production of knowledge on a real-time basis, are predicated on such assumptions. When governments act on analyses derived algorithmically from biopolitical lists, people are targeted not because they have necessarily committed any criminal activity, "but because they show specific behaviors or link patterns, which are regarded by analysts or software designers as suspect or which 'emerge' from the data analysis."[81] In a statement that will echo our subsequent interpretation of Khmer Rouge purges, Weber concludes: "The quantitative methodology cannot make qualitative distinctions between relationships of different 'nodes,' which are easily subsumed into terror networks. Accordingly, relatives, friends and co-workers who have multiple connections to suspects or targets are added to the list."[82]

Understanding lists as inscription devices, as the wherewithal to generate entire networks, draws attention to their strategic functionality: the visceral realities of a perceived threat manifest (e.g., terrorist watch lists) and—supported by narratives of conspiratorial networks—legitimate preemptive action.[83] To this end, an unavoidable corollary of precrime surveillance is preemptive punishment.[84] Preemptive punishment may take any number of forms, including, for example, travel bans or having one's financial assets frozen. Other forms include arrest and detainment, but also torture, political assassinations, and targeted killings.

Preemption is a bureaucratic mode of power that takes threat, which has no actual referent, as its object.[85] As a technique of governance, it has likewise been subject to intensive legal and moral criticism. Laurie Calhoun, for example, describes preemptive predator strikes as examples of summary executions.[86] She calls to question the problems inherent in the algorithmic calculation of suspected terrorists and terrorist networks, noting that "the conviction and sentencing to death of a human being for a capital crime leaves open the possibility of error."[87] For, as Calhoun elaborates, "Human beings are fallible, and the purpose of due process, one of the hallmarks of modern democratic societies, is to minimize the occurrence of the grossest form of injustice, the infliction of penalties upon people for crimes that they did not commit."[88] Preemptive targeted killings are in violation of due process. Guilt is determined not in a court of law but through calculations hidden within the bowels of a faceless bureaucracy. Calhoun continues: "The processes of democratic systems are intended to be transparent. The processes of totalitarian regimes are intended to be opaque. Indeed, the defining characteristics of a totalitarian regime are its lack of due process and arbitrary absolutism, arrived at not through an open dialogue among diversely situated parties but, rather, through a secret decision process that metes out justice in its own arbitrary and unilateral way."[89]

Calhoun's criticism is leveled at the use of drones to terminate suspected terrorists in the global war on terror. It is equally valid in our critique and condemnation of the Khmer Rouge. Throughout Democratic Kampuchea, life-and-death decisions were made in secret, arrests were made in secret, and executions were carried out in secret. Only a small circle of senior officials was privy to these procedures. Those men, women, and children, condemned by the Khmer Rouge security apparatus, were subject to an opaque legal order premised not on an arbitrary execution of justice but instead on a systematic rationale founded upon the threat of traitorous networks and saboteurs. For the Khmer Rouge, evidence was produced in the form of personal biographies, surveillance, and forced confessions. Failures to reach production quotas, disagreements over policy within the inner circle of government, and even the existence of disease, malnutrition, and famine became facts that proved saboteurs and traitors were acting against the Party. For tens of thousands of men, women, and children who would die at the hands of the Khmer Rouge, death began when their names appeared on a list.[90]

The Necropolitics of Bureaucracy

During a meeting held on October 9, 1976, a Khmer Rouge official declared emphatically that within his unit, "Ninety-nine percent of the cadres and combatants . . . are good, although there are some battalion cadres who are not good, but there are only one or two of these." He explained that "Some company cadres behaved inappropriately in terms of eating and communication," and that a man named Soeun "stole a letter from his fellow company cadre and ran away," but was later arrested.[91]

Read in isolation, this text appears rather ordinary. And yet, its simplicity calls to question the everydayness of bureaucratic power. Throughout the reign of the Khmer Rouge, to be identified in a meeting of this sort was to be subjected to an enigmatic yet pervasive security apparatus that functioned primarily through the production, circulation, and consumption of biopolitical knowledge. We read into this text, therefore, not an innocent accounting of organizational activities but the infusion of potential death into the everydayness of life. For within Democratic Kampuchea, what one said, or did, or with whom one associated, was documented, filed, and evaluated. More precisely, we glimpse how bureaucratic procedures constitute a necropolitical form of governance. Here, we see how the labels *criminal* or *traitor* became bureaucratic inscriptions written into the biographic record of countless men, women, and children.

Following Michel Foucault, in the classic conception of sovereignty, the right of life and death was one of the sovereign's basic attributes. In other words, to say that "the sovereign has a right of life and death means that he [*sic*] can . . . either have people put to death or let them live."[92] Life and death, therefore, are removed from the realm of the natural and fall within the field of governance. Foucault suggests also that the sovereign cannot grant life in the same way that he or she can inflict death. The right of life and death, therefore, "is always exercised in an unbalanced way: the balance is always tipped in favor of death." Consequently, the "very essence of the right of life and death is actually the right to kill: it is at the moment when the sovereign can kill that he [*sic*] exercises his right over life."[93]

Gradually, the ancient right to take life or to let live was replaced by a twofold power to foster life or to disallow life to the point of death. On the one hand, there emerged an anatomo-politics of the human body: a micropolitics that sought to maximize the forces of the body and to integrate it into efficient, productive systems. Here, Foucault explains that "it is largely as a force of production that the body is invested with relations of power and domination; but, on the other hand, its constitution as labor power is possible only if it is caught up in a system of subjection . . . the body becomes a useful force only if it is both a productive body and a subjected body."[94] On the other hand, there emerged a suite of regulatory practices that Foucault termed *biopolitics*. This latter development was imbued with the mechanisms, the calculations, of life in its totality: birth, morbidity, mortality, longevity.[95] From this point onward, it became possible to speak of a state's population, as if that population had a transcendental existence and experience above and beyond the government—facets that were intensely managed and analyzed by new and specialized academic disciplines (e.g., demography, sociology, and epidemiology).

The modern state's right to make life or to disallow life, however, never completely erased the classical right to kill. This is seen, for example, when states wage war, when states execute convicted felons, and when states engage in political assassinations and targeted killings. Consequently, what the modern state reveals is a decidedly more nuanced and complex management, or bureaucratization, of life and death.

At this point, it is appropriate to introduce the extension, or modification, of Foucault's work as developed by Achille Mbembe.[96] To begin, Mbembe declares that "To exercise sovereignty is to exercise control over mortality and to define life as the deployment and manifestation of power."[97] This power is manifest in the mundane bureaucratization of society: of the administrative classification of bodies into discrete categories as understood through the lens of security. Indeed, Mbembe postulates necropolitics as the "syntheses between massacre and bureaucracy." As Jamie Allinson explains, "it is the old sovereign power of death, operative in a bio-political setting, implying therefore a division between populations, the making of a 'caesura' between the population worthy of being made to live, and that subject to the right to command death."[98] In the context of Democratic Kampuchea, this caesura appears within the interstices of paranoia politics and the purging of suspected conspiracy networks, a bureaucratic space where everyone is suspect and no one is beyond the lethal surveillance of the Khmer Rouge security apparatus.

It is the knowing and naming of political subjects manifest materially in documents and dossiers that provide the foundation of necrobureaucracies, where the compilation and interpretation of lists is done not for the purpose of life but for death. In the pages that follow, we examine more closely the production of myriad lists: lists of arrests and detainments, of interrogations and executions. We will consider the self-writing of biographies and the routinization of forced confessions. In so doing we understand that Foucault was correct in his assertion that power circulates, but also that power circulates through material documents.

CHAPTER 2

───

A Tale of Two Lists

Surviving documents of the Communist Party of Kampuchea, including reports, memorandums, and telegrams, are replete with lists. Consider for example the following:

1. Pol Touch, female youth;
2. Pol Neang, female youth;
3. Yeu Ong, -ditto—Sap Hoeun, girl.[1]

And:

- Husked "white" rice Number 1 with broken grains of 15 percent. . . . . 5,000 Tonnes
- Peanuts. . . . . 65 Tonnes
- Coffee beans (Robusta variety) Number 1. . . . . 3,240 Tonnes
- Coffee beans (Robusta variety) Number 2. . . . . 2,610 Tonnes
- Coffee beans (Robusta variety) Number 3. . . . . 1,440 Tonnes
- Black pepper Number 1. . . . . 35,125 Tonnes[2]

Taken in isolation these two lists provide little by way of explanation. Read together they provide vital insight into the functioning of the Khmer Rouge bureaucracy. The first list appears in a memo sent to Angkar on September 1, 1977, by a Khmer Rouge cadre named Khun regarding security matters. Khun explains that a man named Chead Han had "said in the morning that he was going to break the hoe's handle, then in the afternoon, he suddenly broke the hoe's handle. After breaking it, he then said if they gave [him] another hoe [he] would break it again until all the hoes were running out." Khun continues that "In the evening of the 31st August 1977, there were 3 female youths and a girl who broke 4 spoons during dinner." Their names were subsequently listed in the memorandum. Khun concludes the letter with a simple but ominous request: "As reported above, what will the Angkar decide? Please provide us an opinion in order that we can take action to solve these matters."[3]

The second list is contained in a letter sent by Vann Rit, on behalf of the Committee for Foreign Trade of Democratic Kampuchea, to the Embassy of the Socialist Federal Republic of Yugoslavia on July 15, 1978. The occasion of the letter was in response to a shipment of rice, peanuts, coffee beans, and pepper, which were to be loaded onto a container ship docked at Kampong Som. Vann Rit explains that Democratic Kampuchea was unable to honor the request, noting that they had waited nearly two weeks for confirmation of the order, but none had been forthcoming. Vann Rit clarifies that "we have in the past arranged goods for sale to Yugoslavia and have been waiting for long without offering them to any other market. We were afraid that if Yugoslavia reversed the decision, we would not be able to make timely arrangements to sell the goods to other market[s] which would therefore degenerate goods quality significantly." To buttress his point, Vann Rit describes a previous order in which 200 tons of coffee, 5,000 tons of husked rice, 45 tons of pepper, and 40 tons of peanuts were requested by Yugoslavia; after considerable delay, however, this request was subsequently reduced to only 200 tons of coffee. According to Vann Rit, "Due to time constraints after such a long wait, we could not make timely arrangements for the sale of the rice and the other goods to other market[s], thus downgrading our goods quality and incurring much loss." He concludes: "We would like to raise this matter for Yugoslavia's information and understanding as to our endeavor and challenges. We are confident that such challenges are temporary and will be overcome, and that both of our sides will continue to cooperate and strive to work out resolutions."[4]

Two features of these documents are remarkable. On the one hand, both documents provide insight into the day-to-day operations of Democratic Kampuchea. The first document addresses security concerns, notably the suspicion of subversive elements who posed a threat to the solvency of Democratic Kampuchea, while the second highlights the difficulties of conducting trade on the global market. On the other hand, these two documents indicate the dialectics of what we may call the political economy of security. In both documents representatives of the CPK express their concern over potential economic losses: broken hoes and spoons or spoiled foodstuffs. More precisely, these documents indicate the interconnections of agricultural productivity, international trade, and the fear of traitorous actions and sabotage.

That both documents were archived by members of the CPK is especially telling. Indeed, the collection of these documents is testimony "to the functions and actions of the dominant political authorities whose transactions they reflected and whose interests and needs were served by their preservation."[5] In other words, these documents constitute the material manifestation of power within Democratic Kampuchea, for it is through the production and distribution of these documents that form is provided to bureaucracies. More properly, an examination of these lists calls attention to the iterative administration of power.

To quote Akhil Gupta, an engagement with the quotidian trappings of bureaucracies "makes evident that the materiality and solidity of the state dissolve under scrutiny."[6] Here, Gupta directs attention to the fact that there is no preexisting, monolithic state but instead an assemblage of material and symbolic practices, all intimately embedded in everyday practices. When a child pledges allegiance to the flag, the state comes into being. When we pay taxes, apply for a visa, or complete the census, the state comes into existence. These activities, moreover, are located in myriad agencies or bureaus, each with its own directives, agendas, and functions. Consequently, "one must inquire into the relation between agencies that regulate different subject areas: departments or bureaus may be responsible for portfolios as diverse as industry, education, defense, policing, medical care, housing, pollution, infrastructure, and the like."[7]

Gupta is correct that we need to think differently about the state and that it is necessary to disaggregate various "agendas, bureaus, levels, and spaces that make up the state."[8] Gupta's argument is all the more relevant for our understanding of the Cambodian genocide. It is nonsensical, for example, to speak of the state of Democratic Kampuchea or even to reduce authority to a singular body, such as Angkar or the Communist Party of Kampuchea. However, it is also necessary to consider specifically how the state may be conceived and articulated not theoretically or academically but instead by those bureaucrats who constitute any particular form of governance. In this chapter I provide an overview of the broader state apparatus as constructed and understood by the CPK.[9] Here, the term *state apparatus*, broadly conceived, refers to the set of bureaucratic institutions through which power is exercised.[10]

A Materialist View of the Communist Party of Kampuchea

Marxist political philosophy understands the state as a material manifestation of a class rule. Karl Marx and Friedrich Engels forward the idea that the modern state is inseparable from capitalism. Thus, as a form of social organization, the state is a concrete manifestation of the ruling class, that is, the bourgeoisie. More broadly, the state for many Marxists is understood as something not imposed on society from the outside but instead a product internal to any given society at a certain stage of development.[11]

The bourgeoisie state, or capitalist state, in particular, is most directly addressed by Vladimir Lenin, notably in his 1917 essay *State and Revolution*, written on the eve of the Bolshevik Revolution.[12] Lenin argues that bureaucracies and standing armies are bourgeois parasites that feed on society and, accordingly, it is necessary for the proletariat to concentrate their forces on the destruction of state power. More precisely, the proletariat is to regard the problem of the state "not as one of perfecting the state machine, but one of *smashing and destroying it.*"[13] As justification, Lenin calls attention to the *Communist Manifesto*, in which Marx and Engels declare: "The proletariat will use its political supremacy to wrest, by degrees, all capital from the bourgeoisie, to centralize all instruments of production in the hands of the state, i.e., of the proletariat organized as the ruling class, and to increase the total productive forces as rapidly as possible."[14]

"If the state is the product of irreconcilable class antagonisms," Lenin continues, "if it is a power standing above society . . . it is clear that the liberation of the oppressed class is impossible, not only without violent revolution, but also without the destruction of the apparatus of state power which was created by the ruling class."[15] It is my contention that the Communist Party of Kampuchea took to heart the sentiments expressed by Lenin; it is necessary therefore to understand the "state" of Democratic Kampuchea not according to conventional terms but rather in Leninist terms.

For Marx, all previous revolutions failed largely because the existing state was appropriated by revolutionaries as opposed to being dismantled. Lenin extends this argument, declaring that "all the revolutions which have occurred up to now have helped to perfect the state machine, whereas it must be smashed, broken."[16] The dialectic transformation of society entails, on the one hand, the complete annihilation of the previous regime and, on the other hand, the establishment of a transitional form of government that, over time, would wither away, resulting in a classless, communal society free of exploitation, oppression, and alienation. The immediate objective of the socialist revolution in Cambodia, therefore, was the material obliteration—the smashing—of the current state. This is made clear in a Khmer Rouge document from 1975: "The immediate goal of the party is to lead the people to succeed in the national democratic revolution, to exterminate the imperialists, feudalists, and capitalists, and to form a national revolutionary state in Cambodia." The document elaborates that "The long range goal of the party is to lead the people in creating a socialist revolution and a communist society in Cambodia."[17]

Key members of the CPK viewed themselves as comprising a vanguard of the proletariat and we must reinterpret the establishment of Democratic Kampuchea as a transitional state in this context. Lenin argues that a vanguard organization "must of necessity be not too extensive and as secret as possible."[18] He elaborates that "A small, compact core, consisting of reliable, experienced and hardened workers, with responsible agents in the principal districts and connected by all the rules of strict secrecy with the organizations of revolutionaries, can, with the wide support of the masses and without an elaborate organization, perform all the functions. . . ."[19] To this end, when Pol Pot and a handful of cadre met in 1960 to replace the KPRP, they in effect formed a dictatorship of the proletariat. Referred to as Angkar, this core group would greatly determine the future state of Democratic Kampuchea.[20] This is well illustrated in numerous minutes of the CPK's meetings. On March 30, 1976, for example, high-ranking officials of the CPK issued a series of directives related to the establishment of state organizations. It was noted that the goal of the revolution was to seize state power and to place it in the hands of the worker-peasants; and that all forms of oppressive state power, presumably of the former regime, were to be eliminated. It was necessary from their vantage point that the CPK establish its own organizations that would reflect the character of the revolution. Disturbingly, the document announced that "The Government: Must be totally an organization of the Party."[21]

Within months of securing military control over Cambodia, the CPK set out to establish Democratic Kampuchea as a transitional state, a mode of social organization that, in principle, would provide a path toward Communism. According to Statutes adopted in January 1976, the Communist Party of Kampuchea held Marxism-Leninism as the foundation of its views and as the compass for all its activities.[22] Consequently, Democratic Kampuchea was to be governed according to the "concrete situation of Kampuchea" and, subsequently, "along the principles and stances of dialectical

33

materialism and historical materialism."[23] This is a remarkable statement that must guide our theorization of the concrete form and function of governance intended by members of the CPK.

A historical materialist approach begins "with real individuals, their activity and the material conditions of their life."[24] At a most basic level, this translates into the obtainment of food, water, shelter, and clothing, which constitute the basic conditions for a living existence. It is noteworthy, therefore, that the first objective identified in the CPK's Four-Year Plan was to "serve the people's livelihood, and to raise the people's standard of living quickly, both in terms of supplies and in terms of other material goods."[25]

Any given society will have its own way of satisfying (producing) these material needs, for example, through self-production, trade, barter, exchange, or even theft. From this, everything else follows, for, as Marx and Engels explain, "By producing their means of subsistence men are indirectly producing their material life."[26] To this end, both Marx and Engels forwarded the proposition that cultural practices and social institutions emanate from satisfaction of the basic necessities of life. Religion, marriage, law itself: these do not precede survivability nor do they emerge apart from the attainment of the conditions of life itself. As Marx explains, "Neither legal relations nor political forms could be comprehended whether by themselves or on the basis of a so-called general development of the human mind." Instead, "they originate in the material conditions of life."[27] This is not to suggest that production determines all facets of social reality. For Marx, determinism is neither teleological inevitability nor a variant of fatalism. Production was determinant only in so far as to say that groups of people (societies) will establish particular institutions and productive relations that are reflective initially of the immediate conditions of existence.

Throughout his writings Marx employs the concept *mode of production*. His clearest exposition of this contested term appears in his *Contribution to the Critique of Political Economy*:

> In the social production of their existence, men inevitably enter into definite relations, which are independent of their

will, namely relations of production appropriate to a given stage in the development of their material forces of production. The totality of these relations of production constitutes the economic structure of society, the real foundation, on which arises a legal and political superstructure and to which correspond definite forms of social consciousness. The mode of production of material life conditions the general process of social, political and intellectual life.[28]

As this passage indicates, the mode of production, on the one hand, is composed of two inner-related components: the relations of production and the forces of production. Combined, these constitute the base or mode of production of society. The superstructure of society, conversely, is composed of those institutions, relations, and practices that make possible the functioning of the base. These include, but are not limited to, political institutions, legal systems, education, and religion. Following Marx, these are not epiphenomena of the base but instead are dialectically related—hence the conception of dialectic materialism.

The relations between any given mode of production and its superstructure have often been oversimplified, both by Marx's admirers and his detractors, into a fixed, deterministic hierarchy. Such a myopic, reductionist interpretation not only does a disservice to Marx's own complex understanding of social relations but also clouds our subsequent understanding of observable political-economic structures. To argue that the superstructure emanates from the base is not to unduly privilege the latter over the former. It does not follow that emanation equates with domination. For Marx, it was essential to consider how the pieces fit together, for example, how productive apparatuses interact with legal systems and how educational systems relate to, and are influenced by, political institutions. He does, unquestionably, afford primacy to economic functions, but only insofar as without the necessary obtainment of food, water, and shelter, all else fades in significance. A society that is unable to feed itself cannot survive. Is it possible, for example, to have law or education without an underlying mode of production?

Marx would argue no, because the mode of production accounts for the processes by which the materiality of day-to-day life is experienced. Does law or education influence how the materiality of social reproduction takes place? Yes, and this brings home the point that the relation between the base and superstructure is dialectic and not mono-causal, that is, the base does not determine the superstructure in a vulgar cause-and-effect manner. For Marx, the basis and superstructure comprise a totality whereby economic, political, legal, and social relations are coconstitutive.

Academically, we may quibble with Marx's interpretation of societal functions and his so-called privileging of productive forces. However, any scholarly evaluation of Democratic Kampuchea must acknowledge that members of the CPK followed Marx in his assessment. Documentary evidence reveals that the CPK approached governance from the standpoint of, first and foremost, securing people's livelihoods. This was to be accomplished, in principle, through a concrete analysis of the basic conditions of survivability throughout the country. That the material conditions conducive to life were not wholly provided must not detract us from the materialist articulations of Khmer Rouge planning. Only through the lens of historical and dialectic materialism is it possible to lay bare the parameters of CPK bureaucracy.

State Functions of the Khmer Rouge Bureaucracy

Following Gordon Clark and Michael Dear, a proper analysis of bureaucracies requires an understanding of state functions, which, in turn, must be derived from an analysis of state form. Form, in this context, refers to how the specific state structure is constituted by, and evolves within, a given social formation. State functions refer to those activities undertaken in the name of the state.[29] Helpful in this regard is Charles Perrow's distinction between "official" and "operative" goals.[30] Official goals are those ideas put forth in public statements by representatives of the state, such as presidents, prime ministers, or secretary-generals. It is common that official goals as exemplified by public pronouncements are "purposely vague and general." These statements, moreover, "do not indicate two major factors which influence organizational behavior: the host of decisions that must be made among alternative ways of achieving official goals and the priority of multiple goals, and the many unofficial goals pursued by groups within the organization."[31] Operative goals, conversely, refer to "the ends sought through the actual operating policies of the organization; they tell us what the organization actually is trying to do, regardless of what the official goals say are the aims."[32]

Throughout Democratic Kampuchea an assortment of goals was forwarded, for example, in public statements, speeches, and radio broadcasts. These include references to building socialism or to launching offensives against nature in an effort to increase rice production. Frequently, such official statements were deceptively simple and laden with hyperbole. Meeting minutes, internal telegrams, and messages delivered by courier, on the other hand, more readily indicate the various options considered by senior leaders. These operative documents, unlike official statements, press releases, and public statements, better provide critical insight into the decision-making processes that took place.

All archival records are incomplete. In recognition of this, Jason Dittmer writes of the "occlusion of documents," that is, archives and historical records are always partial.[33] On the one hand, not all materials survive or are collected while, on the other hand, those materials that are archived are likewise incomplete in their recordings. Many Khmer Rouge documents, for example, provide summaries of discussions as opposed to detailed accounts of what was deliberated. Likewise, it is not always possible to parse out the competing positions adopted by participants. We know, by way of illustration, that on May 3, 1976, Pol Pot, Nuon Chea, Ieng Sary, Penh Thuok, and Khieu Samphan met to discuss foreign affairs, and that Phouk recorded the minutes.[34] We do not know who, if anyone, was absent from the meeting. We know also from the minutes that Ieng Sary prepared a report on an upcoming conference scheduled to take place in Colombo, Sri Lanka. We know that three decisions were made, but it remains unclear if there was any disagreement and, if so, by whom. It also remains unclear how these decisions were derived, or if alternatives were considered.

Beyond these limitations, there is much that remains undocumented. As anyone who has ever worked in a bureaucracy knows, many decisions are made informally—the proverbial hallway or water-cooler conversation. Barring the appearance of these conversations in memoirs, diaries, or related documents, it is simply not possible at this point to provide a complete understanding of the operative goals forwarded by the CPK. The herculean efforts of the staff at the Documentation Center of Cambodia have provided a solid foundation, and my evaluation and interpretation of the Khmer Rouge bureaucracy is indebted to their efforts.

With these caveats in mind, it is possible to provide a broad description of the CPK's bureaucratic structure. Throughout this chapter I employ a modified taxonomy of the state apparatus as developed by Clark and Dear.[35] My intent in adopting this approach is not to unambiguously pigeonhole the myriad ministries, committees, and other political entities established by the CPK into definitive categories. Nor is my purpose to suggest a form of institutional organization of the CPK's practice where none existed. Rather, my approach aims to accentuate, as Andrew Mertha writes, that Democratic Kampuchea "was a state defined by a distinctive network of organizations and institutions, not the absence of them."[36]

The Executive Apparatus

As a dictatorship of the proletariat, the CPK did not attempt to establish a state as this political term is commonly understood.[37] Rather, the leadership of the CPK, on paper, adopted a representative form of governance termed *democratic centralism*. Not found in the writings of Marx or Engels, democratic centralism was first introduced as the organizing principle of both the Bolshevik and Menshevik factions of the Russian Revolution and subsequently elaborated on by Lenin. As a form of political organization, democratic centralism holds that postrevolutionary societies would be governed not by members of the (deposed) ruling class but democratically by the workers themselves. Under socialism, according to Lenin, the functions of state administration become simplified to the point of irrelevance. Accordingly, a separate managerial class was thought to be unnecessary, for the workers themselves would be able to govern. This form of representative democratic politics would extend into other spheres of society, including that of production, whereby workers would assume the decision-making role of bureaucrats regarding production and distribution.

Publicly, the CPK's adherence to democratic centralism was announced in the aforementioned speech by Pol Pot in September 1977. Pol Pot declared, "the implementation of the Party's dictatorship of the proletariat in all areas of our revolutionary activity. We promote broad democracy among the people by a correct application of democratic centralism, so that this immense force will mobilize enthusiastically and rapidly for socialist revolution and construction, at great leaps and bounds forward."[38]

Democratic centralism was also embedded in the Constitution of Democratic Kampuchea, promulgated on January 5, 1976. According to Article 1, "The State of Kampuchea is the State of the workers, peasants and other laborers of Kampuchea."[39] Here, we must not lose sight that the "State" referred to in this article must be understood as a state in the Leninist sense, that is, a communal organization of men and women. This understanding necessarily informs Article 2 of the Constitution: "All important means of production are the collective property of the people's State and the collective property of the communally organized people."[40] In other words, and consistent with the broad coordinates of democratic centralism, economic productivity was to be organized by the workers themselves. That this did not occur should not detract us from understanding, at a theoretical level, how key members of the CPK approached the question of governance.

Governance in practice was centralized among a few important individuals who comprised the Standing Committee. Dominated by Pol Pot, Nuon Chea, Son Sen, and Ieng Sary, the Standing Committee was the true locus of sovereign power and literally held the power of life and death. Membership of the committee fluctuated, in large part because of internal purges initiated by Pol Pot toward other members suspected of traitorous activities. As of April 1975, the Standing Committee included Pol Pot (secretary-general), Nuon Chea (deputy secretary-general and vice-chair of the Military Commission), Ieng Sary (deputy prime minister of foreign affairs, So Phim, (secretary, East Zone), Vorn Vet (deputy prime minister for the economy), Ros Nhim (secretary, Northwest Zone), Ta Mok (secretary, Southwest Zone), and Son Sen (deputy prime minister for defense).

The Standing Committee was a subset of a larger body designated as the Central Committee.[41] By Statute, the Central Committee was the highest decision-making body in Democratic Kampuchea. Likewise, as a more broadly representative body, the Central Committee was theoretically given responsibility to "implement the Party political line and Statute throughout the Party," as well as to "Govern and arrange cadres and Party members throughout the entire Party."[42] In practice, the Central Committee remained subservient to the dictates of the Standing Committee.

The Standing Committee was supported by several governmental bureaucracies essential for the day-to-day operations of Democratic Kampuchea. These included both the Political Office 870 and Office S-71 (this latter entity was known also as Ministry S-71 or simply the Government Office). Political Office 870 was tasked with matters of policy, including the coordination of communication between the Party Center and the various territorial committees (discussed below). S-71, conversely, was responsible for a variety of administrative and logistical functions and included a wide array of suboffices, all code-named with the prefix *K*.[43] K-1 for example, designated a housing compound that contained, for at least part of the time, the residence and workplace of Pol Pot; other key offices included K-3 (Khieu Samphan's residence), K-4 (logistics), K-7 (courier and communications), K-11 (medical affairs), and K-12 (motor pool).

The Standing Committee exercised near total control throughout Democratic Kampuchea through a particular territorial administrative function, itself greatly informed by democratic centralism. Following the coup of 1970, the Khmer Rouge began to build its rank and file through the establishment of a new Communist system throughout the countryside. Modeled after their Chinese and Vietnamese counterparts, small guerrilla units known as *korng chhlorb* were organized to both fight and recruit new members. These military units were under the command of a three-person committee consisting of a chief, deputy chief, and a member.[44]

Throughout the civil war, CPK armed forces were regionally based and largely autonomous.[45] Traditionally, Cambodia was administered following a territorial hierarchy. At the lowest level stood the *phoun* (hamlet) or *phum* (village). Collectively, *phoun* and *phum* would comprise a *khum* (commune), various *khum* would form a *srok* (district), and various *srok* would form a province. The CPK effectively continued the territorial division of Cambodia for administrative purposes, but made a number of modifications. First, the CPK adopted a military administrative unit known as *phumipeak*, or zone. Previously, a *phumipeak* that encompassed many provinces existed only in the military domain under the form of a military region. The CPK, however, elevated all civilian administration to the zone level.[46] These were referred to by cardinal directions, for example, Southwest or East Zone, although all zones were given numeric codes.[47] Second, each zone was to be composed of *damban*, or regions (also translated as sectors). These were largely based on former provinces, but there was no one-to-one correspondence. In fact, many regions of Democratic Kampuchea crossed the old administrative boundaries of Cambodia. Regions were designated by number, often (but not always) indicating a level of systemization. The Northwest Zone, for example, was composed of seven regions, numbered 1 through 7. The East Zone consisted of five regions numbered 20 through 24. Other regions, however, were less straightforward, reflecting in part the ongoing shuffling of regions between zones.[48] Administrative divisions below the zone

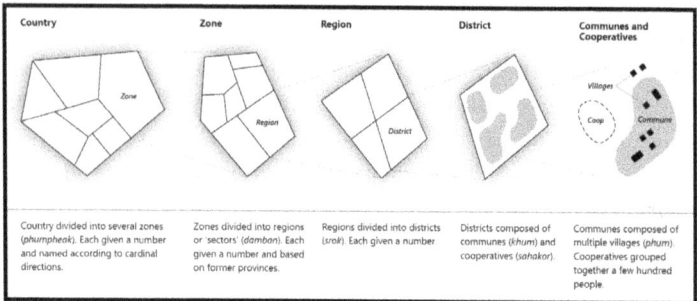

Figure 2.1: Territorial Organization of Democratic Kampuchea

and regional level conformed to prerevolutionary terminology. Each region was composed of several districts (*srok*), each district was composed of several communes (*khum*), and each commune was composed of numerous villages (*phum*). In the Northwest Zone, Region 5, located north of Battambang City, was divided into four districts, identified as Serey Sophoan, Preah Neth Preah, Phnom Srok, and Thma Puok. Each of these four districts was divided into a number of communes. Phnom Srok consisted of five communes while Thma Puok was composed of nine communes. In the district of Phnom Srok, Sreh Chik commune consisted of fifteen villages.

As of April 1975, the CPK divided Cambodia's nineteen provinces into five zones: the Northeast, North, Northwest, Southwest, and East. A special zone was also created to include the area around Phnom Penh. In the ensuing months and years, administrative divisions changed often, usually as a result of internal purges or power plays among CPK leaders. Toward the end of 1975, for example, the Southwest Zone was split into two, forming a new West Zone and a smaller Southwest Zone. The Phnom Penh special zone was also dissolved, thereafter categorized as a distinct territory not within the formal administrative structures. Later, two autonomous regions were formed: Region 106, consisting mostly of

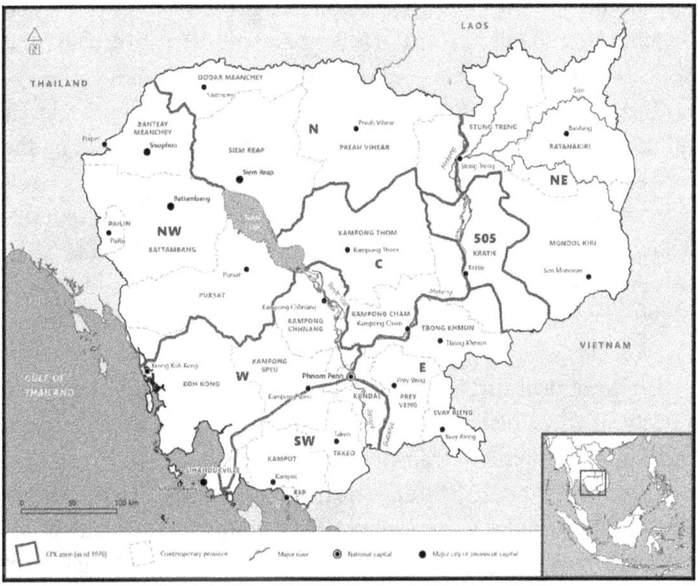

Figure 2.2: Former Provincial Boundaries and CPK Zone-Level Administrative Boundaries, ca. 1976

the former Siem Reap and Oddar Meanchey provinces, and Region 103, composed of the former Preah Vihear Province. The port facility at Kampong Som was also organized as a separate entity. And in late 1976 and early 1977 a seventh zone was created when Regions 103 and 106 were merged to form a new North Zone; the old North Zone was renamed the Central Zone.[49]

Each political division was administered by a three-person committee consisting of a secretary, deputy secretary, and member, responsible for politics, security, and economics, respectively. At the commune and village level, the two senior ranking committee members were usually identified as chief and deputy chief. The CPK's spatial organization of the country was pivotal for its administrative practices. The Zone Committee, for example, was responsible for overseeing the implementation of CPK plans and policies throughout its respective zone and for delegating plans and policies to all other levels (e.g., regions and districts) in its zone.

The committees at the region, district, and commune levels fulfilled similar functions of implementing tasks delegated by the higher levels. The degree of authority, especially among lower levels of governance, remains unclear. In general, "administrative levels below the zone were more akin to implementing bodies than decision-making ones."[50] However, evidence indicates that for some projects, such as the construction of small-scale canals and dikes, local chiefs had a certain degree of leeway.

Each political division from the commune level up included a variety of three-person committees responsible for specific tasks, including economics, transportation, finance, medical, mobile, military, social affairs, fishing, textile, and security. Here, Khmer Rouge terminology is important. The Economic Committee, for example, was responsible for the collection and warehousing of rice, while the Finance Committee was tasked with the distribution of all other agricultural products. Mobile Committees were responsible for the deployment of mobile work brigades to undertake specific projects, such as the construction of a canal, the clearance of forest, or the harvesting of fields. Moreover, not all zones, regions, districts, communes, or villages would include all ten committees. Communes that did not include sizable bodies of water would obviously not have Fishing Committees. In general, most divisions would have an Economic Unit, Transportation Unit, and Security Unit.

Existing apart from, but still administratively connected to, the hierarchical structure of zone, region, district, commune, and village were cooperatives, that is, ad hoc units born of administrative necessity and formed according to specific needs. If, for example, a major construction project was initiated at the zone level, such as the building of a reservoir, the relevant zone secretary would be responsible for assembling myriad cooperatives to undertake the task. Depending on the expected number of workers required, each region may be called upon to arrange for a specified quota of laborers; subsequently, each district would be required to provide a certain number of laborers. This recruitment system continued to the level of the commune, whereby groups of villagers would be assembled. Conversely, if a project was initiated at the district level, laborers would be recruited only from those communes (and hence, villages) of the district involved.

The Consensus Apparatus

The purpose of the consensus-seeking mechanism is to ensure that all social groups have access to the processes of the social contract; in general, consensus apparatuses would include those mechanisms addressing politics, law, and repression.[51] The political subapparatus, more specifically, would incorporate a myriad of parties, elections, and constitutions; the legal subapparatus would include courts, law firms, and legal statutes; and the repressive subapparatus would include various mechanisms of internal and external enforcement of power, such as the police and the military.[52] The repressive subapparatuses of Democratic Kampuchea will be discussed at length in Chapter 4; in this section I address only the first two.

Important for any form of governance are the conditions by which citizens may participate. Consequently, the consensus apparatus entails the mechanisms by which the public participates in governance. Most prominent throughout Democratic Kampuchea was the distinction between new (or after April 17) people and base people. The moniker *base people* refers to those who came under Khmer Rouge control during the civil war, that is, prior to April 17, 1975. In general, these people were considered more loyal and trustworthy. The category of new people, conversely, consists of those who either did not live in liberated areas prior to the date of victory or did not support the Khmer Rouge. Beyond this informal distinction, other, more legal qualifications were applied. According to Article 9 of the Constitution, "Every citizen of Kampuchea has the full right to enjoy material, moral and cultural life. . . . Every citizen of Kampuchea has all his means of existence fully secured."[53] These rights did not extend, however, to full and equal political participation, despite rhetoric that Democratic Kampuchea was a people's state. Indeed, Statutes adopted in 1976 outlined the ideology, membership, structure, and organization of the Party.[54] Article 1, for example, specifies that any man or woman, aged eighteen or older, could in principle join the CPK.[55] However, membership was conditional upon the fulfillment of two criteria. First, prospective members "Must have had good and constantly combative activities, tested in successive revolutionary work in the unions, in the cooperatives, and in the Revolutionary Army, following the Party political line, following the ideological stances of the Party, and following the organizational stances of the Party"; "Must be of good class pedigree, and in particular hold the worker class stance of the Party, which they have successfully strived to build while inside the revolutionary movement under the leadership of the Party"; "Must have[a] good and clean life morals and be good and clean politically, never having been involved with the enemy"; "Must examine, question, and take the measure of the opinions of the popular masses inside the framework that those selected into the Party must live or work in the cooperatives, unions, company-level units, or various other units"; and "Must have a clear personal history with a verified base of origin, place of residence, and work."[56] This last condition is especially noteworthy in that it directs attention to the second criteria, the process of becoming a member. To this point, the Statutes indicate that "Many levels of Party organization must collectively examine, deliberate, and decide before permission to join can be granted."[57] In general, this meant that members throughout the various hierarchies of administration were to decide on one's fulfillment of the first set of criteria; these decisions were based in large part on an evaluation of biographies that were gathered from all people throughout Democratic Kampuchea.

According to the Statutes, a preparatory period was necessary, during which evaluators would (again, in principle) determine whether any specific man or woman was eligible and acceptable for membership. Potential Party members were required to satisfy ten additional criteria for selection into various Party leadership positions. Article 5 clarifies that "To raise the quality of Party leadership and to guarantee its inherent strength and purity of Party politics, ideology, and organization, various criteria must be established as the factors for deliberation in selecting cadre into the various leadership committees of the Party."[58] These included (1) "Strong revolutionary stance on the Party political line"; (2) "Strong Party revolutionary stance on proletarian ideology"; (3) "Strong revolutionary stance on internal Party solidarity and unity"; (4) "Strong revolutionary stance on the lines of organization, leadership, and work of the Party"; (5) "Strong Party revolutionary stance on revolutionary vigilance, maintaining secrecy, and defending revolutionary forces"; (6) "Strong revolutionary Party stance of 'independence, mastery, self-reliance, and self-mastery'"; (7) "Strong revolutionary stance in making and examining personal histories and revolutionary life views"; (8) "Strong revolutionary stance on class"; (9) "Strong revolutionary stance on clean life morals, and politically clean"; and (10) "The capability to build oneself and be receptive to future leadership."[59] Each of these ten criteria contained detailed explanatory remarks as to fulfillment. For example, to demonstrate "Strong Party revolutionary stance of proletarian ideology," a cadre (1) "Must have a correct and strong proletarian class stance in every sector, material, right of power, and life morality"; (2) "Have a correct and strong stance of collective ownership in every sector, materials, right of power, and life morality, and live in a regime of collective organization"; (3) "Have a high and absolute stance of sacrifice of private ownership in every sector, material, right of power, and life morality"; (4) "Have an audacious stance of active combat and endurance of difficulties on all occasions in absolute class struggle in the national defense and national construction of Democratic Kampuchea in the direction of social revolution and building socialism"; and (5) "Must be vigilant regarding the stance of thick and materialistic personal and private ownership, rights of power, and life morality."[60]

The Statute clarifies also that individual members could not make decisions by themselves, but only in concert with other members—a key tenet of democratic centralism. Of particular significance is the designation of rights (Article 3) afforded to Party members. Full-rights status meant that members were permitted to "consider and discuss and join in decision making" on all Party affairs, unlike "candidate" members, who were allowed only to participate in meetings, without the right of decision-making.[61]

Constitutionally, Democratic Kampuchea was to be governed by the Assembly of the People's Representatives of Kampuchea. As specified in Article 5, this body was to be composed of 250 members representing workers, peasants, other laborers, and the Revolutionary Army of Kampuchea. Consequently, on March 20, 1976, elections were held to appoint men and women to this governing organ, and during the first and only congressional meeting of the PRA, held April 11–13, 1976, Khieu Samphan was appointed as chairman of the State Presidium, a position that, under the Constitution, was responsible for representing the State of Democratic Kampuchea, both foreign and domestically. Nuon Chea was to serve as chairman of the Standing Committee of the People's Representative Assembly.[62] Apart from the appointments of Khieu Samphan and Nuon Chea, these elections mattered little, as true political power remained vested in the Standing Committee of the CPK.

The Productive Apparatus

After years of armed conflict, the physical infrastructure of Cambodia was in ruins. Approximately one-third of the country's bridges were destroyed, two-fifths of the road network was unusable, and the railroad was inoperable. Much of the country's productive infrastructure, including its lone oil refinery near Kompong Som, had stopped working. Only 300 of 1,400 rice mills and 60 of 240 sawmills were functioning; and both timber and rubber production, Cambodia's major prewar commercial products other than rice, had declined to only one-fifth of prewar production levels. Moreover, upward of half of Cambodia's livestock had been killed, either through fighting, bombing, or as a food source for the starving people.[63] While not absolving the CPK of responsibility for the brutal conditions that would characterize Democratic Kampuchea, it is necessary to reposition CPK policy and practice within the realities of a postwar environment.

The CPK premised that economic success and, by extension, political success, depended on its agricultural sector.[64] As explained in its Four-Year Plan, developed between July 21 and August 2, 1976, the CPK identified two economic objectives. The first, as we have seen, was "to serve the people's livelihood, and to raise the people's standard of living quickly, both in terms of supplies and in terms of other material goods."[65] This was to be accomplished through the satisfaction of a second objective, namely, to "seek, gather, save, and increase capital from agriculture, aiming to rapidly expand our agriculture, our industry, and our defense."[66] Therefore, to achieve industrial self-sufficiency, including both light and heavy industry, the CPK decreed that they would "only have to earn [foreign] capital from agriculture."[67]

Overall, Democratic Kampuchea's economy was structured around a policy of import-substitution industrialization (ISI), a strategy widely employed by member states of the Non-Aligned Movement.[68] Much has been made of the CPK's rhetoric of self-reliance and self-mastery. For some scholars, this is evidence of a deeply entrenched policy of isolationism. Karl Jackson, for example, explains that "the Khmer revolutionaries were trying to establish total sovereignty and self-reliance in the cultural, economic, and political realms," and that their "application of the doctrine of self-reliance led the revolutionaries to seal Cambodia off from all but a very few close allies."[69] Charles Twining likewise explains that the leaders of Democratic Kampuchea "wanted genuinely to create a country totally independent from every point of view. To achieve this state, Cambodia must be self-contained and self-reliant to the point of autarky."[70] These assessments, however, are grossly inaccurate and only deflect attention from the geopolitical context within which Democratic Kampuchea was organized.

In the aftermath of the Second World War, representatives of many former colonies sought to forge an independent path, free from the Cold War dictates of either American capitalism or Soviet socialism.[71] Known as the Non-Aligned Movement, this movement became a powerful political force that proclaimed a commitment to nationalism, the preservation of national dignity, and the realization of national power.[72] Moreover, the Non-Aligned Movement connoted an alliance with the forces of regionalism, national independence, the struggle for a new economic order, social and economic progress, and self-reliance.[73] The CPK's adherence to the Non-Aligned Movement is codified in numerous speeches and documents, including the 1976 Constitution of Democratic Kampuchea.

In August 1976 representatives of the CPK, including Khieu Samphan, attended the 5th Summit Conference of Non-Aligned Countries, held in Colombo, Sri Lanka. A report subsequently published by the Embassy of Democratic Kampuchea in Berlin, East Germany,[74] expounded that:

> The people of Kampuchea warmly hails the victories of the 5th Summit Conference of Non-Aligned Countries which consolidate the non-aligned principles, enhance the non-aligned movement and strengthen the solidarity within its ranks. . . . In contributing to the revolutionary struggle of the peoples of the world, to the liberation struggle of the brotherly countries of the Third World and to the strengthening of the cause of the great non-aligned family, the people of Kampuchea is determined to carry out the revolution successfully in its own country, to build up its economy and edify its country according to the principles of independence, sovereignty and self-reliance.[75]

Two months later, Ieng Sary, deputy prime minister of foreign affairs, spoke before the 31st Session of the United Nations General Assembly in New York. Following an opening statement, Ieng Sary explained that

> The 31st Regular Session of our General Assembly takes place at a time when all the peoples of the world and especially the peoples of the non-aligned countries and of the Third World

are waging a victorious struggle everywhere against imperialism, colonialism, neo-colonialism, Zionism and all forms of foreign interference, aggression, expansionism and exploitation, for independence, sovereignty, territorial integrity, for the right to determine their own destiny and for the establishment of a new international economic order on the basis of justice and equality.[76]

He continued that:

Dozens of new independent states are arising from the ruins of colonialism, determined to engage in the struggle to defend and consolidate their political and economic independence, their sovereignty and territorial integrity against all acts of domination, exploitation, interference and aggression on the part of the rich great powers. . . . They call forcefully for the establishment of new relations between the peoples and nations, in accordance with the significant changes which have taken place in the world, and based on the principles of mutual respect of independence, sovereignty and territorial integrity, equality, mutual advantage, non-interference in the internal affairs of other states and the right of every people to manage its own affairs.[77]

Democratic Kampuchea, Ieng Sary explained, stood by these principles. Moreover, the people of Kampuchea had participated actively in the struggle against colonialism and foreign aggression. "Together with all the other peoples," he declared, Democratic Kampuchea "has actively taken part in the common struggle against imperialism, colonialism and neo-colonialism in order to liberate itself from all forms of domination, oppression and exploitation."

Ieng Sary's official statements reflect an attitude not of isolationism but of an attempt to establish Democratic Kampuchea as an independent, sovereign state that would interact on the global stage on conditions of its own choosing. Seen in this light, the repeated phrases of self-reliance and self-mastery peppered throughout hundreds of CPK operational documents take on a vastly different meaning than that proposed by Jackson, Twining, and others. CPK officials were not opposed to cultivating foreign relations, as documentary evidence clearly shows. Indeed, throughout 1975 and 1976, key CPK officials were anxious to extend relations, especially with (but not limited to) those governments associated with the Non-Aligned Movement.

Proponents of ISI argued that less-developed countries should initially domestically produce previously imported, simple consumer goods and then domestically produce a wider range of more sophisticated manufactured items.[78] In other words, advocates of ISI promoted an economic strategy predicated on self-sufficiency. Variously understood within broader theories of dependency or underdevelopment, the argument follows: for decades, if not centuries, the economies of colonies were held in check by unfair trade arrangements and production processes that consigned the colonies to subservience within the global economy. Colonies and former colonies historically were forced to import most of their manufactured goods in return for the export of primary products, such as sugar, bananas, coffee, tea, and cotton. Under ISI, these unequal relations were to be inverted. Governments of former colonies would protect their domestic industries and, by extension, encourage the production of domestic consumer goods. Revenue saved from not having to import these goods could then be used to purchase other manufactured commodities that could not be domestically produced given the country's overall level of industrialization.

A CPK document from May 8, 1976, for example, specified that "We will decrease importing items next year, including cotton and jute, because we are working hard to produce ours. We will import only some important items such as chemical fertilizer, plastic, acid, . . . and other raw materials."[79] According to this document, such a strategy was deemed most appropriate. Indeed, to solve the currency problem, it was determined that solutions were not to be found "by taking loans from the West or Eastern Europe," for in so doing the CPK would lose their "self-reliant stance."[80]

Having adopted a policy of import substitution, the CPK concentrated on items that could be effectively produced, both for domestic consumption and foreign trade. On the home front, plans called for the production of items necessary to facilitate the people's livelihood: plates, pots, spoons, mosquito nets, shovels, hoes, and so on. In practice, most of these industries never materialized, although textile factories and some machine shops were in operation. Archived documents indicate also that the CPK was receptive to any number of imported goods, but that a combination of economic and political considerations would determine the conditions of foreign trade.

As specified in Party documents, CPK officials premised Democratic Kampuchea as replete with "such things as land, livestock, natural resources, water sources such as lakes, rivers and ponds," and that these "natural characteristics have given [Democratic Kampuchea] great advantages compared with China, Vietnam, or Africa."[81] However, the Khmer Rouge leadership determined that agriculture, primarily rice, was to be the country's comparative advantage. During a speech delivered in June 1976 at an assembly of cadres of the Western Zone, the speaker (most likely Pol Pot) discussed the importance of rapid agricultural development. The speaker explains, "National construction proceeds along the lines laid down by the Party. The important point of this is building up our agriculture, which is backward, into modern agriculture within ten to fifteen years."[82] Consequently, as detailed in the Four-Year Plan, "We stand on agriculture as the basis, so as to collect agricultural capital with which to strengthen and expand industry." This was no desire to construct an agrarian utopia, but instead a pragmatic course of action based on capitalist principles. Indeed, it was simply a continuation of policies advocated by the former French colonial government and that of Sihanouk. From a competitive standpoint, rice was the clear choice. And while other agricultural products were identified, including rubber, corn, beans, fish, and forest products, these were largely gratis. The CPK argument was profit-based: "For 100,000 tons of milled rice, we would get [U.S.] $20 million; if we had 500,000 tons we'd get $100 million. . . . We must increase rice production in order to obtain capital. Other products, which are only complimentary[,] will be increased in the future."[83]

Policy decisions were based on calculations of expected economic productivity. Foremost was the proposed increase in rice production, an objective that was pivotal to the CPK's overall strategy of state-building. This is vividly illustrated in a series of remarks prepared and delivered by Pol Pot at a special meeting of the CPK center, held August 21–23, 1976. Here, Pol Pot considers the production of rice as it relates to Democratic Kampuchea's physical geography. He explains:

> We have greater resources than other countries in terms of rice fields. Furthermore, the strength of our rice fields is that we have more of them than others do. The strength of our agriculture is greater than that of other countries in this respect. . . . It is the Party's wish to transform agriculture from a backward type to a modern type in ten to fifteen years. A long-term strategy must be worked out. We are working (here) on a Four-Year Plan in order to set off in the direction of achieving this 10–15 year target.[84]

It was determined by the CPK that Democratic Kampuchea would need to triple rice productivity to a national average yield of three tons per hectare per year. Only by obtaining such a surplus could the CPK raise sufficient revenues to import necessary goods and commodities, notably ammunition. The strategy for increased rice production was predicated on the introduction of more rational and efficient agricultural techniques. Thus, the CPK classified rice fields into two categories: those harvested once a year and those harvested twice. Calculations provided by the CPK indicate that in 1977 there would be an anticipated 2.4 million hectares of land suitable for rice production; of these, 1.4 million hectares could sustain a single harvest per year; the remaining would be conducive to two harvests. Over the next four years, according to Pol Pot, the land devoted to single harvests would remain constant, while the amount of double-cropped lands would progressively increase from

200,000 hectares in 1977 to 500,000 in 1980. However, it was determined that all new agricultural lands would generate two harvests per year.[85]

For the CPK, an overriding difficulty associated with increased rice production and, by extension, the economic development and defense of Democratic Kampuchea, was that of water. According to the Four-Year Plan, it was necessary to "increase the degree of mastery over the water problem from one year to another until it reaches 100 percent by 1980 for first-class rice land and reaches 40–50% for ordinary rice land."[86] Following a table of calculations indicating the annual percentage increase projected between 1977 and 1980, the text continues: "In order to gain mastery over water there must be a network of dikes and canals as the basis. There must also be canals, reservoirs, and irrigation pumps stationed in accordance with our strategy."[87] The rapid and massive development of irrigation was thus paramount, necessitating the completion of thousands of dikes, dams, canals, and reservoirs throughout the country. This necessitated in turn the constant resettlement of men and women through forced movements to satisfy ever-changing labor needs.[88] In time, railroads would emerge as the principle means of resettling populations from areas of labor surplus to areas of labor shortage.[89]

To achieve these operational objectives, on October 9, 1975, the Standing Committee began delegating key members to specific tasks. Koy Thuon was appointed to oversee domestic and international commerce, and Vorn Vet was responsible for industry, railroads, and fisheries.[90] On the surface, these committees seem arbitrary and perhaps devoid of internal logic. Indeed, Boraden Nhem concludes that Democratic Kampuchea comprised an "empty government," noting that the CPK established ministries for specific and ad hoc tasks.[91] This is partially accurate, but carries an important caveat. Closer inspection begins to shine light on the consonance between CPK operational objectives and the resultant bureaucratic structure. These ministries, while seemingly disparate, did align with an overall economic strategy predicated on the production and distribution of rice that would, in principle, facilitate the overall industrialization of Democratic Kampuchea. To achieve this goal required the management of a host of related activities, including the expansion of irrigation to provide water for agriculture, improvements in transportation to facilitate the movement of labor and commodities, and financial institutions to assist in the international exchange of commodities. Thus, through the course of CPK rule, countless committees and ministries would form and reform in response to changing political-economic conditions but also to the ongoing purges that decimated the bureaucracy.[92]

Five bureaucracies comprised the core production apparatus. These included three ministries—the Ministry of Commerce, Ministry of Industry, and Ministry of Public Works—and two separate, but related, institutions: the State Warehouse and the Transportation Committee. The Ministry of Commerce, referred to as K-51 and initially headed by Koy Thuon, was responsible for the coordination of economic production and trade. Operationally, K-51 was divided into two sections, domestic and foreign. On the domestic side, the Ministry of Commerce was charged with the oversight of various production facilities, while on the foreign side, it was tasked with handling foreign banking matters. To accomplish these tasks, a number of subunits were established, including BOTRA and FORTRA, devoted to foreign trade; IMEX, to coordinate foreign exchange; the Ren Fung Corporation, responsible for a variety of financial arrangements, especially as these related to China; and the Poipet Gate, in charge of governing trade with Thailand.[93]

The Ministry of Industry, headed by Vorn Vet, was responsible for a variety of economic functions that spanned industry, agriculture, electricity, public works, and railroads. Paramount was the oversight of countless factories, Logistical Units, and Technical Units that operated throughout Democratic Kampuchea. Within Phnom Penh there were at least two dozen factories, although some estimates place this figure as high as seventy.[94] These factories produced everything from thread to plastics, soap to soy sauce; however, the precise industries to be developed were to align with the overall operational objectives of facilitating agricul-tural and industry within a context of import substitution. The factory code-named A-1, for example, produced thread; wooden bobbins were manufactured by at least six lathe factories; and these semifinished goods were combined at the various textile and clothing factories.[95]

The spatial distribution of production facilities indicates considerable continuity with economic activities in existence during the previous regime. Elsewhere colleagues and I refer to the socio-spatial organization of production along two factors: conversion and continuity. On the one hand, it was CPK practice to convert preexisting structures for new uses. For example, the Khmer Rouge frequently converted *wats* (temples) into warehouses and granaries. On the other hand, the CPK retained preexisting uses—a practice of continuity. Many pre-1975 warehouses, for example, continued to be used as warehouses; sawmills continued to function as sawmills; and textile factories continued to produce textiles. By way of illustration, Khmer Rouge garment factories located in Phnom Penh were concentrated in the areas of Chak Angre, Tuol Kok, Stung Mean Chey, and the O'Russei Market. Historically, these locations were the sites of various textile factories and they remain so today.[96]

To facilitate the distribution of goods both within and beyond Democratic Kampuchea, it was necessary to repair and, if possible, expand the country's physical infrastructure. To a large extent this fell under the jurisdiction of the Ministry of Public Works (S-8), headed first by Tauch Pheuan. Early on, this ministry employed upward of three thousand workers—testimony to its importance. Key operations included bridge construction, dam building, roads, transport, and water. An exceptionally nebulous bureaucracy, the Ministry of Public Works apparently aligned with the Energy Committee (under the supervision of Vorn Vet) to coordinate three power plants and an oil refinery.[97] After several purges, however, the Ministry of Public Works, like many other bureaucracies within Democratic Kampuchea, effectively ceased to function. Craig Etcheson finds that the equipment needed to build, maintain, and repair infrastructure, such as power stations and the electrical power grid, did not exist within Democratic Kampuchea, thus making it difficult to carry out many projects. Moreover, without the ability to adequately maintain those systems that were in operation, it was inevitable that more and more problems would arise. For example, the electrical system steadily deteriorated, leading CPK's senior leaders to accuse the Public Works employees of sabotage.[98]

All commodities produced or repaired in the many factories throughout Democratic Kampuchea, as well as goods imported into the country, or scheduled to be exported, required warehousing at some point. Most warehouses were located near major transportation arteries (e.g., riverfronts, railroad stations, and highways). Especially important was an area known as Kilometer 6, located at the intersection of a major rail line and the riverfront along National Highway 5, just outside Phnom Penh. A sprawling complex of steel and cement warehouses, Kilometer 6 warehoused any number of goods, including textiles, rubber, and cement. Other warehouses were of a more specific nature. Surrounding any given hospital, for example, were various warehouses used to store both raw materials used in pharmaceutical factories as well as medicines and medical equipment imported from China and other countries.[99]

The State Warehouse, located in Phnom Penh, was responsible for the overall distribution of commodities. Supervised by Ta Reoung, the State Warehouse contained several subunits, each accountable for particular tasks or commodities. Andre Mertha details that the distribution of goods between and within administrative zones followed specific procedures. He writes, "For everyday goods and commodities, amounts were calculated based on the number of people in a zone. Zone commanders would send their requests for non-regular items directly to 870, which would consider the request and then issue a letter to the State Warehouse, which would coordinate with the zone 'commerce' office in Phnom Penh and the central transportation unit."[100] These procedures highlight a final component of the broader production apparatus of Democratic Kampuchea, namely, transportation.

Throughout late 1975 and 1976, transportation-related issues were apparently conducted on an ad hoc basis. It was not until 1977, according to Mertha, that a Transportation Committee was formally established, itself subdivided into river, land, and rail sections. The Water Transportation Unit, for example, oversaw ship-assembly factories, a fuel-transportation section, a printing house, a Marine Transportation Unit, and a ship-piloting company; the land transportation section was tasked with the repair and expansion of roads; and the railroad branch was responsible for rebuilding and expanding the country's railroad network. This latter unit was assisted greatly by Chinese engineers; over time, they would complain about the difficulties of accomplishing any project, given the lack of personnel following repeated purges in the Transportation Committee.[101]

The Integrative Apparatus

In an ideal setting, the integrative apparatus includes (but is not limited to) those functions related to health and education.[102] Accordingly, specific bureaucracies oversee the establishment of hospitals and schools, the provision of medicines and textbooks, and the staffing of doctors, nurses, and teachers. Also included are media-related bureaucracies, including newspapers, television studios, and radio stations. These latter institutions may, in theory, be either public or state-run. In authoritarian states such as Democratic Kampuchea, there is no difference.

For some readers, it may seem incongruous that specific bureaucracies charged with education and health existed in Democratic Kampuchea. It is commonplace, for example, to describe the Khmer Rouge as anti-intellectual and antiprofessional and to believe that anyone who was literate or trained in Western forms of education was summarily executed. In actuality, the CPK forwarded an integrative apparatus that conformed to their Leninist understanding of a socialist state. This does not lessen the brutality evinced by the Khmer Rouge, for many professionals were murdered. Rather, this accentuates the pragmatism forwarded by the CPK in their attempt to reintroduce schools, hospitals, and pharmacies.[103]

Education, even for revolutionary parties, is vital in that it provides support and legitimacy for associated political and economic programs. That the Standing Committee of the CPK understood this necessity is evident in the Party's Four-Year Plan. However, the Standing Committee was equally clear that it would not simply resume the preexisting structure but instead transform education in conformance with Party dictates. "Continue the struggle," it is reported in the Four-Year Plan, "to abolish, uproot, and disperse the cultural, literary, and artistic remnants of the imperialists, colonialists, and all of the other oppressor classes. . . . Continue to strengthen and expand the building of revolutionary culture, literature and art of the worker-peasant class in accordance with the Party's proletarian standpoint."[104]

Prior to the CPK's rise to power, Cambodia was home to 5,276 primary schools, 146 secondary schools, and 9 institutes of higher education.[105] However, Prince Sihanouk perceived education as an important step to break the chains of neocolonial dependency and, accordingly, promoted professional and technical skills.[106] Under the CPK, this infrastructure was violently demolished. According to Thomas Clayton, the Khmer Rouge destroyed 90 percent of all school buildings, emptied libraries, burned their contents, and destroyed nearly all school laboratory equipment.[107] Those buildings left standing were often converted into other uses, such as warehouses or security centers. Apart from destroying much of the physical infrastructure, teachers were also targeted for elimination. It is estimated that upward of 90 percent of all teachers at all levels died throughout the CPK regime. As one example, of the one thousand academics employed at the Royal University of Phnom Penh prior to 1975, only eighty-seven are known to have survived.[108]

From 1976 onward, the CPK planned but never completely implemented a sweeping overhaul of the country's educational system. As detailed in the Four-Year Plan, the CPK proposed curricula that would provide a system of learning that would nurture culture, political awareness, and socialist consciousness. Three years of primary education were to be offered, followed by three years of secondary education composed of general and technical subjects, and three years of tertiary education. Details for primary education are conspicuously vague, apart from the intonation to "give attention to abolishing illiteracy among the population." At the secondary level, however, subjects were to include reading and writing, arithmetic, geography, natural sciences (e.g., physics and chemistry), the history of the revolutionary struggle, and the Party's politics, consciousness, and organization. There were to be no examinations and no certificates; the system of education proposed by the CPK was to be concrete rather than abstract, learned through participation within the cooperatives, factories, and military units. Educational methods accordingly were to include equal time spent on academic study and material production, for example, agricultural-related activities.[109]

There was no overarching system in place to train teachers. Nor was access to education guaranteed for the children of Democratic Kampuchea. Rather, teachers were recruited among the most loyal Party members; most, in fact, had either very little or no training. And for those students who did participate in education activities— that is, when they were not tending cattle or collecting manure—lessons were held in improvised classrooms, in stables, or in the fields. Educational materials were largely nonexistent, with lessons consisting mostly of rote memorization of war-related songs and slogans.[110]

The CPK leadership professed a concern with the overall health and well-being of its citizenry. Throughout 1975 and 1976, for example, numerous documents call attention to the living conditions of base people, new people, and Khmer Rouge cadre. According to a report of conditions in the Northwest prepared by the Standing Committee in August 20–24, 1975, it was noted that overall "shelters have been prepared for the people everywhere" and that the "base people are stable. There are not yet shortages of livelihood." However, "remote districts are still in need and many [base] people are also suffering from disease." Conversely, the "new people are experiencing shortages, shortages of food supplies as well as shortages of medications."[111] In a telegram sent to Office 870 in November 1975, the secretary of Region 23 described a situation in which many fish had died and were found floating in the lakes and streams. Subsequently, people from the region gathered, cooked, and ate the fish. Soon thereafter, many people suffered from diarrhea, with some dying. The secretary explained that people were therefore informed that they were not permitted to gather dead fish and were instructed to eat only cooked food and to drink boiled water. Men and women were also to report to the medical staff any ailment they experienced. In concluding his report, the secretary did note that sufficient medicines were not available in his region to treat people, and that they were especially lacking the means to treat malaria and intestinal diseases.[112]

In general, the Standing Committee was aware of the appalling conditions experienced by men, women, and children throughout Democratic Kampuchea. The Party was also aware of the inequality of conditions experienced between base people and new people. However, the provision of adequate food and medicine was tempered by the broader operational objectives of economic growth. Perhaps most telling is a document dated March 8, 1976. The agenda of the meeting was twofold: to address the forthcoming elections of March and the situation in the North Zone. With respect to the latter, Comrade Sot reported that Sector 106 was beset with numerous health-related issues. He explained that there were many sick people and that this resulted in a loss of approximately 40 percent of the labor force. Outbreaks of chicken pox and cholera were also reported. Comrade Hang, reporting on the situation in Sector 103, likewise informed the Standing Committee of widespread illnesses. In response, Angkar offered the following opinion: "Today, we think much about the livelihood of the people, but expenditures for material purchases to solve the livelihood of the people are limited because we must purchase many other things as well, and our funds are few. Therefore, we must understand concentrating on solving the livelihood of the people at the base to the maximum extent."[113]

Angkar's response evinces a peculiarly utilitarian attitude toward the people of Democratic Kampuchea. The hardships experienced by the people, notably the prevalence of diseases, were duly noted, but any redress would require an investment of resources. The Standing Committee did not say that resources were unavailable, but rather intimated that materials were needed elsewhere. In other words, villages, communes, districts, and regions would have to fend for themselves. This often meant making do with locally produced medicines and treatment by locally recruited medics.

Prior to 1975, Cambodia had two coexisting medical systems: traditional forms of medicine were widely practiced, and Western-based medical practices were also available. The indigenous system centered on the role of *kru khmae* (Khmer-style teacher) and the healing process consisted of a diagnosis dialogue. The *kru khmae* and the patient would enter into a mutual relationship that covered physical, social, and cosmological components. Specifically, diagnosis and therapy were derived from a consensus between the *kru khmae*, the patient, his or her relatives, and the spirits.[114]

The arrival of French colonialism brought with it Western-based medical practices. Initially, these were coordinated by the French military and focused on curative aspects and some preventive practices. As civilian authorities assumed principle responsibility for the health of their colony, medical practices shifted. Preventive health care—principally for French citizens—assumed center stage, as officials were more concerned with preventing the spread of infectious diseases such as cholera, smallpox, and the plague. In time, these preventive practices, albeit on a limited scale, were extended to the Cambodians. Concurrently, throughout the colonial period French authorities viewed indigenous medical practices mostly with indifference. In effect, as long as traditional practices did not negatively impact French policy or practice, they were tolerated.

Following independence, Western-based medicines were actively promoted through the establishment of hospitals, clinics, medical-related schools, and pharmaceutical companies. Between 1955 and 1969, for example, the number of hospitals and district clinics increased from 16 to 69 and the number of community dispensaries increased from 103 to 587. More specifically, in 1959 the French opened the Calmette Hospital in Phnom Penh; this was followed by the opening of the Khmer-Soviet Friendship Hospital (also known as the Russian Hospital) in 1960. Domestic production of pharmaceuticals began in 1963 with the establishment of the Khmer Pharmaceutical Factory.

Similar to their approach to education, the Standing Committee of the CPK sought to replace the preexisting health-care system with their own. During the evacuation of Phnom Penh in April 1975, all hospitals, including doctors, nurses, and patients, were forced to leave; so too were medical practitioners throughout the country. Most (but not all) would never return. Some estimates indicate that by 1979, fewer than fifty medical doctors who had practiced in Cambodia prior to 1975 remained alive. To fill the void, the CPK recruited and trained, often with the assistance of Chinese doctors, their own medical personnel.

A Khmer Rouge slogan held that "Daughters should grow up to be medical staff, while sons, to be soldiers."[115] In part, there is a kernel of truth to this sentiment. Many young girls, mostly between twelve and fifteen years of age, volunteered or were recruited among the base population to train as nurses or to serve in other medical-related positions.[116] Moreover, many senior positions within the medical sector were filled by the daughters of high-ranking CPK officials. The four daughters of Ta Mok, for example, became nurses.[117] That being said, Democratic Kampuchea's gendered division of labor was slightly more complex and, in fact, often conformed with that of more traditional patriarchal societies. On the one hand, men frequently served as medics and women served as soldiers. On the other hand, most senior positions were occupied by men. Indeed, no woman served on the Standing Committee or occupied the position of zone secretary. Only two women, Ieng Thirith and Yun Yat, served on the Central Committee.

Most of those women and men who worked as medical staff were uneducated; medical training was hurried and rudimentary, lasting at most a matter of weeks. Nurses were taught how to give injections and to administer pills and other medicines. And since most of the trainees could not read, they were instructed in how to recognize the words printed on the bottles.[118] Collectively, these medical personnel were known as *pet padevat* or revolutionary medics.

Medicines and pharmaceuticals were available throughout Democratic Kampuchea, as the CPK continued to import supplies from other countries. Thus, alongside the importation of axes, knives, sickles, and plows, sizable quantities of penicillin, quinine, serum, and vitamins were brought into the country. The aforementioned Ren Fung Company, for example, facilitated the shipment of penicillin, nivaquine, quinine, and chloroquine. The CPK likewise accepted so-called gifts from abroad, including approximately US$12,000 worth of antimalarial drugs provided in 1976 by the American Friends Service Committee, with Washington's approval, via China.[119] Upon arrival, imported medicines and medical equipment, dental equipment and dental supplies, and pharmaceuticals of all sorts were generally stored in warehouses in Phnom Penh, the port at Kompong Som, or around the town of Poipet. Later, these would be distributed to the various zones, sectors, districts, and communes, according to procedures adopted by the Standing Committee and the State Warehouse Committee.

The CPK also established factories to produce their own medicines and pharmaceuticals. Many of these were located throughout Phnom Penh and produced penicillin, serum, setropharine, and vitamins B1, B6, and B12. The former Pasteur Institute, located in the Chroy Changvar area of Phnom Penh, was reopened to manufacture vaccines.[120] The efficacy of these medicines was dubious at best. Often Chinese doctors monitored the production of Western-based medicines. These were produced from raw materials imported from Thailand, Hong Kong, and elsewhere. Other indigenous medicines were produced. Manufactured also under the supervision of

Chinese doctors, but with the assistance of local *kru khmae*, these medicines were used to treat fever, headaches, stomachaches, and fainting spells. Raw materials included plant roots, tree bark, sap, and other natural compounds. Young girls would mix these materials together and shape them into small pills, which became widely known as rabbit-dropping medicine, both because of their appearance and effectiveness.[121]

The health system of Democratic Kampuchea was administered by Ieng Thirith, wife of Ieng Sary, through the Ministry of Social Affairs. Identified by the code K-2, the ministry also coordinated and managed a hierarchy of hospitals, clinics, and other health facilities throughout the country. Within Phnom Penh, both the Calmette Hospital and Russian Hospital, although initially evacuated and ransacked, were put into operation. These hospitals were better supplied and better staffed; accessibility was also restricted, as these hospitals catered predominantly to senior officials and their families. Provincial hospitals existed outside the capital; these generally had a few fully trained doctors, at times Chinese advisers, and some Western-based medical supplies. Conditions deteriorated as one proceeded down the hierarchy. At the district level, health clinics were rarely staffed by trained medical practitioners and medicines consisted mostly of domestically produced pharmaceuticals—the rabbit-dropping medicines. The lowest level of health care was the *munti pet* (small clinics). Most often, these were converted school buildings, *wats*, or even someone's house. *Munti pet* were staffed by *pet padevat* and were poorly provisioned. According to Mertha, the Ministry of Social Affairs had no direct authority over medical services in the country beyond those located in Phnom Penh.[122]

Beyond the functions of health and education, the integrative apparatus consists of those bureaucracies responsible for media and the dissemination of information. Within Democratic Kampuchea, these were also to align with the overall operational objectives of promoting economic growth and the political task of building socialism. As enumerated in the Four-Year Plan, media technologies, including radios, films, and magazines, were to facilitate the dissemination of propaganda and information. Because of the low levels of literacy, the first two media assumed great importance; as to the latter, pictorial magazines were preferred. Caution, however, was necessary in the propagation of information. The Four-Year Plan warned to "Be careful in building, strengthening and expanding the ranks by choosing [people of] backgrounds close to the revolutionary movement [who] can apply the Party's policy to instruct the people and disseminate propaganda and information."[123]

The salience of propaganda long preceded the establishment of Democratic Kampuchea, however. Throughout their long revolutionary struggle, the CPK routinely engaged in propaganda activities. As detailed in Chapter 2, the Khmer Rouge capitalized on both the United States–led bombing campaign and the coup against Sihanouk. To this end, the institutionalization of the media had a strong foundation upon which to build. Prior to 1975, for example, two journals had already been established: *Revolutionary Flag (tung padevat)* and *Revolutionary Youth (youveak chon youveak neary padevat)*. These would, until the fall of Democratic Kampuchea, serve as important conduits through which the CPK disseminated official and operative objectives.

At a meeting held on January 9, 1976, members of the Standing Committee discussed Party propaganda and reeducation goals. It was asserted that propaganda and reeducation practices had, and would continue, to serve the revolution. Key advances, it was claimed, had been made in all communication sectors: radio, the arts, and magazines. Collectively, these efforts had "incited the spirit of national defense and the restoration of the economy" and had contributed to "the spirit of solving the livelihood of the people." However, several "deficiencies" were also documented. Performances, for example, did "not yet reflect the heroism of the people" or of "the Revolutionary Army." Nor did these channels of communication "demonstrate for all to see [the] great force of solidarity between the workers and the peasants, between the people and the Army, and [did] not yet reflect in a lively way their daily lives."[124]

Two months later, on March 8, 1976, the Standing Committee met again to discuss ongoing propaganda work. The occasion of this meeting was the forthcoming elections scheduled for March 20, 1976. It is clear from the discussion that the Standing Committee perceived the radio broadcasting of the elections not only as salient for the citizens of Democratic Kampuchea, but also for the international community. Indeed, it was imperative that the elections be broadcast lest other countries, notably France and Vietnam, might see the CPK as "dictators" and that "there is no democracy" in Democratic Kampuchea. It was important, however, that "content" be broadcast, but that it must not be too strong on explanation. It would be necessary to praise their accomplishments, but not excessively brag, thereby generating negative publicity.[125]

Beyond monitoring its own content, the Standing Committee determined that foreign news be monitored so as to keep Angkar informed. Following the meeting of March 8, 1976, for example, it was decided that news would be sent to Angkar every day, but that news should be reported in summary outline, together with some opinion and analysis. In general, these reports would be collected by messenger daily, at 5:15 p.m. In the event of something "especially important," the Standing Committee should be telephoned immediately.[126]

By mid-1976, the Ministry of Information and Propaganda, headed by longtime revolutionary Hu Nim, was in operation.[127] A complex bureaucracy, Office K-33 (as it was designated) consisted of more than a dozen subunits. Office K-25, for example, produced the journals *Revolutionary Flag* and *Revolutionary Youth*, while K-26, K-27, and K-28 were printing houses responsible for various newspapers, magazines, or official documents. Radio broadcasts were administered through Office K-33, and K-34 oversaw the production of propaganda films. Functionally, therefore, the Ministry of Information and Propaganda was a key conduit between CPK policy and implementation at lower levels.[128]

Conclusions

In this chapter I have sketched the broad coordinates of the Khmer Rouge bureaucracy. My objective has not been to provide an exhaustive historiography of any particular apparatus, a task that is needed, but rather to provide a necessary context within which we may better understand the materiality of power as it was administered behind the scenes. Democratic Kampuchea was not an empty government, but instead comprised a particular form of bureaucratic rule heavily informed by Leninist principles. Accordingly, our attention must consider more concretely how the administrative structure of Democratic Kampuchea facilitated the production of biopolitical knowledge, manifest materially in invoices and inventories, memos and meeting minutes, and how this knowledge was subsequently made actionable in the form of arrests, interrogations, and executions. In short, through an engagement with the complexities of administrative functions, this chapter provides an institutional grounding for a more sustained engagement with the necropolitics of bureaucratic rule.

Power, following Foucault, circulates, but it does so through the inscription and transmission of knowledge in the form of bureaucratic writing. As Gupta suggests, "Writing is one of the chief activities of bureaucrats; it is not secondary or subsequent to bureaucratic activity."[129] Indeed, the voluminous materials archived by the Khmer Rouge and later collected at the Documentation Center of Cambodia provide insight into the functions of a government that was anything but empty. To this end, the documentary record is itself reflective of the power of rule by desk. "Interpreting the act of writing as functioning merely to record or commemorate real bureaucratic activity," Gupta elaborates, "prevents one from seeing that writing is not just a by-product of the routes of state officials but is constitutive of states."[130]

The implications of such an approach are far-reaching. As illustrated by the two lists that opened this chapter, we begin to grasp the salience of bureaucratic procedures on day-to-day life within

Democratic Kampuchea. Issues of trade relations and foreign policies interact in complex ways with the physical labor involved in agriculture, and both presented immediate security concerns for the CPK. Hence, invoices of peanuts and coffee beans, when juxtaposed with lists of suspected malcontents, call attention to the everyday scalar politics that connect bureaucracies both within and beyond Democratic Kampuchea. Without this contextual understanding, particular institutions that comprise the Khmer Rouge security apparatus, such as S-21, appear indeed as ad hoc organizations within a chaotic political environment. Conversely, by repositioning the nascent ministries and departments of Democratic Kampuchea within a materialist framework—as understood by the CPK—it becomes possible to more fully articulate the calculative power of bureaucratic rule.

CHAPTER 3

Into the Darkness

When the Khmer Rouge stood victorious on the streets of Phnom Penh in April 1975, they constituted neither a centralized, efficient political party nor military force. Their victory was the haphazard by-product of the culmination of a series of concurrent revolutions, armed conflicts, and geopolitical machinations. The leadership of the CPK understood their tenuous hold on power and lack of widespread popular support, let alone loyalty. More to the point, after five years of struggle, not only was the Party still a formal secret, but most of the population was unaware of the main leaders or overarching objectives of the Khmer Rouge.[1] To this was added a pervasive layer of mistrust among senior leaders of the CPK with respect to the Cambodian citizenry. This is seen most clearly in the fundamental distinction between so-called new people and base people put forward by the Khmer Rouge.

In a series of meetings held August 20–24, 1975, members of the CPK discussed the status and future of their socialist revolution.[2] Minutes of the meetings reveal four broad topics of discussion, followed by a series of recommendations. First, it was noted that unequal living conditions between base and new people were clearly apparent. For the base people, shelters had been prepared and, for the most part, there was no shortage of food or medicine, except for those living in outlying districts. Here, it was noted, many base people were suffering from diseases. For the new people, conversely, there was a lack of both food and medicine. Overall, the minutes conclude: "Most people feel warmth being with the revolution and are active in [the] country's building movement and crops diversification movement."[3] Second, regarding the enemy situation, it was noted that there had not yet been any military action on behalf of

Thailand, although some "Thais illegally came about 3 kilometers into our territory to cultivate rice."[4] To this, an unnamed cadre stated, "We are seeking to smash them." More pressing were possible internal activities, as the report explains: "They have their secret connections contacting each other from one place to another. . . . There are still some persons in our line who have not been completely screened. And they use those individuals to lead people to escape. We have successfully arrested some of them and are carrying out more searches." Third, an update on the Khmer Rouge's military situation is provided. It was noted, for example, that from a political standpoint, consciousness and solidarity of the soldiers was not a problem, but there was a lack of hammocks and mosquito nets. Fourth, the economic condition is discussed. Rice was actively being planted, both on old land (meaning existing rice fields) and on new land. Water management remained a concern, as fields around Pursat were badly short of water while the area around Sisophon was receiving too much water. Beyond rice cultivation, cotton and hemp were planted and hemp-weaving factories were established. Tractor-repair factories were also becoming operational in Mongkul Borei and Thmar Kol.

Angkar's guiding opinions are presented in the second half of the minutes. With respect to national defense, the resolution of the political situation of people is deemed crucial. Echoing Lenin's remarks that "our task is not to degrade the revolutionaries to the level of an amateur, but to exalt the amateur to the level of a revolutionary,"[5] the CPK determined that "the importance is to settle [the] political situation of people by making them stable-minded and become united with revolutionary authorities."[6] The meeting minutes continue that "The revolutionary authorities must . . . control people in all areas—politics, consciousness, and assignment."[7] The means to this end was through the continued use of collectives: "People are strong only when collectives are strong."[8] Accordingly, "the issue of people's living standards within collectives must be resolved. Even with new people, we have to help improve their living conditions so that they will be satisfied with the revolution."[9] The building of socialism, in other words, was to be an ongoing process. Recommendations were provided also for economic activities, ranging from the need to relocate workers to areas suffering from labor shortages to the continued need to manage water more effectively.

The meeting minutes of August 20–24, 1975, provide insight into the CPK's day-to-day concerns and practice, but especially the prevailing security concerns about two interrelated threats. Externally, CPK officials worried about armed intervention by outside powers, notably Vietnam or the United States, and internally by suspected traitors and saboteurs. The security fears articulated by the CPK were viewed as mutually reinforcing, in that the CPK leadership feared the presence of spies working from within. To a certain extent, these concerns are understandable, although not necessarily justifiable. The long years of revolution were marked by repeated instances of betrayal. The Vietnamese Communists continually expected their Khmer counterparts to work with Sihanouk; Sihanouk, in turn, supported Lon Nol in the targeting and killing of Khmer revolutionaries. It is perhaps expected, therefore, that treasonous activities would emerge as the most dreaded security threat facing the fledgling CPK. What is remarkable are the methods employed by key officials within the CPK in their pursuit of traitors, for behind the massive death toll is a rudimentary bureaucracy that systematized the arrest, detainment, torture, and execution of hundreds of thousands of men, women, and children. It is this bureaucratic element that warrants closer scrutiny.

In this chapter I consider broadly the Khmer Rouge security apparatus and, in so doing, accentuate the necropolitics of bureaucratic governance that came to typify Democratic Kampuchea. I do so with a particular purpose in mind: to articulate more precisely the CPK legal order as a mode of governance buttressed by the practice of lethal surveillance.[10] Following Katherine Kindervater, lethal surveillance marks the imbrication of myriad surveillance techniques with the sovereign right to kill. Practices of lethal surveillance thus appear at the intersection of knowledge production—of monitoring, classifying, and codifying suspected enemies—and the practice of law enforcement, that is, the arrest, detainment, interrogation, and execution of enemies.

Law, Legal Orders, and the CPK

What distinguishes legal order from spontaneous social order?[11] Many scholars of Democratic Kampuchea have formed a consensus that the country had no law or legal system. Helen Fein, for example, states that when the CPK came to power, "they imposed totalitarian rule without law."[12] Anthony Barnett concludes that "there was no public law or Party regulation to safeguard, even by process let alone appeal, the lives of ordinary Cambodians from the authority of their local rulers."[13] These assessments are not necessarily mistaken as they are incomplete. To be certain, there were no judges, juries, or lawyers. Nor did the CPK establish courts of law or even lawbooks. The absence of these, however, does not necessarily correspond with the conclusion that the country was lawless. Consequently, our interpretation of the Khmer Rouge security apparatus must necessarily grapple with our understanding of law and the legal order.

Such an approach is not a gratuitous exercise in semantics; labels matter. Thus, we may agree on the aforementioned observable facts—that throughout Democratic Kampuchea, there were no judges or juries, no lawyers or courts of law; and that people were arrested without due cause, were not put on trial, and had no chance for appeal. For some, the conclusion is straightforward. There was no law in Democratic Kampuchea and, by extension, we surmise that the country experienced a condition of lawlessness. Stated thusly, we are obliged to evaluate and interpret all activities, for example, the arrests, tortures, forced confessions, and executions from this vantage point.

Other observers point to Democratic Kampuchea's Constitution, written between December 15 and 19, 1975, and promulgated on January 5, 1976. Likewise, one might identify the CPK's Statutes, also promulgated in January 1976. From this vantage point, a different legal landscape begins to appear. Here, an incipient legal order is perceptible, thereby altering our subsequent analysis. Indeed, rather than conceding that chaos reigned throughout Democratic Kampuchea, one is forced to ask why the legal system was not fully developed and why the fundamental rights, however minimal, established throughout the Constitution and Statutes, were not upheld.

How we define the Khmer Rouge legal order matters greatly. For many scholars, a "legal order is defined by the existence of the institutions that characterize modern western democracies; namely, centralized production of legal rules by legislatures and courts combined with centralized coercive enforcement of those rules by duly constituted governments."[14] However, following Gillian Hadfield and Barry Weingast, it is possible "to develop an account of legal order that does not presume that legal order is characterized, necessarily, by the types of institutions we see today in modern developed nation states: courts, legislatures, police, and so on."[15] The benefits of doing so include a more robust analysis of both policy and practice. Accordingly, I begin with the presumption that an operational objective of the CPK was to establish a legal order. By extension, this legal order was, from the position of the CPK, to be derived dialectically with the overall materialist grounding of Democratic Kampuchea's political economy. In effect, Democratic Kampuchea's legal order must be contextualized within a framework of historical materialism.[16]

There is no singular Marxist legal theory. That being said, certain commonalities exist, especially among those theories informed by Lenin. Both law and the legal order are held as epiphenomena of a capitalist society; accordingly, the legal order—much like the state—is a bourgeois institution that represents the class rule of society. The Soviet Marxist theorist Evgeny Pashukanis, for example, held that law was the codification of capitalist social relations in legal form. Law was thus distinct from administration, which, under socialism, emphasizes duties rather than rights, the common good rather than formal equality, the collective rather than individuals, and unity of purpose rather than resolution of conflicts of interests.[17] Notable also is the assertion among certain

Marxist legal theorists that law itself will cease to be necessary following the collapse of the capitalist state.

The Constitution as drafted by members of the CPK included both duties and rights. Article 12, for example, declares that "Every citizen of Kampuchea enjoys full rights to a constantly improving material, spiritual, and cultural life."[18] It continues that "Every citizen of Democratic Kampuchea is guaranteed a living. All workers are the masters of their factories. All peasants are the masters of the rice paddies and fields. All other laborers have the right to work. There is absolutely no unemployment in Democratic Kampuchea."[19] Inalienable rights were apparently guaranteed also in Article 13: "There must be complete equality among all Kampuchean people in an equal, just, democratic, harmonious, and happy society within the great national solidarity for defending and building the country together."[20] The question of religious rights was ambiguously stated in the Constitution. Article 20 states that "Every citizen of Kampuchea has the right to worship according to any religion and the right not to worship according to any religion." However, the article continues that "Reactionary religions which are detrimental to Democratic Kampuchea and Kampuchean people are absolutely forbidden."[21] It is perhaps no surprise that the phrase "reactionary religions" was undefined in the Constitution. In practice, it is clear that any religion, including Buddhism and Islam, were considered reactionary and therefore prohibited. Justus van der Kroef writes that "Yun Yat reportedly told a group of visiting Yugoslav journalists in April 1978 that 'Buddhism is incompatible with revolution' because it was an instrument of exploitation."[22] Particular duties were also specified in the Constitution. Article 14 declares that "It is the duty of all to defend and build the country together in accordance with individual ability and potential."[23]

Two articles pertain specifically to justice or what we may term the legal order. Article 9 states that "Justice is administered by people's courts, representing and defending the people's justice, defending the democratic rights and liberties of the people, and condemning any activities directed against the people's State or violating the laws of the people's State. The judges at all levels will be chosen and appointed by the People's Representative Assembly."[24] At least two issues related to Article 9 are problematic. First, the PRA never met following its initial establishment in April 1976. Whether the CPK intended the PRA to be purely symbolic, or that when the Constitution was drafted in December 1975, it was the CPK's intent to hold elections is not known with any degree of certainty. Article 5 of the Constitution did affirm that legislative power would be invested in the representative assembly of the people, the PRA, and that members of the assembly would be "elected by the people through direct and prompt general elections by secret ballot to be held throughout the country every five years."[25] Democratic Kampuchea, of course, collapsed in less than four years. Second, there is no indication that people's courts were established or that judges were appointed throughout the administrative hierarchy of Democratic Kampuchea. Again, it is unclear if the CPK ever intended for these procedures to be followed or if the purges that transpired especially from 1976 onward negated an initial commitment to a people's democracy. In effect, one is left unsure as to how the Constitution should be assessed: Is this document illustrative of an operational objective or an official objective? Does the Constitution give weight to the argument that an embryonic legal order was developing, or that the leadership of the CPK drafted the document as an elaborate form of propaganda?

Article 9 condemns activities that are directed against the people's state and in violation of the laws of the people's state. Article 10, curiously, does not specify what these activities may be, although certain forms of punishment are indicated: "Dangerous activities in opposition to the people's State must be condemned to the highest degree," and "Other cases are subject to constructive re-education in the framework of the State's or people's organizations."[26] Article 10, in other words, provides the clearest exposition of the CPK's approach to justice. Those activities determined to be in opposition to the state are to be "condemned to the highest degree." The Constitution is conspicuously silent as to the form of such opposition; however, regardless of how opposition is defined, one can only interpret Article 10 as a codification of capital punishment. The second clause indicates that punishment beyond the highest degree involves constructive reeducation that would take place at some undetermined level of authority.

Taken together, it is possible to see the coordinates of a particular legal order emerging, namely, we see evidence that the CPK sought to utilize the legal system to facilitate a productive and efficient economic system; implement an effective system of governance based on democratic centralism; and ensure the protection of the rights of individuals and groups to decent treatment, security, and opportunity.[27] No doubt these elements were tinged with a draconian sense of fairness and equality. However, it is this budding legal order, and its bureaucratic manifestation, that underscore the purges that transpired. This is made clear through an investigation of the CPK Statutes developed concurrently with the drafting and adoption of the Constitution.

The Statutes reaffirm and elaborate on the ideas expressed in the Constitution. Statute 6, for example, holds that "The Party must have high-level revolutionary vigilance toward all enemy activities and trickery, direct or indirect, overt or secret, which have the intent to destroy the Party by every means. All Party organizations and every Party member, must always be good and clean and be pure politically, ideologically, and organizationally, by building a clear, clean, and pure personal history, consecutively and constantly."[28] This Statute is informative in that it provides greater detail as to the form of dangerous activities and accentuates the importance of personal biographies. Indeed, the direct reference to one's personal history indicates that biopolitical data would serve as prima facie evidence. In practice, of course, there was no opportunity for those men and women arrested to establish their innocence. As to the dangerous activities, Statute 6 clarifies that "The Party absolutely opposes any political, ideological, or organizational violation of organizational discipline through independentism, liberalism, sectarianism, or nepotism, which destroys Party solidarity and unity, and absolutely opposes any creation of cliques to break up the Party."[29] A cursory reading of this statement leaves one with the impression that any disagreement, however slight, of the Party would be construed as a grave violation. Security for Democratic Kampuchea was predicated thusly on an extreme form of either being for or against the Party. There was no middle ground. If any word spoken or action taken was determined to be in contradiction to the Party, swift punishment to the highest degree would be meted out.

There is also a subtler significance to Statute 6. The clue is found in the phrase that the CPK "absolutely opposes any creation of *cliques* to break up the Party."[30] I read in this statement an explicit admission that even as of January 1976, the CPK feared the existence of organized social networks. To be so clearly articulated in the Statutes provides insight into the conspiratorial fears expressed by certain members of the CPK. When read in concert with the need to establish clear, clean, and pure personal histories, the administrative dimensions of the CPK's legal order are further established.

Hadfield and Weingast suggest that, at a minimum, a legal order exists if (1) there is an identifiable entity that deliberately supplies a normative classification scheme that designates some actions as wrongful (punishable, undesirable); and (2) actors, as a consequence of the classification scheme, forego wrongful actions to a significant extent.[31] Both the Constitution and the Statutes establish to a limited degree a normative classification scheme that designates acceptable and unacceptable behaviors. To what extent and how were these norms transmitted throughout Democratic Kampuchea? The answers are embedded within the territorial structure of CPK administration. As detailed in the previous chapter, governance in Democratic Kampuchea was premised on democratic centralism and organized hierarchically. Both of these parameters are spelled out in the Statutes. The aforementioned Statute 6 explains that "The Party absolutely respects and implements democratic centralism. The Party has a single firm organizational discipline, with each individual being self-aware, aiming to incite the combat spirit of the Party members and aiming to well-maintain Party solidarity and internal unity absolutely and firmly, politically, ideologically, and organization-ally."[32] In other words, each Party member was to adhere in strict obedience to the Party line. Such an approach, theoretically, departs from more traditional understandings of democratic centralism, in which workers within society, for example, are to have equal input into decision-making processes. For the CPK, democratic centralism translated into the dissemination of decisions made predominantly (but not always exclusively) by the Central (or, more precisely, the Standing) Committee.

The transmission of Party policy and planning documents—in short, the circulation of information materialized—occurred through the hierarchy of branches, communes, district, sectors, and zones. Each territorially based division had, according to CPK Statutes, its own operational objectives and bureaucratic functions. Article 9 of the Statutes stipulates that "Each revolutionary cooperative, factory, military company-level unit, worksite, and Ministry-Office may organize a Party Branch."[33] Branch-level units were important as these entities had the most direct contact with the populace of Democratic Kampuchea. For that reason, the tasks of any branch-level unit was first to "Proselytize the popular masses with specific plans and programs in its areas, in the unions and cooperatives and in the Revolutionary Army, regarding political lines, ideological principles and stances, and organizational lines, according to the task of national defense and the construction of Democratic Kampuchea, in the Party stance of class struggle of socialist revolution and in building socialism."[34] Effectively, branch-level units were to transmit Party policy to base people, new people, and Party members; crucial also to this function was to situate political education within the broader political economy and security of the Party, the revolution, and the state. In this manner the legal order was in principle to be disseminated throughout the country. In this manner all men, women, and children were again, in principle, to be informed of normative behaviors, of actions deemed right or wrong. Operationally, officials at the branch level were to continually screen Party members, maintain a system of reporting to upper echelons, and hold regular meetings in order to attend to their tasks.

District-level units were given similar responsibilities. Officials from the district level were to make regular visits to the branch-level units, provide guidance as to the implementation of policy, and remain vigilant in their pursuit of national defense and building socialism. Article 13 states also that district-level officials were to "Constantly and tightly grasp the Branches, cadres, and Party members along with all the core organizations of the District in regards to personal histories. . . ."[35] From this we see the deepening of the CPK's legal order, but especially how biographies were inter-woven throughout society. Branch-level units were to observe, monitor, and evaluate those people under their jurisdiction. Information on suspicious behaviors, conceived as anything in opposition to the Party line, was to be documented in telegrams and letters, to be sent up the chain of command. These procedures of information transmission, of relaying decisions from officials above to subordinates below, and of reporting on conditions below to superiors above, were replicated at both the sector level and zone level. Sector-level committee members were to regularly visit district and branch units, facilitate in the implementation of tasks, and monitor and report on security risks through the compilation and evaluation of personal biographies. Zone-level committees were to regularly visit sector-, district-, and branch-level units for the same reasons.

The socio-material organization of Democratic Kampuchea was a direct reflection of democratic centralism.[36] As Herbert Schurmann explains, "The operation of the principle of centralism has seen the creation of a web of organization with vertical chains of command which ultimately merge, like the apex of a pyramid, at the very top."[37] In theory, throughout Democratic Kampuchea, each political division, including cooperatives, was to be self-reliant and autonomous—a structure colleagues and I identify elsewhere as integrated autonomy.[38] In practice, flows of information, supplies, and so on were channeled hierarchically through respective three-person committees, with ultimate control overseen by the Standing Committee of the CPK. Lower-level cadre—for example, those governing at the district level—were required to channel all requests via messenger or telegram to their immediate supervisors at the regional level; these cadres, in turn, would forward the requests to the zone level, where they would then be routed (often via telegram) to the relevant ministries of the CPK. In broad strokes, zone-level committees communicated with the Central Party by telegraph and courier; face-to-face meetings also occurred, as zone-level officials were required to engage in various meetings in Phnom Penh. As one moved down the chain of command, however, forms of communication became more interpersonal. Telegraphs and couriers were still employed, especially between zone-level and sector-level members; below this, however, communication was conducted mostly face to face. Indeed, Etcheson notes that relatively few examples of written communications between the district level and lower echelons exist. Particularly at the branch level, communication was largely oral. On the one hand, officials working at the branch levels were generally in close proximity; on the other hand, there was a high degree of illiteracy among these officials, making written communication difficult. Written communication, transmitted usually by messenger, did take place, however, including the forwarding of biographies or queries regarding the disposition of detained enemies. One may speculate, therefore, that information deemed most crucial to the security of the Party and the state was inscribed in written form.[39]

There were to be no horizontal relations. For example, a district secretary in the Northwest Zone was not permitted to request supplies from a neighboring district secretary, also located in the Northwest Zone. He or she would (in theory) have to route the request through the Zone Committee (and hence to the Standing Committee) before it would be rerouted to the other district cadre. This form of socio-spatial organization appears exceptionally inefficient and cumbersome, but also belies the common misperception that the CPK disdained bureaucratic procedures. The importance, both in practice and in theory, should not be overlooked or discounted. On a practical side, the Standing Committee of the CPK was able to keep tabs on almost everything that happened throughout the country. This enabled the top echelon to more effectively centralize its authority and to enact sweeping transformations of the country, for the centralism of democratic centralism "arises from the fact that decisions of a higher-level party organization are always binding on lower party bodies and every party member."[40]

As in the Soviet Union and China, leaders of the CPK recognized the inherent problems and contradictions of democratic centralism, notably the disconnect between democracy (understood as free and full participation of the masses) and centralism (that is, the concentration of decision-making power by those at the apex of the political hierarchy). How, for example, are disagreements between levels resolved? What democratic or participatory roles are provided for the majority of citizens who are not Party members?[41]

The CPK's awareness of these problems is evidenced in various documents, notably a December 20, 1976, report on activities of the Party Center. In reference to efforts to build political consciousness, the report reads: "We have nourished political consciousness, proletarian patriotism and proletarian internationalism. We have also nourished dialectical materialism as a basis. . . . Proletarian patriotic consciousness and proletarian internationalism can transform people's nature into something new. As for the problem of nurturing a Marxist-Leninist viewpoint, we should allow this to seep in according to our chosen methods."[42] The report indicates, however, that "complete mastery" was not yet attained, as "We have struggled to institute a leadership stance consistent with democratic centralism."[43] What was the cause of these struggles? The report clarifies that "We have purified the surface of the Party and the key organizations to a large extent"—a clear reference to the ongoing purges that had taken place over the previous twenty months. The problem was that the Party was unable to "expand key organizations or . . . only expand them slightly."[44] Party leaders, as evidenced by this report, expressed concern with the expansion of members who exhibited the proper political consciousness. The concern was that insufficient numbers of citizens had attained the political maturity necessary, from the CPK's vantage point, to fully participate in governance. Solutions proposed included the widespread use of life histories and mandatory study sessions. According to the report, it was thought that membership could expand by 40 percent within the first half of 1977; however, the report cautioned that "If someone's life history isn't good, don't enroll him in the Party, no matter what size [is in his favor]."[45]

The enforcement of the law, so to speak, assumed a decidedly more nebulous process. Andrew Mertha finds that zone leaders appear to have significant control over their jurisdictions. Indeed, these officials "were extraordinarily powerful right up until the moment they were not."[46] Mertha concludes that administrative levels below the zone were more akin to implementing bodies than decision-making ones.[47] Arguably, the most important decision was that of capital punishment: the right to execute an individual deemed guilty of the most serious crimes. Here, caution must be taken. We know what the documents indicate; we are less sure when it comes to actual practice. The Constitution, for example, specifies that judges were to be nominated and appointed at all levels of governance; presumably, these judges would have determined the guilt or innocence of those accused. This did not happen. Indeed, no concrete evidence exists that any judges were ever appointed. Rather, decision-making power remained in the hands of the tripartite committees that were in place at all levels. Evidence suggests, furthermore, that zone-level officials were considerably more autonomous in their ability to make decisions, and that officials occupying the lower echelons implemented the decisions rendered from above.

It is apparent that the Central Committee was well aware of the problem—especially as it related to capital punishment. On March 30, 1976, the Central Committee authorized "The right to smash, inside and outside the ranks."[48] This document is generally considered to be the clearest example of a smoking gun in that it purports to establish the bureaucratic hierarchy by which people could be executed. Accordingly, the ability to smash—that is, to execute people—was "to be decided by the Zone Standing Committee."[49] In other words, targeted killings were to be determined by the three-person committee at the zone level. Significantly, no specific protocols are provided that might shed insight into the decision-making process. The accused person was not to stand before the committee, nor was there any form of legal representation. It appears that decisions were made primarily (if not exclusively) on the paper trail that accrued and circulated throughout the various bureaucratic levels.

The March 30, 1976, memo thus indicates but does not readily explicate myriad protocols for the sanctioned killing of suspected enemies. For those accused men and women who staffed the various units, offices, and ministries in support of the Party Center, decisions were to be rendered by the Central Office Committee. Conversely, those accused who worked in other sectors were to be judged by the Standing Committee. Lastly, the fate of those in the military accused of crimes was to be decided upon by the General Staff.[50]

Documentary evidence indicates that members of the zone level had the authority to smash people. Further evidence details that those members holding office in the upper echelon, notably the Standing Committee, were kept abreast of these actions. On July 18, 1976, for example, the secretary of Sector 103, Bu Phat (alias Hang), sent a telegram to "Beloved and Missed Brother," and copied it to Nuon Chea, Son Sen, and Ieng Sary. The telegram states that ten men "were already smashed" based on a preliminary investigation, and that sector leaders would be conducting "a further detailed investigation." The telegram also details the activities of a man named Yeuang, who was allegedly part of a larger conspiratorial network, all of whom were themselves suspected of traitorous activities and trickery.[51] Relatedly, Etcheson cites a weekly report from "401" (an alias for West Zone Secretary Chou Chet) to Angkar dated August 4, 1978, whereupon "100 Vietnamese people—small and big, young and old—have been smashed" along with 60 other ordinary people who have been smashed. And as a final example, on May 11, 1978, Moul Sambath (alias Ros Nhim), secretary of the Northwest Zone, reported to Office 870 that numerous enemies suspected of assorted offenses had been smashed, and that other problems had been "solved." Several measures were in place to combat the criminal elements, including ongoing investigations and the additional smashing of even more enemies.[52] In total, these documents confirm that the zone leadership had the authority to carry out mass executions, and that the zone kept the upper echelon informed of these decisions.[53] Evidence further reveals that officials at lower levels of governance, including both district-level and commune-level members, were given, or assumed, the authority to smash people, in violation of the memo of March 30, 1976. In June 1977, for example, a *chhlop* unit in the East Zone's Sector 22 detained a man accused of being a former military officer under Lon Nol and arrested his wife. The telegram reports that the man was "taken out" and presumably smashed.[54]

Secrecy and Surveillance

The political economy of Democratic Kampuchea placed the majority of the population between the grasp of two powerful forces: a demand for surplus rice and agricultural inputs that justified draconian labor policies on the one hand and a rationing system that winnowed away every excess grain of rice on the other.[55] For workers, the result was an institutional arrangement that could not (and would not) respond to deteriorating conditions as these became more pronounced. As people became weakened through malnutrition, starvation, and disease, their work productivity declined. When productivity declined, local cadres were forced to appropriate ever greater quantities of rice to satisfy quotas established by officials at the upper echelons. Cooperative chiefs had to answer to district superiors; district secretaries had to answer to sector secretaries; and sector secretaries had to answer to zone secretaries. It was inevitable that perceived failures occurring at one level would reverberate up and down the administrative hierarchy. The subsequent uneven conditions and mortality rates across Democratic Kampuchea reflect in part the varied responses of zone-, sector-, district-, and branch-level officials.[56]

While members of the Standing Committee made statements of abundance, militias and members of the Santebal (secret police) arrested, tortured, and executed those who complained about lack of food.[57] Documents describe people being arrested for stealing food or merely complaining about insufficient rations. Such punishment was not confined to the masses. CPK leaders purged local officials who admitted that starvation was occurring in their areas. As the food crises deepened, the CPK blamed traitorous and inept cadres across the hierarchy of undermining the food production apparatus. This security discourse of internal enemies and traitors and saboteurs seemingly justified the CPK's intensification and expansion of surveillance, imprisonment, and execution.[58]

As surveillance practices became entrenched throughout Democratic Kampuchea, so too did paranoia and the circulation of conspiracy theories among the upper echelons of the CPK.[59] In Chapter 1 I introduced Anne McClintock's analytical usage of paranoia as "a way of seeing and being attentive to contradictions within power, a way of making visible . . . the contradictory flashpoints of violence that the state tries to conceal."[60] Thus, while it is commonly understood that paranoid fantasies form a constant marker of the urge of absolute power, the paradox is that such paranoia emanates from a position of insecurity.[61] Jonathan Bach explains that the "archetype of the ruler is . . . also always an archetype of a survivor. Practically speaking, the ruler is always more vulnerable if left exposed, and thus must constantly create the conditions that forestall a likely death at the hands of enemies, rival, and troublemakers."[62] It is no small leap to see how the survival of the ruler may be transferred to the survival of the Party, the revolution, and the state. Indeed, a common refrain among members of the Standing Committee was to ensure the continuance of revolution and the security of the Party. While addressing a meeting of secretaries and deputy secretaries of military divisions on August 30, 1976, for example, Son Sen explained that it was necessary to "Give additional education about the spirit of vigilance. Do not allow pacifism. Give education about the enemies' tricks so that brothers and sisters will be informed thereof and will not be fooled by them." He continued that "it is imperative to take further educational measures and to administer and organize well. Enemy situations will exist one after the other but they won't be at all powerful; as long as we are vigilant we will certainly be able to fend them off."[63] Later, when meeting with officials of Division 703 and staff from S-21 on September 9, 1976, Son Sen warned that it was necessary to "Heighten the outlook of revolutionary vigilance in view of the increasingly very sharp contradictions and the ever strong class hatred of the enemies of the Kampuchean revolution." Organizationally, comrades were to "firmly grasp biographies and ideologies" and to increase "surveillance of enemy situations."[64]

A series of meeting minutes between division and regiment secretaries and members of the upper echelon of Angkar illustrate not only the deepening suspicion of Party cadre but also the vigilance by which cadre performed their duties. Overall, the minutes present an overview of "enemy activities" and subsequent opinions and directives issued by Son Sen. On September 16, 1976, for example, Comrade Voeung reports that three days earlier, a female cadre named Moeun was arrested for committing a "moral offense with a guard." Comrade Pin likewise informs the leadership that eight people suspected of attempting to flee were captured. Comrade Nat recounts that three soldiers from Division 502 had been detained and requested they be sent to Phnom Penh. Comrade Tat, lastly, confirms that a man named Neou was arrested. In response, Son Sen provides his own assessment and interpretation of various enemy activities, including the existence of traitorous networks, many of which had connections with Soviet, Vietnamese, and American intelligence agencies. He notes that during the war, the Party did not always "select good people." The deputy prime minister for defense then implores the division secretaries to "Investigate soldiers' biography carefully, especially the new members."[65] On that same day Son Sen met with other cadres, including Duch, commandant of S-21; Ieng Sary, deputy prime minister of foreign affairs; and Sam Huoy (alias Meas Tall), secretary of Division 290. Comrade Sam Huoy opened the meeting with a report on enemy activities. He notes that near the village of Neak Loeung, a person "coming to steal rice" was detained. Later that night the prisoner attempted to escape and was shot and killed. And while Sam Huoy laments that they were unable to interrogate the prisoner beforehand, he is pleased to provide updated information on additional arrests and of people under observation. Son Sen replies that these activities were connected to the existence of various suspected traitorous networks. Accordingly, Son Sen provides a list of four names to Sam Huoy, who was instructed to conduct additional investigations. Duch also provides a list of twenty-nine men and two women, all of whom were to be arrested and sent to S-21. These named individuals were in addition to another eleven people, whose fate had been determined at a meeting held the day before. Secrecy was essential, Duch reminded everyone, explaining that it is necessary to "Do whatever to take these people without making their unit fall into chaotic situation, learn and understand about the situation, and do it secretly." On a practical note, Duch concludes that guards from S-21 and Division 690 would "collaborate and arrest those [forty] people from their unit and load them onto the truck." Almost as an afterthought, Duch mentions that "As for the two women, we can deal with them later on."[66]

These documents are telling in that they demonstrate the deliberations that took place behind the purges. Key officials throughout the bureaucratic hierarchy met and discussed events, exchanged lists, and made decisions as to the fate of suspected men and women. Orders would subsequently be issued and disseminated, possibly through telegram or courier, or, perhaps more likely, face to face. These orders would specify which unit was responsible for coordinating arrests and how precisely the moment of capture would take place. Collectively it becomes apparent how the materiality of information facilitated subsequent actions and, in principle, would enable lower-level functionaries to claim later that they were simply following orders. However, many of these ordinary bureaucrats would also find themselves at the mercy of the same documents they prepared, filed, and circulated.

Over time, fear would permeate the CPK's governmental hierarchy: zone-level committees would watch sector-level committees; sector-level committees would watch district-level committees; and so on down the chain of command. In this manner paranoia diffused spatially throughout society, contributing to a peculiar geography of suspicion and mistrust. As Harper explains, "When suspicion is a condition of surveillance, any comment on that surveillance embroils the speaker in suspicion—their own—and they are thus positioned as paranoid." This is fatally revealed in the testimony of Kim Vun. During the period of Democratic Kampuchea rule, Kim Vun worked in various subunits associated with the Ministry of Propaganda and Information. His wife, Chim Nary, also occupied many positions that placed her in regular contact with high-ranking officials, including Yun Yat, then deputy secretary of the Ministry of Education. At some point, in late 1977 or early 1978, a number of associates, including three men named Pang, Kat, and Chhay, disappeared. Kim Vun recalls telling his wife, "You need to be careful because you worked with them; be careful not to get involved." He also told her, perhaps naively, that because both of them worked with members close to the Party Center and were known by so many senior officials, she could never be taken away and killed. Kim Vun was wrong in his assessment of Party loyalty, and his optimism that the Khmer Rouge bureaucracy would look after its own was gravely misplaced. Chim Nary and their twelve-month-old daughter were approached by a man on a motorbike. Kim Vun remembers waiting throughout the night for his wife and daughter to return, but when morning arrived, his family was still missing. At the Ministry of Propaganda and Education offices, Kim Vun asked about his wife and child, and was informed that they had been taken to attend a study session. Dissatisfied with the vague response, Kim Vun went up the chain of command to Yun Yat. She replied simply that he had "No need to know about that now." Perhaps because of his questioning, Kim

Vun was himself sent to attend a political study session for two weeks. It was only after this period of bureaucratic purgatory that Yun Yat informed him that his wife had been arrested because she was linked to a CIA network. Kim Vun would never see his wife or daughter again.[67]

Secrecy, surveillance, and violent enforcement of the Party and revolution predated the CPK's victory on April 17, 1975. However, documentary evidence illustrates a deepening of biopolitical concerns, especially throughout 1976. My sense is that having attained victory, the CPK leadership became even more insecure in not wanting to lose what they had already achieved. Consequently, we witness an expansion of the scale and scope of direct violence. As Bach suggests, "power as survival consists not only of forestalling death, but of creating it."[68] It was incumbent upon the upper echelon to be vigilant in the compilation of personal biographies, in the education of proper political ideology, and in the surveillance of its population for indications of betrayal or sabotage. Those holding positions of authority were to be anticipatory in their outlook, in order to forestall any possible enemy activity before it took place.

The ability to command the death of others enhances the effect of survivorship.[69] In Democratic Kampuchea, the public display of torture and execution at the branch level served to reify the authority of Angkar. This is succinctly described by Haing Ngor: "The soldiers took captives morning and afternoon. Instead of marching them away immediately, the soldiers made public examples of them, tying them to trees and shouting to anyone who would listen what they had done wrong."[70] However, not all acts were visible. Many, in fact, took place in secrecy—a procedure that elevated a sense of fear and insecurity among the populace. Indeed, it was commonplace that men, women, and children simply disappeared. Sreytouch Svay-Ryser was only seven years old when the Khmer Rouge came to power. Forced to leave Phnom Penh and move to a collective in Battambang, Svay-Ryser recalls the constant fear that Angkar would discover her brother had previously served in the Lon Nol army. She writes: "We knew that any time or at any hour Angkar could come to get him. Angkar usually came and took people away during the night. So when it got dark, we couldn't sleep."[71] Roeun Sam was a teenager; she recalls the terror: "When night came I always worried. I stayed up even when they told us to go to sleep. Angkar walked around with a flashlight at night to see who was asleep and who wasn't. I was afraid that maybe next time it would be me. I would die before I saw the sun rise. I had little rest, and then I heard the whistle and inside I sighed, 'Oh, I'm alive!' I got up and got in line. From one night to the next it was the same."[72]

"In a system of ubiquitous spying," Hannah Arendt writes, "everybody may be a police agent and each individual feels himself under constant surveillance."[73] Indeed, throughout Democratic Kampuchea, an inescapable paranoia operated at multiple levels, as those who were watching themselves became increasingly paranoid of being watched. As Ngor writes, "People carried within them an unspoken fear. They worried about their own survival, and they didn't trust anyone else, even their spouses."[74] Ngor's experiences relate to what Mark Andrejevic describes as lateral surveillance: not the top-down monitoring of employees by employers, or of citizens by the state, but rather the peer-to-peer surveillance of spouses, friends, and relatives.[75] At this point, the policing of society and securing the state is off-loaded onto the citizenry. Such lateral surveillance, however, continues to be tied to the monitoring of authorities, who establish the bureaucratic guidelines for subjects responsible for their own security, a responsibility that includes keeping an eye on those around them.[76]

One consequence of feeling watched is to render the subject self-conscious and fearful. Knowledge of an omnipresent system of surveillance is to induce paranoia whereby individuals begin to monitor themselves. Hence, the paranoia evinced by those in positions of authorities permeates society, but it is a decidedly unequal paranoia. In effect, those individuals who are subjected to practices of surveillance engage in what Michel Foucault called "technologies of the self."[77] Here, technologies of the self include those practices "which permit individuals to effect by their own means or with the help of others a certain number of operations on their own bodies and souls, thoughts, conduct, and way of being."[78]

It is beyond the scope of this section to fully explicate the nuances of Foucault's argument. For our present purposes, I consider the implications of Foucault's argument within the context of the bureaucratic governance of a surveillance society. In such an environment, prison walls are not necessary to enforce discipline. Rather, the threat of being watched, or of maintaining social contacts with others, may be sufficient to induce a sense of personal paranoia. Democratic Kampuchea was, in this sense, a terror society. It was a society in which no one, including the senior leaders of the CPK, felt secure. In short, the massive scale of state surveillance meant that not only were all people aware of the possibility of others being informers, but also that others would view them as potential informers.[79] In the beginning, men and women like Kim Vun may have expressed optimism that Angkar would protect them. In the end, few (if any) people would feel that way. With their lives inscribed on paper, form-based prisoners to the ever-present compilation of even more information on daily behaviors or social relationships, they all came under suspicion and were subjected to the possibility of arrest and execution.

If Democratic Kampuchea was a terror society, it is not simply because of the specter of physical violence, of random killings, rape, and torture. It was also because Democratic Kampuchea was very much a bureaucratic society. And it was this administrative component that conditioned everyday life. According to Foucault, the development of administrative structures and bureaucracies increased the amount and role of writing in the political sphere. Foucault elaborates that "Taking care of oneself became linked to constant writing activity. The self is something to write about, a theme or object (subject) of writing activity."[80] Viewed from this perspective, the obligation of everyone throughout Democratic Kampuchea to prepare, on a repeated basis, personal biographies assumes an added element of significance. For it was through the composition and compilation of biographies that bureaucrats throughout the governance structure maintained tabs on those people under their jurisdiction. There was a legal order throughout Democratic Kampuchea predicated upon a particular technology of the self whereby all men and women were to divulge not only the social networks in which they were allegedly embedded, but also their thoughts and attitudes.

In the next chapter I discuss in greater detail the torture-induced confessions extracted from detainees at S-21 and other security centers throughout Democratic Kampuchea. Before doing so, however, it is necessary to emphasize that confessions were but one form of documentary evidence the Khmer Rouge produced in support of their conspiracy theories of traitorous networks. For before any man or woman was arrested, tortured, and forced to confess to crimes they did not commit, they were pressed to cast suspicion upon themselves and others through acts of self-incrimination. Drawing on Foucault, Ian Burkitt explains that the experience of the self becomes intensified and widened in writing, which is a technique for more detailed introspection. Through the act of writing (or, in the case of illiteracy, transcription), the self can become objectified in a different way than in speech, for the act of writing sets down on paper one's self. Burkitt concludes that "writing is a technique of the self in which the self becomes more stabilized as an object that can be set out in detail before oneself and others and, in such an objective form, studied and analyzed."[81]

To summarize my argument thus far: through displacement, forced labor, the imposition of inadequate food rations, and other deprivations, the CPK negatively affected the material conditions of the population and reduced their potential to survive. These tactics of social reorganization established a structure of violence and a condition of rule that contributed to the deaths of upward of two million people. This systematic coproduction of violence—through technologies like the food ration, the reorganization of Cambodia's space economy, and the instantiation of a security apparatus—sub-jugated life to the threat of death, an expression of what Achille Mbembe terms *necropower*: "The generalized instrumentalization of human existence and the material destruction of human bodies and populations."[82] The CPK implemented these policies not out of insanity or impulsive cruelty, but because such policies were rational to the imperatives of their particular political economy based on the expansion and intensification of agricultural productivity and import substitution industrialization.[83] In the process, the bureaucratic structure of governance throughout Democratic Kampuchea induced myriad strategies of surveillance: a managerial strategy, whereby superiors monitored the actions of their subordinates; a lateral form of surveillance, whereby spouses, friends, relatives, and coworkers monitored each other; and a form of auto-surveillance, a technology of self, whereby men and women self-surveilled through the writing of personal biographies. Consequently, the structure of rule came to imitate the symptoms of paranoia, which included a slowly developing mistrust, suspicion of others, theories of a highly organized system that appears as a conspiracy, fear of loss of autonomy, projective thinking, and violence.[84] It is now possible to consider in greater detail the infrastructure of the Khmer Rouge security apparatus.

The CPK's Security Apparatus

In conventional accounts of CPK security, including but not limited to those of S-21, scholars draw heavily on the writings of Erving Goffman. In his influential study on asylums, for example, Goffman defines a total institution as "a place of residence and work where a large number of like-situated individuals, cut off from the wider society for an appreciable period of time, together lead an enclosed, formally administered round of life."[85] Operationally, the concept of a total institution speaks to a condition where one's life is dominated by faceless bureaucracies: an isolated, dehumanized existence whereby one is subjected to myriad rules and regulations.

Goffman's work has been widely applied in the social sciences, including studies not only on asylums, but also schools, the military, and prisons. It is not surprising, therefore, that scholars of Democratic Kampuchea would do likewise.[86] Most well known is the pioneering work of David Chandler, who describes Democratic Kampuchea as "a total institution par excellence" and S-21 as "an extreme example of a total institution."[87] The problem, conceptually, is that the documentary evidence reveals a more nuanced understanding. Indeed, given the plethora of archived meeting minutes, telegrams, reports, and letters, the concept of a total institution as heuristic device rapidly breaks down. Democratic Kampuchea was not a closed society. Nor did the CPK attempt to impose complete isolation throughout society. Adhering to the principles of the Non-Aligned Movement, for example, the CPK selectively engaged with foreign governments, as senior leaders cautiously participated in trade relations or accepted foreign aid. To be sure, accessibility to the so-called outside world was limited, but it is simply not the case that the CPK leadership attempted to wall off Democratic Kampuchea and become entirely self-reliant.

Is it possible, though, to conceive more narrowly of the Khmer Rouge security apparatus as a total institution? Certainly S-21 and the many other security centers throughout Democratic Kampuchea were walled off, surrounded by armed guards and barbed wire. Secrecy was of the utmost importance. Such banal statements, of course, can be applied to almost any prison throughout, say, the United States. To avoid such platitudes, it is necessary to consider more precisely, and supported by documentary evidence, the form and functions of the Khmer Rouge security apparatus within the broader context of CPK bureaucracy. It is essential, in other words, to resituate the socio-materiality of security centers within the hierarchical and territorial parameters of the Khmer Rouge bureaucracy. It is for this reason that I turn to recent developments in carceral geographies.

Broadly conceived, the field of carceral geography, on the one hand, is concerned with the spaces and practices of incarceration but, on the other hand, seeks to critique the carceral as something more than the spaces in which individuals are confined, that is, to conceive of the carceral as a social and material construction relevant both within and beyond the physical sites of incarceration.[88] Carceral geographies, in effect, move beyond the limitations of the total institution to address the totality of institutions in all their complexity. To this end, geographers, criminologists,

sociologists, and other social scientists have challenged two fundamental aspects of Goffman's conception of a total institution as it
applies to prisons. First, scholars have stressed the need to place
prisons and other sites of detention within a wider political
economic context. Prisons are more than simply sites of incarceration or places designed to impose discipline and punishment on
inmates. Rather, prisons are being reevaluated as crucial nodes in
the functioning of political and economic processes. Building on
this, a second challenge is the caution against promoting an uncrit-
ical understanding of prisons as "impervious, closed-in on
themselves and cut-off from the wider world."[89] Keith Farrington,
for example, calls attention to "diverse transactions, exchanges and
relationships, which connect and bind together (a) the prison institution, (b) its immediate host community, and (c) society more
generally." He elaborates that "When looked at from this perspective, it appears that Goffman's notion of the prison as a total
institution might best be rejected in favor of a somewhat different
theoretical conception—that of the prison as a 'not-so-total' institution, enclosed within an identifiable-yet-permeable membrane of
structures, mechanisms and policies, all of which maintain, at
most, a selective and imperfect degree of separation between what
exists inside of and what lies beyond prison walls."[90] Jennifer Turner
agrees, writing that "Despite their often secluded physical locations,
which position them in geographically outlying or isolated sites, the
inter-linkages between prisons and society are numerous and
complex."[91]

Security centers within Democratic Kampuchea were physically
barricaded and heavily guarded, and visitors most definitely were
not admitted. But this is not the same as implying there was no connection between any given center and the broader society. Telegrams
and reports were circulated within and between security centers;
other written documents entered and left via couriers and messen-
gers; and key members of the CPK would personally visit various
security centers that fell under their jurisdiction. Indeed, if these
institutions had been so completely shut off, the purges throughout
Democratic Kampuchea would not have happened. Simply put, it

was the *circulation* of information through a bureaucratic chain of command that was essential to the administration of violence enacted by the CPK. Accordingly, a conception of the porosity of security centers provides a more accurate accounting of the Khmer Rouge security apparatus than that of Goffman's total institution.

We need to rethink Khmer Rouge security centers not as walled enclosures sealed off from the rest of Democratic Kampuchea, but instead as key nodes in the transmission of information. For example, as discussed in Chapter 4, confessions obtained through interrogation were crucial for the manufacturing of strings of traitors whom the CPK perceived were infiltrating society. Confessions were used not only or even necessarily predominantly to establish guilt of the detainee but rather as biopolitical data to identify other suspected traitors for subsequent arrest, interrogation, and, most likely, execution. As Heder elaborates, "It appears that the confessions were produced for a larger purpose: to convince some skeptical individuals in the CPK leadership, and to confirm the suspicions of others, that the 'conspiracies' alleged by the Party existed, that these conspiracies explained the regime's failures, and that further arrests were required in order to give proper effect to the regime's policies."[92]

A hierarchical network of approximately two hundred security centers, mirroring the overall bureaucratic structure of Democratic Kampuchea, was established throughout the country. Each zone in theory was to maintain a zone-level security center, each sector a sector-level security center, and so on.[93] In practice, the resultant security apparatus proved exceptionally adept at introducing the myriad techniques of surveillance throughout society. As Meng-Try Ea concludes, the "operational methods of these centers were uniform and employed widely." Moreover, "there was coordination among all levels of security centers, with communications going both up and down the chain of command."[94]

The lowest level of CPK governance, as explained earlier, was composed of branch-level entities, including villages, communes, cooperatives, and mobile work brigades. The salience of this level is that cadre had immediate access to the general population. The

compilation and review of personal biographies was vitally important. Information in this way routinely circulated throughout the
administrative structures. Local officials would inform their superiors at the district level on the enemy situation; they would also
implement directives sent from above, such as requests to investigate suspected networks of traitors. Commune-level officials also
were responsible for deciding who should be refashioned, in other
words, deciding who would be sent for harsh labor and political
education in special work camps. This was generally punishment
for failing to achieve work quotas, committing minor infractions
such as stealing food, or, in some cases, simply behaving strangely.[95]
A youth named Kap, for example, was arrested on July 8, 1978.
According to the accompanying letter, sent by Thuok, a member of
the Committee of the Cooperative of the Trapeang Thom North
Commune, Kap had become insane and, during a period of hospi-
talization, began singing a traitorous song.[96]

A crucial function of the security apparatus at this level was the
provision of concrete observations of suspected enemy activity,
notably the presence of traitorous networks. One local official
named San, for example, arrested two men—Hul and Sean. These
men were subsequently transferred to a higher-level security center,
along with a letter with the request to "Interrogate the contemptible
Hul, Second-Lieutenant, and ask him to find out his network. When
he fled Phnom Chruos Chrey . . . , whether he had his network in
Chamcar Sieng or not? What are their names? Concerning the
named Sean, who was sent there yesterday, I would like to also ask
Comrade elder brother to interrogate to find out his network of
assignment, and ask him who else has been assigned?"[97]

Branch-level security centers were normally small structures,
perhaps a wooden shack or converted building. Generally, these
would hold only a few prisoners at a time, most of whom would be
released after a period of detainment. Those detained were most
often accused of minor crimes, perhaps stealing food. More important prisoners would be transferred to higher-level security centers.
Executions at the branch level did take place, although written documentation is scarce.[98] It is also known that local officials would

directly order the execution of detainees. On some occasions, however, officials would request guidance from officials higher up the chain of command. Policing functions were most often conducted by the armed militias known as *chhlop*. These cadres would guard the forced labor units, spy on people, make arrests, and, if needed, execute dissidents.[99]

To a certain extent, higher-level security centers functioned as collection points for those accused of more serious crimes, such as theft or immoral sexual relations. Frequently, soldiers and civil servants of the former Lon Nol regime, arrested at lower levels, would be detained at district- and sector-level security centers.[100] For example, on July 6, 1978, a man named Nun was arrested from Trapeang Thom North Commune. He was accused of serving in the Lon Nol army. This was "according to the statement of his wife who was sent over . . . by the Trapeang Thom North Commune's base, because his wife had also committed activities to destroy the cooperative."[101]

One step removed from the branch level, district-level security centers served an important function in the initial gathering and evaluation of information collected from the disparate units within their jurisdiction. For example, one document indicates that a woman was to be arrested and sent to the district-level security center. She was a farmer and wife of a military officer and had three children. According to the report, the woman in question allegedly said, "Doing the revolution is very difficult, we have to do the works days and nights, and are given gruel to eat; we cannot bear this sort of living. During the old regime, I had never been working, but still I had a car to take me when going down from my house, wherever I went, I always had a car to take me. But now, I have to do rice farming, it's very difficult!" The report further specified that the accused "had many more conflicts."[102]

In effect, district-level bureaucrats provided the fundamental material link between agricultural cooperatives and work projects and the wider governmental bureaucracy.[103] District-level officials "were responsible for ensuring that every Cooperative continuously identified and eliminated enemies in order to build socialism quickly."[104] Officials at this level were also required to keep the upper echelon informed of ongoing work efforts, and prepare and transmit situation reports on the progress of work activities and enemy activity. District Committees were also required to draw up lists of those to be executed. These lists were subsequently transmitted up the chain of command. Etcheson concludes that "CPK leadership at the District echelon had broad authority over personnel and organizational matters, security, and economic matters within their respective Districts."[105]

Illustrative of a district-level security center is the Kraing Ta Chan security center, a fenced-in compound composed of several wooden buildings. Located in District 105, Sector 13, Southwest Zone, the site was first established as a meeting place for Khmer Rouge officials during the revolution. In mid-1973 it was converted by the Sector Committee into a detention office under the control of the District 105 Committee; it remained in operation until the collapse of Democratic Kampuchea. It is not known precisely how many people were detained throughout the existence of Kraing Ta Chan.[106] Archived documentation indicates a capacity of approximately 100 detainees per month. One document from July 1977, for example, indicates that 18 new prisoners arrived that month, bringing the total to 81; however, 39 were executed and 2 others died from diseases, thus dropping to just 40 detainees at the end of the month. A similar report for November 1977 specifies that 75 people were admitted to the security center; 92 were purged; 6 died of illness; and 1 was transferred to another location. Overall, by month's end, the prison population stood at 85. Also included in the report was a tally sheet of "food production" and "economic expenditures." Thus, on the one hand, the security center planted 7 cabbage plots, 2 garlic plots, 200 tobacco plants, 270 tomatoes, and various other fruits and vegetables. The security center used 860 cans of paddy rice, 34 gasoline cans, 80 cans of salt. An additional 95 bags of rice were issued to Samrong Subdistrict, 1.5 bags of manioc to Toteung Thngai Village, and 2 bags of seed rice and 2 horse carts of manioc plants were sent in support of District 106.[107] This tally sheet added to the list of detainees is significant in that it highlights an additional material flow that bridged security centers and the broader society. Many security centers were designed to be places of production. And while not rising to the level of the slave-labor camps of Nazi Germany, the security centers of Democratic Kampuchea were expected to produce much of their own foodstuffs and indeed produce sufficient surpluses for distribution. It is important to acknowledge, therefore, that more than just prisoners entered the security centers. Other products, including clothes and tools, were also brought in. This illustrates that security centers were very much connected within the larger circuits of Democratic Kampuchea's political economy.

Kraing Ta Chan demonstrates many of the security functions of district-level security centers. For example, confessions were often the fundamental building blocks of CPK conspiracy theories. At Kraing Ta Chan, confessions were obtained as a means of identifying subsequent traitors, and this information was subsequently transmitted up and down the chain of command. Customarily, the chairman of Kraing Ta Chan would report and send confessions to the District Committee; they, in turn, would transmit these to the Sector Committee. At the end of the month, the district secretary would send a written report on its activities to the sector. Some witnesses recall that if the matter concerned only the sector, information was possibly sent directly to the zone level or Central Party, bypassing the District Committee.[108]

Unlike branch-level security centers, district-level security centers, such as Kraing Ta Chan, were more permanent in structure and often located in or near larger towns and cities. Operationally, prisoners would arrive night and day, either individually or in groups. Some of these prisoners were transfers from branch-level security centers while others were sent directly. Men, women, and children were detained at Kraing Ta Chan. Most were new people, but base people, former Khmer Republic soldiers, CPK cadre, Chinese, Vietnamese, and Cham were also imprisoned at the facility. Men and women were shackled together in large cells, usually comprising two rows of twenty to twenty-five people each. Children under ten years of age were not shackled, but kept near their mothers.[109] Conditions were horrific, with detainees dying of disease, starvation-related conditions, and maltreatment. There is no record of medical facilities being present on-site. [110]

Detainees were tortured, with both physical and psychological forms applied to extract confessions. Physical forms of torture included beatings and suffocation. Eyewitness accounts suggest that water boarding was also used. There is also evidence that acid may have been thrown on people.[111] Initial confessions were hand-written. These were subsequently typed and used as a basis for additional rounds of interrogation. Once completed, confessions were channeled to the district secretary, who would, after reviewing the document, forward it to the sector secretary. In turn, the sector secretary would advise the District Committee of which individuals were to be killed and those who were to be released. These names would subsequently be forwarded to Kraing Ta Chan for implementation.[112] For example, on August 25, 1977, a report was filed summarizing the conclusions of three men, all former military officers, who had been interrogated. They were allegedly "against the cooperative" and "were not happy with labor work." All three confessed to being "upset in the cooperative . . . because they had always been in the positions of ordering people; and with their [former] titles, they had money and fancy life." An annotation on the report, dated August 27, 1977, reads: "As to these three traitors, the Party decided to have them smashed."[113] This and other documentation suggest that the Sector Committee was primarily responsible for determining who was to be executed.[114] The Central Party, in turn, was informed of these actions. In total, these procedures illustrate how notations written by senior leaders grant the confession official status. Confessions as documents are "accepted as evidence that a designate official saw and touched the paper" and that this "is read to verify that the official has knowledge of the information the document conveys, that it is information that he or she knows to be true."[115]

Those prisoners scheduled for execution were usually taken at night to one of the many mass graves in the surrounding area. Here, deceptive practices were used, in part to ensure docility among the prisoners. For example, it was not uncommon that Khmer Rouge guards would tell the condemned men and women that they were being returned to their former unit. In reality, they were blindfolded and transported to the execution site by foot, oxcart, or truck, depending on the distances involved and the number of prisoners taken at any given time. Oral testimonies indicate that some prisoners were forced to dig their own burial pits while other accounts indicate that the pits had already been excavated by guards. The moment of execution was swift. Prisoners were forced to kneel in front of the pit. From behind they were struck by a blow to the back of the neck with a cart axle, a digging hoe, or some other blunt object. This was followed by a slash of the throat. Murder was rudimentary and brutal. Estimates as to the total number of victims vary, with upward of fifteen thousand men, women, and children thought to have died at Kraing Ta Chan.[116]

The Sang security center provides another example of a district-level security center. This facility was located in District 145, Sector 25, Southwest Zone, and came into operation around 1976 or 1977.[117] It too remained in operation until the collapse of Democratic Kampuchea. The Sang security center was formerly a teacher training center. Having been converted to a prison, it consisted of several concrete structures, including special detention cells for CPK cadres who had committed serious offenses. Other buildings included a kitchen, guardhouse, and a blacksmith.[118]

Similar to Kraing Ta Chan, the Sang security center detained men, women, and children. Most detainees were local, having been arrested from the surrounding area. Prisoners included CPK cadre, new people, base people, and former Khmer Republic soldiers. Consequently, most crimes for which people were arrested included expressing loyalty toward or sympathy for the former regime, engaging in traitorous activities, or sabotage. This latter crime could include not following orders, breaking shovels or plows, or stealing food. Countless others were arrested simply because their names appeared in other prisoners' confessions.[119] Torture was also used to extract confessions, and the attendant information was circulated up and down the chain of command. Indeed, it was very

important that information derived from confessions was transmitted to the cooperative or mobile unit where the detained was
previously assigned. In this way, branch-level officials could conduct
further investigations into alleged enemy networks.[120]

Sector Committee members who held jurisdiction over the Sang
facility would decide on the fate of detainees. And similar to the
procedures at Kraing Ta Chan, prisoners at Sang were taken away at
night, often under false pretenses. Some were released, others transferred to neighboring district-level security centers because of
periodic overcrowding, and still others were transferred to higher-
level prisons. Many were simply killed. For the Sang security center,
the main execution site was a grove of bamboo, located approximately one kilometer away. Accordingly, most condemned
prisoners walked to the killing grounds, where they were blindfolded, stripped of clothing, and forced to kneel by the edge of a pit
to await the fatal blow. It is estimated that upward of five thousand
people processed through the Sang facility were executed.[121]

Sector-level facilities operated much as district-level security
centers. Prisoners by and large were either sent to these security
centers directly on the orders of zone-level or sector-level officials,
or were transferred from lower-level facilities, most often regionally
based district-level prisons. Also prevalent were sector-level reeducation centers. In the Southwest Zone, for example, the Region 33
security center functioned more as a forced labor camp than the
prototypical security center. At Region 33, prisoners, many of
whom were arrested for having committed theft or for not meeting
production quotas, were by and large not shackled. Rather, they
lived in six cooperatives, one each for the elderly, widows with or
without children, male and female youth, and children. In general,
detainees were forced to perform physical labor, such as working in
nearby agricultural fields. That being said, detainees could be subjected to torture and interrogation and even execution.[122]

Region 33 illustrates the exception to the rule. In general, sector-
level security centers were for men and women deemed to be guilty
of the most serious offenses, such as traitorous activities or their
association with traitors. Prisoners arrived at sector-level security

centers via one of two main pathways. Detainees could be transferred from district-level or perhaps even branch-level facilities. It appears as if the precise route of transfer depended on geography. Prisoners, for example, could be transferred directly from a branch-level to a sector-level facility, bypassing the district level altogether. Or prisoners could be arrested and sent initially to a sector-level security center.

Sector-level committees, including those who ran the security centers, had a high degree of autonomy in their decision-making. Documentary evidence indicates that sector-level officials could and did execute prisoners on their own volition, provided (ostensibly) that the upper echelon was kept informed. Earlier, I made reference to a telegram sent on July 18, 1976, by Bu Phat (alias Hang) informing the Standing Committee of recent traitorous activities and that ten men had been smashed.[123] Likewise, in a telegram dated March 21, 1976, Suas Nau (alias Suas Son alias Chhouk), secretary of Sector 24, reported to the East Zone secretary, So Phim (alias Chhon), that a number of Vietnamese had been captured in recent days. Suas Nau explained that at least one man had been beaten during his interrogation in an attempt to learn more about "his organizational links." So Phim, in turn, forwarded the telegram to Pol Pot, Nuon Chea, Son Sen, and Ieng Sary.[124] In other cases, especially if the accused was an important Party member, sector-level officials would specifically request from the zone or Party permission to execute people under their control.[125]

Another example of a sector-level facility is the Phnom Kraol security center, a multifaceted complex that included the Phnom Kraol Prison, Sector 105 Office K-11, and the Sector 105 secretary, headquartered at Office K-17. In existence since before 1975, the security center was initially under the command of the Northeast Zone until, at the end of 1976, it became autonomous and thereafter reported directly to the CPK Center. The prison proper was a one-room wooden structure, although prisoners were occasionally detained at K-17.[126] Executions took place at Trapeang Pring (also known as Tuol Khmaoch), located about 4 kilometers from the prison.

More than simply a place of detainment and execution, the security center, but especially K-17, was an important conduit of information. Evidence reveals a constant flow of communications between the Party Center and this facility. K-17, for example, would regularly send information to the District Committees under its jurisdiction. It would also report directly to the Party Center. Surviving documents establish a chain of information between the Phnom Kraol security center and both Office 870 and K-3 (Khieu Samphan's residence). Monthly meetings with high-ranking Party officials were also held at K-11 (medical affairs).[127]

Witness testimony suggests that the majority of prisoners at Phnom Kraol were accused of treasonous activities. Party members would be arrested directly by Khmer Rouge cadre after having been called to a meeting. Others were arrested at their home units, usually under order of the sector secretary. Still others were transferred from district- or branch-level facilities following an earlier period of detainment, torture, and interrogation. Procedures were similar to those found at other sector-level and district-level prisons. Upon arrival, prisoners were required to write down their personal biographies and these documents would, subsequently, be used to identify contradictions in the accused person's background. Detainees were shackled and held in large communal cells. Those criminals considered more serious, or those holding more senior-level positions, were often kept in isolation. The Phnom Kraol security center, similar to other sector-level facilities, had a capacity of approximately four hundred.[128]

Given that sector-level security centers most often held prisoners accused of the most serious crimes, interrogation procedures, including torture, were widely employed. Center 15, a sector-level security center located in Sector 25, Southwest Zone, is instructive. First established sometime in 1973, during the revolution, Center 15 was initially located at Rokakroam Village, Sa-ang District. It was then relocated sometime in 1974 to Khbal Chroy Village, Koh Thom District, before it was moved to Koh Thmei Island sometime in 1975. A converted *wat* was used to detain male prisoners while female prisoners were detained at the former Koh

Thmei elementary school. A nearby house was converted into a residence for prison guards, and another structure was used for interrogation. Condemned prisoners were executed in the nearby fields.[129]

Center 15 is notable in that it sits at the center of a major conspiracy network that was purged by the CPK. Meng-Try Ea, in his book *The Chains of Terror*, reconstructs what happened.[130] In mid-1976 a Khmer Rouge cadre exploded a grenade near the Royal Palace in Phnom Penh. He was subsequently arrested and interrogated. In his confession he implicated his superiors, So Phim and Suas Nau (alias Suas Son alias Chhouk). This was a remarkable revelation. So Phim was secretary of the East Zone and member of the Central Committee; Sous Nau was secretary of Sector 24. Confronted with this information, Pol Pot and other members of the Standing Committee began to suspect their associates of plotting a coup against the CPK leadership. Soon, Party officials from Sector 25 came under suspicion.

In due course, Chan Chakrei, chief of military Division 170, was arrested and sent to S-21. His confession implicated several other sector officials, including Huot Se, security chief, and Riel Lenh, district chief. Arrested and dispatched to S-21, these officials implicated still other people.[131] On August 30, 1976, at a meeting of secretaries and deputy secretaries, Son Sen explained that "more than 100 persons" thought to be connected with Chan Chakrei had been arrested; this came on the heels of the previous arrest of "more than 60 persons." Son Sen warned that these individuals "had been getting ready for [a] major unrest." It was necessary, therefore, to "Be conscientious about patrolling and do not allow enemies to make contact with one another." More specific measures included ongoing examination of "no-good elements" and the physical separation of people under suspicion.[132] On September 9, 1976, Son Sen explained further that "A lot of the links are connected to Division 170, either in that unit of organization currently or 170s that were sent to the [Ministry of] Industry." He also identified that linkages existed between members of Division 170 and divisions 180, 220, and 703. Son Sen admonished those in attendance to "Heighten the outlook of revolutionary vigilance" because "these activities are part of an overall enemy plan." He declared, "We have to be on guard against an enemy assassination of the Organization." To this end, Son Sen stated that it was necessary for division leaders to be "constant [in promoting] political and ideological education," but also to "firmly grasp biographies and ideologies." To ensure security, it was necessary to increase "surveillance of enemy situations." He concluded with the foreboding pronouncement: "The 170s should be rounded up in one place."[133] Eight days later, on September 17, 1976, 42 members of Division 170 were arrested. All would be executed by the end of the year. So "successful" was the operation that Son Sen could announce, on October 11, 1976, "We clearly see the conflict now. The leaders have been basically smashed." This was followed with a warning, though, that "their hands and arms still remain."[134]

Perhaps more than any other level, zone-level security centers were tasked with the function of smashing those considered most treasonous. Torture was the order of the day, and eventual execution all but a certainty. Similar to facilities administered at the sector level, reeducation camps were also in operation at the zone level. However, the ultimate security function at this level was to identify and punish criminal networks. Seated atop the administrative hierarchy and just below the Central Party, zone-level officials were required to disseminate operational objectives to the lower echelons while gathering and summarizing information from below. Zone Committees, coupled with their respective zone-level security-center commanders, had explicit authority to smash enemies, including Party members, prisoners of war, Khmer Rouge cadre, and both base and new people. And they did so with considerable regularity.

Conclusions

Pol Pot, Ieng Sary, and Nuon Chea, among others, believed in their own infallibility. Revolution was achieved against all odds because they alone, as members of a vanguard party, followed the correct line. The subsequent transformation would likewise be accomplished if and only if their operational objectives were conducted properly. Any deviation, any setback, could only be interpreted as betrayal by traitorous elements. In this way, the specific coordinates of the revolution contributed to the deepening of a conspiracy culture. Past betrayals were projected forward, demonstrating an expansionary logic to mundane reason brought about by the assumption that objects and events are characterized by qualities of coherence, consistency, and determinateness.[135] If the Khmer Communist revolution was betrayed in the past, so also it might be betrayed in the future. If once-loyal associates betrayed the Party in the past, so might others become disloyal in the future.

Bureaucratic violence does not stand outside of more spectacular forms of genocidal violence. Rather, the power of pens, paper, and filing cabinets facilitates violence of all forms to become manifest. And it is this twist, as Ian Shaw and Majed Akhter write, that "complicates our understanding of what a bureaucracy is: no longer the 'pen arm' of the sovereign as opposed to the 'sword arm.' Rather, both act in concert to fuel a deadly and alienated rule by Nobody."[136] The Khmer Rouge bureaucracy engaged in a low-tech practice of lethal surveillance, whereby mechanisms of surveillance and knowledge production and decisions of life and death became one and the same.[137] Certainly, real-time information was not assembled through the collection of digital information. Biopolitical information was, however, collected through the routine collection and compilation of revolutionary biographies, prisoner biographies, and forced confessions extracted through torture. To date, very little scholarly attention has been directed toward the production of these documents, that is, the biographies and confessions, by the Khmer Rouge. Such a conceptual shift, however, provides a radical way forward in understanding the security apparatus of Democratic Kampuchea. In an effort to resituate these data collection procedures as an early form of data mining, it becomes possible to accentuate the underlying bureaucracy that enabled purges to take place. For as Amoore and de Goede explain, "it is not the collection, monitoring or 'sight' of data that is significant, so much as the way decisions are made on the basis of a risk analysis that 'foresees.'"[138] In the end, before Kim Ham Bin and Chhim Sak were brutally murdered, they were killed by executive fiat.

CHAPTER 4

─────

Mortal Accountings

All that remains of Kiet Sophal is a photograph (Photograph 4.1). We know little about her death and even less about her life. Prison records indicate that she was arrested on April 13, 1977. Five other men and women were arrested on the same day: Mao Hok, a combatant assigned to the Ministry of Energy; Nuon Prang, a member of Division 920 and wife of Khun; Ping Chun, a combatant from the Ministry of Energy; Prakk Nat, squad member of Division 920; and Seam Ho, squad chief of the Ministry of Energy.

The entry for Kiet Sophal indicates that her alias was Phal; she was female, but no age is recorded. She was arrested from the Ministry of Public Works, where her job was to take care of children. There has been no information about her family or what she did prior to the revolution. We do not know why she was arrested. Was she accused of traitorous activities or found delinquent in her duties? Or was she arrested simply because she was associated with someone else charged with a crime? It is also not known if Kiet Sophal was interrogated. Perhaps she was tortured. Perhaps she was raped. All that is known is that Kiet Sophal was detained for ninety-nine days and was scheduled to be executed, along with eighty-one other men and women, on July 22, 1977.[1] None of the other five prisoners who entered S-21 were killed on this date.[2]

Since the fall of the Khmer Rouge, a surfeit of materials has been collected, archived, and analyzed. Many of these documents originated from S-21 and afford considerable opportunities for scholars, lawyers, and other concerned people to engage in fine-scaled and aggregate study of Khmer Rouge activities. Equally, if not more important, these documents have facilitated the efforts of staff members at the Documentation Center of Cambodia to

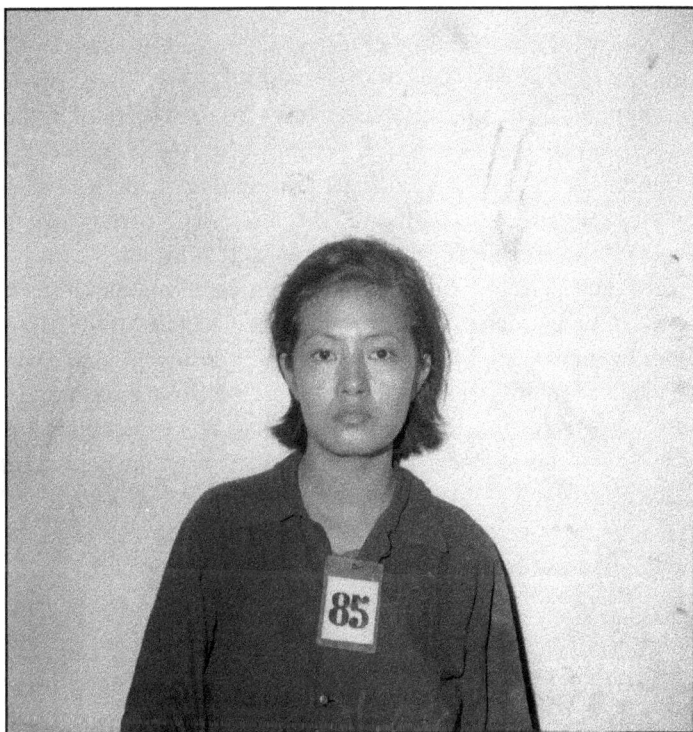

Photograph 4.1: Mug shot of Kiet Sophal *(Courtesy of Tuol Sleng Genocide Museum)*

help provide closure to countless men and women seeking information on friends and relatives who disappeared at the hands of the Khmer Rouge.

Records are incomplete, however, as the story of Kiet Sophal illustrates. Nevertheless, the documents provide an invaluable glimpse into the day-to-day bureaucracies of a genocidal regime. Any analysis of these records, though, must be firmly grounded in the concrete procedures by which they were originally produced and compiled. In this chapter I document the bureaucratization of violence. In so doing, I partially redress a lacuna surrounding the scholarly analysis of the Khmer Rouge security apparatus. Innumerable studies have focused on S-21 with much work concentrated on the memorialization of genocide as reflected by the conversion of the security center into a museum.[3] As well, a voluminous amount of scholarship has addressed the mug-shot photographs associated with S-21. This research, in particular, has explored the afterlife of S-21 photographs, that is, how we are to receive and perceive photographs of men, women, and children about to be murdered.[4] Apart from David Chandler's pioneering work, minimal empirical analysis of S-21 documents has been conducted.[5] In this chapter I step inside the S-21 security center. My intent is twofold: first, to interpret S-21 not as a total institution but instead as a bureaucratic center of calculation within a broader carceral geography of lethal surveillance; and second, to analyze the patterns of arrests and executions, thereby providing insight into the corporeal manifestation of administrative violence.

S-21 Security Center

Prior to assuming power in April 1975, the CPK had established a security apparatus known as *santebal*. The term itself is a contraction of the Khmer words *santesokh* (security) and *nokorbal* (police). According to Chandler, the santebal functioned similarly to the East German Stasi and even the American Federal Bureau of Investigation (FBI) and Britain's MI5, in that it was a national security police.[6] However, unlike these other security forces, the santebal had no central policy-making office and did little in the way of primary investigations. Rather, the primary function was simply to arrest, detain, and execute both external and internal enemies of the state.

From 1971 onward, security centers were established in those areas liberated by the armed forces of the Khmer Rouge. In July of that year, for example, a facility code-named M-13 was set up in Kampong Speu Province. Chaired by a former mathematician named Kaing Guek Eav (alias Duch), M-13 was divided into two parts: M-13A and M-13B. Prisoners detained at the former site were interrogated, tortured, and executed, while those at the latter were reeducated and released. In August 1975 high-ranking officials of the CPK determined that a security center was necessary to detain suspected Khmer Rouge cadre. Son Sen appointed In Lorn (alias Nat) as chairman of S-21 and Duch as deputy.

The overarching Khmer Rouge security apparatus was tasked with three functions: to reeducate, refashion, or purge men and women determined to be guilty of having committed, or likely to commit, criminal activities. Within the broader administrative structure, S-21 was unique in that it was established not to reform or rehabilitate but to specifically document and punish perceived criminal offenses against the Party. In other words, S-21 was administratively a state-level security center designed to eliminate principally those who allegedly committed treason or otherwise betrayed the Party, the revolution, and Democratic Kampuchea. In this way, S-21 was to function not as a concentration camp or extermination camp, such as those found throughout Nazi Germany, but instead as an integral component of the overall Khmer Rouge bureaucracy. Consequently, the targeted groups for S-21 were neither base people nor new people but instead Khmer Rouge soldiers, cadres, Party members, and their relatives. Effectively, S-21 was established by the Communist Party of Kampuchea to surveil and punish its own members—men and women such as Kiet Sophal.

Initially S-21 was located in Boeng Keng Kang 3 Subdistrict, Chamkar Mon District, Phnom Penh, and was composed of a series of buildings used for detention and interrogation. In late November 1975 the facility was moved to the building of the former National Police Headquarters, the Police Judiciaire compound on Street 51, located near the Central Market. However, due to concerns that visiting Chinese visitors might witness activities associated with the security center, it was relocated back to its original site. In March 1976 Nat was transferred and Duch was appointed chair and secretary of S-21 (Photograph 4.2). One month later, Duch ordered S-21 to be moved to the site of a former high school (Ponhea Yat

Photograph 4.2: Communal dining of S-21 staff. Duch is standing at the right. *(Courtesy of the Documentation Center of Cambodia Archives)*

Lycée), located between streets 113, 131, 320, and 350. S-21 remained at that location until the fall of Phnom Penh on January 7, 1979.[7]

The central compound of S-21 was surrounded by an outer barrier consisting of a 2 meter-high zinc wall, topped with barbed wire; an inner wall, also 2 meters in height, was formed of concrete and wrought iron. It too was lined with barbed wire. Two separate guard units were responsible for patrolling the perimeter. Within the main compound were five buildings. Building A functioned as the special prison for important prisoners, where they were most often tortured and interrogated in their individual cells. Buildings B, C, and D contained both common cells, where upward of twenty to forty prisoners might be detained, and individual cells, measuring about 2 meters by 1 meter (Photograph 4.3). These latter cells,

Photograph 4.3: Single prisoner cell at S-21 *(Courtesy of James A. Tyner)*

constructed of brick or wood, were used primarily for important prisoners awaiting interrogation. Building E, a one-story wooden structure, occupied the center of the compound and was used for registration and documentation purposes. Various other buildings outside the main compound were also used throughout the existence of S-21; these included former residences used for administrative purposes, political education classes, reception of prisoners, communal cooking and dining, interrogation, execution, medical facilities, S-21 staff housing, developing of photographs, and warehousing.[8]

Coupled with S-21 was a facility designated as S-24 (also known as S-21Kh). Located in Prey Sar Subdistrict, Dangkao District, Phnom Penh, S-24 was established to reeducate and rehabilitate those men, women, and children who came under suspicion but whose activities did not (yet) rise to a sufficient level of security risk. For example, those who exhibited dubious backgrounds or enemy tendencies might be sent to the Prey Say facility instead of S-21.[9] Detainees were divided into three groups: those considered to be better elements; those classified as fair elements; and those determined to be bad elements. Prisoners designated as fair or bad received comparatively harsher treatment and were subjected to more severe penalties.[10] Regardless of classification, all detainees at S-24 were forced to perform physical labor in an effort to correct them of their perceived offenses. Forced labor included the growing of food to support S-21 and other units. Detainees were also required to attend political training sessions and to provide detailed biographies.[11]

Prey Sar was supervised by Nun Huy (alias Huy Sre), who reported to the chairman at S-21. Immediate responsibilities included the oversight of food production, policy implementation, and investigations of prisoners. Huy Sre did not apparently have full authority to determine whether detainees were to be executed. Rather, Huy Sre would solicit advice from his superiors regarding the disposition of prisoners, as he did on January 19, 1976, when he forwarded a report regarding three combatants: "These youths are carefree and lazy; they are not doing any work. Two combatants of Unit 13 were detained, while the other one was kept in the 'release group.'"[12]

Key officials of the Standing Committee of the CPK retained oversight of S-21 and S-24. From its inception in 1975 to August 1977, S-21 was directly supervised by Son Sen (minister of defense), who, in turn, reported to Nuon Chea (deputy secretary of the CPK) and other members of the Standing Committee. During this period, Son Sen and Nuon Chea received confessions extracted at S-21, reviewed and commented on the confessions, and conveyed orders back to Duch. Such instructions might include specific avenues of questioning to pursue, or a determination that the confession was satisfactory.[13] They would also hold regular meetings with secretaries and deputy secretaries of various units. During these meetings, senior officials, notably Son Sen and Nuon Chea, would evaluate specific situations and recommend specific courses of action. In response to reports of enemy activity, on October 9, 1976, Son Sen surmised that the "traitorous links we have arrested one after the other compromised three networks, but at the end of the day, there is but a single network." Overall, Son Sen concluded that cadres needed to understand that "trivial activities attacking the Revolution such as stealing and speaking" are "all issues that stem from such traitorous links." Consequently, it was necessary to "solidly grasp our duties." Son Sen clarified that grasping meant "Grasping the Party, grasping core organizations, grasping male and female combatants, grasping their biographies clearly, and grasping their standpoints and ideology clearly. This is the main problem, the core problem, the key link in measures to defend our country." National security, in other words, was predicated on concrete assessments of all people, male or female, through continual evaluation of their political stance as inscribed on their personal biographies. Son Sen continued that "Continuous education is imperative" and that "It is imperative to purge no-good elements absolutely in the sense of an absolute class struggle." To this end, for the minister of defense, purges are premised on three principles: (1) the dangerous category, who must be absolutely purged; (2) the ordinary liberal category, who must be reeducated; and (3) the category of those who were merely incited by the enemy and who should undergo refashioning.[14]

On August 15, 1977, Son Sen was reassigned to administer the growing conflict with Vietnam. From that point onward, Duch reported directly to Nuon Chea. The two men met regularly, usually every three to five days, to discuss matters related to S-21. In addition, Nuon Chea would send written communiqués to Duch by messenger. These were usually short letters containing "brief, urgent orders."[15] Nuon Chea would also communicate with Duch through various intermediaries, including Chhim Sam Aok (alias Pang), secretary of S-71, or his deputy, Khan Lin (alias Ken). As a key component of the greater Khmer Rouge security apparatus, S-71 was responsible for the arrest and transfer of prisoners to S-21 or possibly to S-24. These logistics were often coordinated through Office K-7. Significantly, S-71 was also responsible for monitoring suspected CPK members.[16]

Procedural Operations at S-21

S-21 was a complex bureaucracy that, over its life-span, had a staff of approximately twenty-three hundred men and women.[17] Collectively, staff members at S-21 kept meticulous records of their activities. Surviving documents include arrest forms of individual prisoners; personal biographies of prisoners; day-by-day arrest schedules; mug-shot arrest photographs; daily charts on the prison population; handwritten or typewritten confessions; typed summaries of confessions; daily schedules for interrogation; summaries of torture methods used; photographs of tortured prisoners; postmortem photographs of prisoners who died or were executed during torture; reports on medicines administered to prisoners; signed execution orders; signed daily execution schedules; elaborate diagnostic flow charts of conspiratorial networks; and summaries of suspected plots uncovered to overthrow the Party. Various other documents include photographs and personal biographies of S-21; notebooks indicating procedures for conducting interrogations; notebooks from political education sessions; work schedules for guards; and correspondence between S-21 and the Standing Committee.[18]

Overall, a Supervisory Committee, composed initially of Nat, Duch, and Khim Vat (alias Hor), oversaw activities at S-21. Upon Nat's transfer, Duch was appointed secretary, Hor promoted to deputy secretary, and Huy Sre appointed as a third member. As supervisor of S-24, Huy Sre was not present at S-21 on a day-to-day basis. Consequently, most operational decisions at S-21 were made by Duch or Hor. Functionally, S-21 was composed of nine primary units. The Defense Unit was the largest subunit at S-21. Supervised by Hor and assisted by Phal, the Defense Unit was subdivided into three subunits. First were those guards responsible for outer security. This group was initially headed by a cadre known as Him Huy. It was their duty to restrict all access to the compound. Second were the inner guards, supervised by Peng. These men were responsible for guarding prisoners and preventing them from escaping or committing suicide. A third subunit, known as the Special Unit, was responsible for traveling outside of Phnom Penh to make arrests, guarding the special prison cells used to detain high-ranking cadre, transporting prisoners from S-21 to the execution site at Choeung Ek, and carrying out executions. This subunit was initially led by Peng, then by Poch, and finally by Him Huy. These supervisors would report directly to Hor, although Duch would also intervene when deemed necessary.[19]

At S-21 staff routinely performed a number of essential tasks. Arguably, no task was as critical as that performed by those assigned to the Interrogation Unit. Tellingly, as with any bureaucratic functionary, these men and women received training, followed established procedures, worked according to daily schedules, were supervised in their tasks, and, if found wanting in their performance, subject to disciplinary action. The Interrogation Unit, supervised by Duch and managed by Mam Nai (alias Chan alias Pon), consisted of two main subunits, with further divisions based on type of interrogative methods. One was the special subunit of interrogators; these men were responsible for interrogating high-ranking Party members and other important prisoners. The second was the general subunit. These men were responsible for extracting confessions from so-called ordinary prisoners. The general subunit was further divided into three groups, classified by torture methods used. These included a Cool (*trocheak*) Unit, which used verbal and psychological methods of interrogation; a

Hot (*kdau*) Unit, which beat and tortured prisoners; and a Chewing (*angkiem*) Unit, which conducted longer interrogations and utilized various forms of interrogative and torture methods.[20] Each subunit was composed of four to six people.[21]

At some point in 1977, Duch requested and received permission from his superiors to establish an all-female team of interrogators. In 2009 Duch testified at his trial that the idea of forming an all-female team of interrogators came about after a female prisoner was sexually abused by a male interrogator.[22] Five women were selected as interrogators; all were wives of male interrogators serving at S-21. And all would be executed before the fall of the Khmer Rouge. Duch acknowledged that these women had not committed any offenses but were smashed only because their husbands had come under suspicion and were also arrested and executed.[23]

Perhaps no department epitomizes the bureaucratic nature of S-21 as does the Documentation Unit. Supervised by Suos Thy, this unit was responsible for transcribing tape-recorded confessions, typing handwritten notes, preparing summaries of confessions, and maintaining the prison's files.[24] The unit was also responsible for the compilation of both prisoner biographies and staff biographies. Within this unit was the photography subunit. Also under the supervision of Suos Thy, but on a day-to-day basis headed by Nim Kimsreang, the photography subunit was tasked primarily with photographing prisoners upon their arrival (Photograph 4.4). Photographers were also required to take photographs of prisoners who died in captivity and of "important" prisoners after they were executed (Photograph 4.5). The subunit also took identification photographs that were included in the files of all staff members.[25]

Many other subunits ensured the day-to-day functioning of S-21. These included the Medical Unit (headed by Try), tasked with keeping prisoners alive—at least until they were scheduled to be executed; a Messenger Unit, responsible for transmitting information between S-21 and other bureaucratic entities, including the Standing Committee, zone-level secretaries, and the heads of various ministries; the Economics Unit, responsible for the preparation of food for S-21; and the Logistics Unit, whose function was

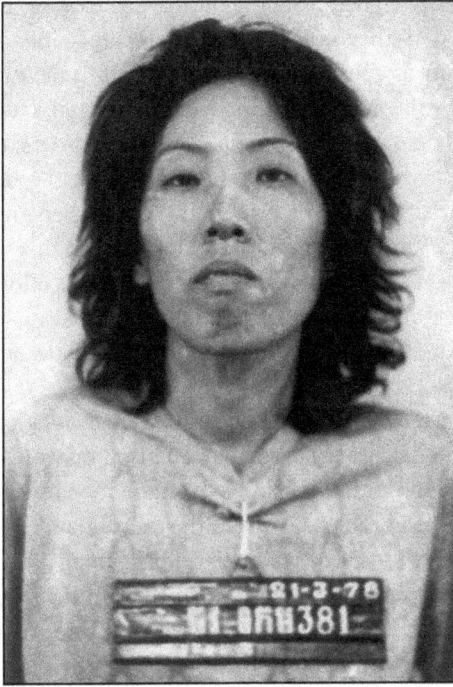

Photograph 4.4: Mug shot of Char Kem *(Courtesy of Tuol Sleng Genocide Museum)*

to oversee telephones, telegrams, vehicles for prisoner transportation, and water and electricity.[26]

How did S-21 function day to day? How did the various units and subunits administer the arrest, transportation, interrogation, and execution of more than twelve thousand men, women, and children? Michelle Caswell suggests that the "bureaucratic records that order and document mass murder are what, in part, enabled Khmer Rouge bureaucrats to authorize mass murder by isolating them from the consequences of their actions."[27] She elaborates that "through recordkeeping, Khmer Rouge bureaucrats like Son Sen and Duch were alienated from the murderous fruit of their labors in that the orders they issued would designate someone further down the chain of command to torture and kill prisoners."[28] To this, I am in partial agreement. Throughout his trial, Duch repeatedly made the case that he was simply following orders; that Nuon Chea or Son Sen were ultimately responsible for the decision to execute any prisoner; that he personally never killed anyone; and that he tortured only one person—and even then, it was not too extreme.[29] As Caswell concludes, "Such documents allowed Duch to efficiently monitor the daily operations of Tuol Sleng, while distancing and ultimately alienating him from the gruesome acts he ordered."[30]

Documentary evidence complicates this interpretation, including Duch's own defense. In particular, archived materials illustrate that neither senior leaders nor lower-level functionaries saw themselves as distanced or alienated from the task at hand. More to the point, documents indicate a concerted effort among participants to amass sufficient materials to justify (in their minds) the guilt of suspects. Annotated comments scrawled on copied confessions, telegrams sent between members of the Standing Committee and S-21 staff, and other written records linking myriad other units expose an exceptionally engaged bureaucracy, not an alienated one. Often it would begin with inscribing a name on a list or the recording of suspicious behavior.

Before any decision to arrest an individual was rendered, there needed to be some form of actionable evidence and there were all too many Khmer Rouge bureaucrats ready to provide documentation. And regardless of how flimsy that evidence may appear now, it does not belie the observation that from the CPK's point of view, biopolitical information was essential. For example, considerable evidence was derived from the compilation of firsthand observations: a man may have been overheard complaining of inadequate food rations; a woman may have been seen stealing a coconut. Often branch-level cadres would evaluate this evidence and make an initial decision regarding punishment. Rudimentary interrogative techniques may be applied, and following some level of physical or

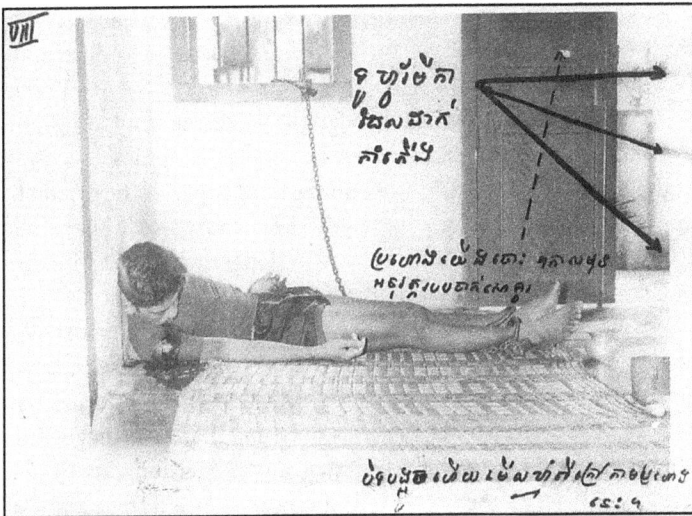

Photograph 4.5: Postmortem photograph of prisoner at S-21 (*Courtesy of Documentation Center of Cambodia Archives*)

psychological abuse, a list of suspects may be forwarded to the upper echelon for additional interrogation. Furthermore, cadres at various levels would generate lists of associates through these confessions. Any person whose name appeared on a list immediately came under suspicion and was subsequently observed, questioned, and possibly arrested. For example, on October 30, 1977, Ren, a staff member of the Revolutionary Army of Kampuchea, informed S-21 that thirty-six "bad elements" were removed. Of these, ten people were named specifically. A female comrade named Yean was accused of committing moral offenses and encouraging other cadre to steal; a man named Saroeun was listed as a militiaman, but "worked in a liberal manner"; while another man, Hok, was considered a "malingerer" and considered "very liberal." Both Makara and Keu Ly were deemed "dishonest and slothful." Twenty-six others went unnamed but were to be sent to S-24. The letter stated: "We are tracing them. Their offenses have not yet been categorized." In signing off, Ren requested further comments to help determine how to proceed.[31]

Evidence was also gained through the gathering, compiling, and evaluation of personal biographies. Personal biographies, especially at the branch level, were written on sheets of paper. If the person in question was illiterate or could not write, a cadre would transcribe the relevant information. Other institutions, such as the Ministry of Commerce or S-21, would provide prepared forms that would be filled out either by the man or woman or a staff member. For example, a brief biography of Khim Met was prepared when she was transferred to S-21 as a staff member. The document indicates that she was twenty years old and was born in Chonlus Village, Tuol Kreul Subdistrict, Kampong Svay District, Kampong Thom Province. Prior to the revolution, she worked as a farmer and was classified as a "middle class peasant." She joined the revolution on November 3, 1974, introduced by a person named Den. Her father, Khim Chin, was deceased and her mother, Pen Morn, worked at a cooperative. Khim Met was not married and had no children. She was transferred to S-21 on October 12, 1977.[32]

The biography of Khim Met is telling in that it reveals how the bureaucratic procedures initiated by the CPK facilitated the construction of social networks that were so vital to the purges. Precise information was requested not only of family members but also of other individuals with whom one may have been associated. Information was routinely gathered on previous units in which one served, thus establishing potential guilt when other units came under suspicion. Prior to her transfer to S-21, for example, Khim Met had served in both Unit 450 and Unit 17. If either of these two units came under suspicion, so too would Khim Met.

Personal biographies were material documents that became actionable objects. Authorities who held jurisdiction over the compilation of biographies, such as district- or sector-level secretaries, would review these documents for contradictions. If, for example, a cadre preparing his biography in 1976 specified his prerevolutionary occupation as farmer, but while preparing a biography in 1977 specified his former occupation as a factory worker, he would come under suspicion. If a cadre listed her birthplace as Phnom Penh on one document but indicated Battambang on another, she would come under suspicion. Authorities could also use biographies to identify social networks. Lists of known associates, for example, could be compiled and matched with other lists, including those provided by cadre serving at either higher or lower echelons.

Confessions of detainees at lower-level security centers were used to initiate additional investigations. On August 10, 1977, Sou Met, secretary of Division 502, wrote to Duch requesting information on the confession of a man from Battalion 512 named Sem. Sem had previously been sent to S-21 for interrogation. Sou Met writes: "I sent this person, whose name had been extracted from the confession of A Sa Um to you for a long time. I would like to have his confession shortly because in the confession of A Sa Um this person was alleged to have betrayed the party, with the instruction from a political assistant, Phal. Phal is working with me. I would like to know whether A Sa Um has provided thorough and precise answer, or we need to take Sem confession into further consideration."[33] This letter highlights not only the crucial role of confessions and how these were used to construct elaborate theories of conspiratorial strings of traitors but also the iterative component of investigations throughout the bureaucratic hierarchy.

The decision to arrest and ultimately send a person to S-21 was a multifaceted process that included innumerable individuals. According to Duch, the "right to arrest was vested with the people who had the right to smash." These guidelines, it will be recalled from Chapter 3, were detailed in a meeting held on March 30, 1976. Duch elaborates that "if the people made such a decision then the subordinates had to arrest them, and also arrest them in order not to allow them to fight back and also to keep the arrests secret."[34] The procedure was not simply a decision rendered by members of the Standing Committee. Senior cadres, most notably those serving on the Standing Committee, did not develop a priori lists of people to be executed. The scale and scope of purges required the active involvement of functionaries from the branch level through the highest echelons of governance. On October 9, 1976, a division secretary reported to Son Sen that a thirteen-year-old girl in the vicinity of Toek Sap was seized, and that she confessed to being a member of a group of three staying at Ou Phos. Another cadre reported that a man named Pring had been arrest by the local militia. When confronted, Pring allegedly admitted that he had left the Prateah Lang Commune without permission to participate with other confederates in a subversive demonstration.[35]

To be sure, the authority to decide the fate of any person was held largely by Nuon Chea, Son Sen, and other senior leaders of the Standing Committee, often in conjunction with considerable input from Duch and Hor. Testimony provided by Duch indicates that if the Standing Committee had made a decision to arrest a person, anyone who failed to respect such an order would in turn be subject to punishment, quite possibly even arrest and execution.[36] Members of the Standing Committee, but most especially Nuon Chea and Son Sen, reviewed confessions or summaries of confessions provided by Duch. These officials would assess the compiled names of suspected traitors and request follow-up information. Frequently, information derived from confessions would be forwarded to the relevant ministries, military units (such as Unit 703), or administrative committees to inform them of "enemy activities within that unit" and to allow them to "contemplate the arrest of the implicated persons." Consequently, information gathered by these lower-level functionaries would then be sent back to the Standing Committee and, often in consultation with Duch, a final decision was rendered as to who would be arrested.[37] Mok Sam Ol (alias Hong), chairman of the Ph-5 Anti-Malaria Hospital, for example, implicated cadres from both the Ministry of Social Affairs and the East Zone. Copies of the confession were sent to the relevant committees for further evaluation.[38]

A picture emerges whereby there was not a single, unidirectional chain of command or kill chain that extended from the Standing Committee to the lower echelons. Rather, significant input could be provided by, for example, a district-level secretary or a zone-level committee member. Undoubtedly, members would be mindful and tread cautiously so as not to call unwarranted attention upon themselves. That being said, the procedures involved in calling for the arrest of someone illustrate a complex bureaucratic system that required input and evaluation at multiple levels of governance.

It would be unfair to conclude that the Khmer Rouge security apparatus was a well-oiled machine. It is not the case that all villages, communes, or cooperatives routinely compiled and analyzed personal biographies or similar documents. Many units, especially those in remote locations, did not always have paper, so the documentation of suspicious activities was communicated orally. Furthermore, many cadres at the lower echelons were illiterate. And lastly, as the purges swept through the country, many administrative procedures, including both the documentation of men and women and the invoicing of goods produced, became increasingly sporadic. As the purges progressed throughout Democratic Kampuchea, the entire Khmer Rouge bureaucracy progressively began to implode because of the lack of personnel.

To be implicated in a confession did not always mean that arrest was certain. For example, of the twenty people named in Mok Sam Ol's confession, archived records of which I am aware indicate that only six were eventually sent to S-21.[39] This is not to minimize those six people who were killed because of the confession. Rather, it is to highlight that key functionaries did engage in evaluative procedures. From the CPK's perspective, there was a legal order in place and that evidence, however loosely defined we understand this term, was assessed. The most important decision was that of arrest, for once a decision was made that someone was to be arrested and sent to S-21, his or her fate was effectively sealed. It was then simply a matter of transporting that person to the security center.

On paper, the logistics of prisoner transport seems straightforward: an order is issued to arrest someone; guards are dispatched to make the arrest; and the prisoner is subsequently transported to S-21. In practice, the administration of prisoner transport to S-21 was more complex and varied, depending in part on the prisoner in question. Senior officials would often be summoned to a particular location, where an arrest would be made. Nuon Chea, for example, would send a telegram or letter to a district- or sector-level cadre requesting that they travel to Phnom Penh for political studies or some other meeting. Vin, chairwoman of the Ministry of Industry Hospital and wife of Vorn Vet, along with Phoas, wife of Vorn Vet's deputy, Chim An, were both summoned to Nuon Chea's office under false pretenses. Upon their arrival they were immediately arrested and transferred to S-21. Likewise, Ney Saran (alias Men San alias Ya), secretary of the Northeast Zone, was told he was being taken for medical care.[40]

For so-called less important prisoners, secrecy and deception were still utilized, if only to minimize potential disruption. In Chapter 3 I detailed a meeting that took place on September 16, 1976, when twenty-nine men and two women were to be arrested. Duch expressed considerable concern that secrecy be maintained to avoid any potential disruption from the unit in question. The arresting guards, Duch explained, were to "consult and discuss with S-21 as regards operational methods for taking them and making assignments to administer the unit of organization while these guys are being removed." Duch cautioned that the "Division must have men in hand and have a solid grip on warehouse and weapons in order to be on guard against the enemy seizing weapons from us."[41]

Members of the Special Guard Unit were sometimes required to collect and transfer prisoners from lower-level security centers to S-21. Duch recalled that these guards would travel either along National Road 5 toward Pursat and Battambang; alternatively, they would take National Road 1 to Prey Vang and Svay Rieng.[42] This suggests the possibility of standardized procedures to arrest and transport prisoners, perhaps even a system whereby prisoners would be assembled at a collection point prior to the arrival of guards from S-21. At this point these procedures remains somewhat conjectural.

Apart from those special prisoners who were arrested after having been summoned to Phnom Penh under false pretenses, prisoners were probably most often transported by truck or some other vehicle. They would be handcuffed and blindfolded; some were shackled together. It was the guards' responsibility to make sure that no one escaped, but also to keep the prisoners docile. Guards were required to report any incident.[43]

Documentation workers at S-21 were responsible for recording daily the number of prisoners entering the facility. On November 24, 1977, for example, a total of 151 prisoners were recorded as having entered S-21 the previous day. The vast majority of these men and women were taken from either Division 920 or Sector 105.[44] This information was important in that it provided a gauge to the overall scope of operations and would inform the upper administration of both the size and composition of the prison population. Apart from this aggregated accounting, staff also processed individually the entering prisoners. Normally, prisoners were first registered at a building outside the main compound, located on Street 360, before being bound together in a human chain and escorted to Building E within the central compound.[45] There, a member of the Documentation Unit would prepare a personal biography for each of the prisoners, a member of the photography subunit would take mug-shot pictures of the detainees to be included in their files, and another cadre would assign each prisoner either to a communal room or individual cell. Those prisoners considered important, such as higher-ranking Party members, would be assigned to individual cells; more ordinary prisoners would be assigned to one of many communal rooms. The most important prisoners—for example, zone-level secretaries or members of the Central Committee—would be held in buildings outside the main compound.[46] As the purges intensified, many prisoners were immediately processed for execution. On May 31, 1978, for example, seven women and one man entered S-21, only to be smashed that same day; of these individuals, all were listed as spouse, daughter, or son of other prisoners.[47] Innumerable other prisoners were never recorded, especially if they were associated with mass executions, which became more prevalent throughout 1977 and 1978.

Detainees endured considerable privation while in captivity. Male prisoners were required to remove all their clothes, save their underwear. This was done ostensibly to prevent suicide attempts. Prisoners assigned to communal rooms were kept shackled together, lying prostrate in rows. Diseases were rampant and hygiene lacking. Only when the stench became unbearable would guards hose out the room while prisoners remained chained to the floors. Food consisted of watery gruel and medical care was virtually nonexistent. Prisoners were kept alive only until they were to be taken away for execution. Those confined to single cells fared no better.[48] Female prisoners, according to Duch, were detained separately from male prisoners. They were also apparently not shackled continuously but rather required to perform work around the compound.[49] Information is limited and I have been unable to confirm specific tasks that they may have been assigned.

The registration of prisoners was a vital part of the administrative function of S-21. Duch and Hor would usually classify arriving detainees into two broad groups: those to be taken away immediately for execution and those to be kept for interrogation. Duch would regularly receive updated prisoner lists. These reports would often include the detainee's name, alias, title, unit, and place of arrest. Armed with this information, Duch would make annotations, specifying the fate of the prisoner. When Sie Mien was arrested, for example, her position was described as "wife of contemptible Hong." An annotation next to her name simply said "Take away for execution." Heng Vy (alias Kha) likewise appeared on a prisoner list. She was described as "Female combatant at the Cement Factory, wife of Pan Chhan." Noted next to her name was "Daughter of contemptible Hong. Keep her for interrogation." Other examples of annotations on prisoner lists include "Keep for a while" or "Do not take outside." It was not uncommon that preliminary interrogation questions were suggested, as in the annotated remarks next to Chab Saren (alias Rem). Identified as a "New person from Sambour Commune, Pursot District, wife of Srei Ung, [former] municipality policeman," annotated instructions were to "Keep for interrogation. Ask [her] for former civil servants who lived near her."[50]

Why would Duch decide that some prisoners were to be kept and not taken for immediate execution or interrogation? During his trial, Duch explained that "at S-21, and probably at other security offices across the country, the committee of the office could make a decision to keep someone for helping the work at the office. . . . [W]e kept them to use them to help in our offices, we were liable for the life and death of those people, so we would be accountable for anything that happened by way of keeping those people alive and use them at our location."[51] Duch's testimony is important in that it provides further clarification of the bureaucratic functions of S-21 and other security centers. Staffing was an ongoing problem, especially as various units began to cannibalize their own members.

The initial compilation of personal biographies upon entry was an important part of the process. These documents could inform the decision whether to hold a prisoner for interrogation or to be sent directly to be executed. Furthermore, if interrogation was deemed necessary, such documents could provide an entry point for questioning. For example, Phal Va (alias Nat), a thirty-five-year-old woman, was arrested and sent to S-21 on December 30, 1978. Her prison biography reveals that prior to her arrest, she was a member of the Committee of State Commerce stationed in Hong Kong; that her parents were Hor Lim (father) and Phal Van (mother); that she was married to San Sok and had one son and two daughters. The report indicates also that Phal Va was 1.6 meters in height.[52] Lim Kimari was a thirty-eight-year-old man arrested on October 25, 1975. Prior to the revolution he was employed at a commerce bank. After April 1975, he was evacuated to Tuol Trea Village, Kandal Province, where he was arrested. His wife's name was Tioulong Rainsy and they had one son and two daughters.[53]

If it was determined that interrogative procedures were to be utilized, Duch and Hor would often consult with the Standing Committee to establish the broad contours for subsequent interrogations, including the line of questioning, the particular interrogative techniques to be applied, and when the interrogation could be concluded. It was up to Hor to coordinate the precise workload, that is, who was to be interrogated on any given day, the interrogator assigned to the detainee, and the type of interrogative methods to be used. By way of illustration, on April 27, 1978, Hor compiled a list of prisoners to be interrogated. Prisoners were specified by position and date of arrest and were further classified by type of torture to be applied (e.g., cold, hot, or chewing) and who was to conduct the interrogation. Sao Saron (alias Saran), for example, was secretary of the 115th Regiment, Sector 23, East Zone; he had been arrested on March 26, 1978, and was to be interrogated by Ros Ouen using cold methods. Conversely, Yin Vorn (alias Lun), deputy hospital chairman of Sector 23, was to be interrogated by Phan Khon using hot methods.[54] A list from February 2, 1978, specifies fifteen prisoners who were to be interrogated; this list also provides some insight into the workload of S-21 in that Comrade Chhin was scheduled to interrogate three separate prisoners, while Comrade Ly was responsible for three prisoners and was to assist in the interrogation of two others.[55] Interrogation lists might also indicate the status of ongoing investigations. On April 11, 1978, for example, Khoeun provided updates on thirty-one prisoners. The confession of Im Mon, former chief of the West Zone Office, was being "recorded" by an interrogator named Chea Vuth; the confession of Am Sokhon, a member of Office K-33 of the Ministry of Propaganda, was "clear"; and Chung Huy Sean, a female combatant and translator from Division 502, had provided "no response" yet. Furthermore, as reported by S-21 staff member Tit, an additional seventy-two confessions were either being documented or in the process of being recorded.[56]

Throughout their captivity, prisoners' names routinely appeared on various documents. Daily reports of detainees, for example, were regularly compiled by Hor and his staff working in the Documentation Unit. In time, these became standardized to the extent that by 1977, daily logs resembled balance sheets found in many bureaucracies the world over. These daily logs would indicate how many prisoners were currently detained, disaggregated by place of arrest, such as a specific military sector, autonomous region and zone, or branch of the government, such as the Ministry of Foreign Affairs or the State Warehouse. A daily report of April 25, 1977, signed by Hor, indicates that 1,203 prisoners were currently being detained; a footnote at the bottom of this biopolitical balance sheet remarked that an individual named Khheang Sek "croaked"; he was killed by torture.[57] Other lists might indicate individual prisoners who were to be detained for various reasons. A list from February 1, 1977, for example, provides information on 74 men and women who were to be "put on hold." Thus, Kim Iem was "sick" and had "not yet confessed" while Lem Tith reportedly had fever and constipation.[58] Another undated report, presumably from early 1977, provides a list of 56 male and female prisoners who were to be "kept." This list provides information on the prisoner's name, alias, position and function, and date of entry at S-21. It does not indicate when, or if, any of these prisoners had been interrogated thus far.[59]

The principle objective of S-21 was not to exterminate prisoners, although this was the eventual result. Rather, it was to extract confessions through interrogative procedures. To what end, though, did the CPK need confessions? Caswell suggests that

> by documenting confessions (obtained through torture), Duch and his staff at S-21 were able to prove to the upper echelons that their own top-level decisions regarding arrests were prudent, thereby reaffirming the omniscience of the highest-ranking Khmer Rouge leaders; while the use of the records was to document killings, the purpose was to flatter the upper echelon. In this tautology, when high-ranking Khmer Rouge leader suspected someone of being a traitor, that person had to be tortured so that he would confess, so that his confession would serve as written proof confirming the original suspicion.[60]

Documentary evidence, however, does not readily support this conclusion. Security practices under the CPK were not tautological. The administrative process was not driven by initial suspicions expressed by the Standing Committee, with all lower-level functionaries down the bureaucratic hierarchy simply following orders. As noted, the path to S-21 assumed many different forms. Lower-level officials could, and did, inform their superiors of suspected individuals; requests could be made to enact specific investigations; confessions were corroborated with other confessions; personal biographies were evaluated at all levels in an effort to identify individual traitors or conspiratorial networks. It is simply not the case that members of the Standing Committee were omnipotent in their actions and that this was the catalyst of ongoing purges.

The process of interrogation was not to justify predetermined decisions rendered by infallible Party leaders but instead instituted to provide evidence among bureaucrats working from the lowest of levels through to the highest. The mere observation that not all people implicated in a confession were ultimately arrested should give pause to the notion that no evaluative procedure took place. We may question how so-called evidence was weighed, and we may certainly take issue with the lack of judicial review. We must acknowledge, however, that many (most?) decisions to arrest did not emanate from the upper echelon and, subsequently, confessions were not used to document the all-knowing power of these individuals. To this point, we should also keep in mind that interrogation and forced confessions were not unique to S-21 and that information circulated constantly throughout S-21 and the myriad other security centers throughout Democratic Kampuchea. Prisoners were arrested at all levels of the administrative hierarchy and they were interrogated and forced to confess to crimes at all levels. On this point, an untold number of people would have been arrested, interrogated, forced to confess, and executed without any input from the Standing Committee. Moreover, information derived from these lower-level procedures could and did provide the impetus for subsequent investigations, thereby bringing to the attention of the Standing Committee suspicious behaviors and activities. In other words, the search for traitors, the evaluative use of confessions and personal biographies, was both a top-down and bottom-up procedure. The functioning of the Khmer Rouge bureaucracy is considerably more multifaceted than generally acknowledged.

I do agree with Caswell that certain members of the Standing Committee—namely, Pol Pot, Nuon Chea, Ieng Sary, and Son Sen—viewed their policies and programs as unswervingly correct. Within the broader administrative apparatus, these men largely determined the myriad operational objectives that were subsequently disseminated throughout Democratic Kampuchea. Members of the Standing Committee essentially appointed, or at the very least monitored, the appointment of lower-level apparatchiks; they supervised the implementation of Party policy; and they assessed the effectiveness of these policies. On this account these members did assume an aura of sagacity that subsequently permeated the entire administrative hierarchy. Thus, when confronted with evidence of economic or political failings, these members could only conclude that bad elements throughout the ranks were conspiring against them. It was on this level that paranoia marked the search for traitors. The upper echelon did not necessarily know a priori who those men and women were. They did presume that turncoats did exist, though, and guided their subordinates accordingly in the effort to root out the conspirators. In this process, fears of betrayal did disseminate in a top-down process. Once established, however, the actual investigative procedures, including that of interrogation, were a combination of top-down and bottom-up ways. Duch testified, for example, that during the early months of S-21, he and Nat met with Son Sen. A piece of paper was presented, reportedly providing evidence that cadres at Sector 32 had exposed a network of CIA agents. Son Sen questioned why the interrogative procedures at S-21 had not yet uncovered similar evidence of CIA activity. Upon their return to S-21, both Duch and Nat informed members of the Interrogation Unit to find evidence of CIA involvement. Not surprisingly, subsequent confessions revealed extensive CIA activity.[61]

Interrogative procedures at S-21 must be understood as a crucial node of the larger security apparatus, itself intertwined within an even greater administrative structure. The circulation of biopoliti-cal data, manifest in confessions and personal biographies obtained throughout the entire bureaucracy, was essential for the conduct of policing practices at S-21. This is a point affirmed by Son Sen. During a meeting with divisional secretaries and deputy secretar-ies, Son Sen addressed the "problem of analyzing or discovering the enemy." He explained that "if phenomena already exist, you must find the reason, the source, where they come from." Furthermore, "Wherever an incident takes place, you must look there" and "If there is evidence, then you must follow up." Effort, though, was required beyond simply responding to reported incidents; instead, cadres were to take a more active role in ferreting out enemies. Thus, "all biographies must be grasped again" in an effort to examine links between named suspects. Investigative procedures, however, were to be clandestine: "The problem arises of the names of all these traitors: we do not disseminate them. It is imperative to maintain absolute secrecy. In educating the brothers and sisters, educate them only in terms of perspective and standpoint."[62]

As with other administrative functions within S-21, interroga-tive procedures appear to have become more sophisticated, more routinized, and more efficient over time. Indeed, the act of interro-gation was approached as any other function, so much so that Alex Hinton can write that "interrogation . . . apparently sometimes involved a degree of boredom or aversion."[63] Hinton finds evidence that cadre fell into "clock watching" or worked "irregular hours."[64]

Bureaucrats were required to undergo training as would any other staff member. At S-21, training was conducted largely by Duch. According to Alex Hinton, Duch's interrogative techniques seem to have been inspired by two different but reinforcing moral underpinnings. Hinton explains that on the one hand, Duch appeared to have a commitment to truth and knowledge and the scientific principles by which they might be discerned; and on the other hand, his approached resonated with Buddhist rationalism, which emphasized the analysis of evidence to discern truth from falsehood and moral right from wrong.[65] In total, Hinton con-cludes that for Duch, S-21 reports, including confessions, were not merely passive bureaucratic filings but instead helped drive the process.[66]

Training would normally last from two to four weeks, approximately two hours per day, with interrogators required to attend "follow-up" training.[67] Ever pragmatic, Duch explained that he trained interrogators to use politics and to study the prisoners' backgrounds by way of asking questions instead of simply resorting to physical means.[68] When torture was permitted, Duch instructed his staff to employ one of four procedures: beatings and whippings, electrocution, simulated suffocation, and a variant of water boarding. The actual technique of applying torture, Duch explained, was not taught, for "You do not need to teach a crocodile how to swim."[69] More important, for Duch, was to accentuate the political importance of torture and of how torture would be carried out. He stressed that detainees were not to be beaten to the point of unconsciousness. This was not done out of humanitarian concerns but again reflected the pragmatism by which torture was employed. If prisoners were beaten until they were too weak to respond, the interrogative process was prolonged. Thus, out of a desire for efficiency, interrogators were to inflict pain, but not so much as to impinge the investigation. It was absolutely essential that detainees were not "accidentally" killed before the interrogation was completed to Angkar's satisfaction.

If prisoners did die in captivity, those S-21 staff members responsible were not necessarily subject to swift and severe punishment. It was necessary, however, that the incident be reported. It was also not uncommon that postmortem photographs of the prisoners were taken as confirmation of death (photographs 4.6 and 4.7). Duch explained that this was done primarily in case members of the Standing Committee requested additional information from the prisoner in question. Without proof that the detainee had died in captivity, suspicion among Angkar might arise, such as the unauthorized release or escape of the prisoner.[70]

The day-to-day procedure of interrogation became routinized. For any given shift, the interrogator would inform the guard on duty as to which prisoner was to be interrogated. The guard would

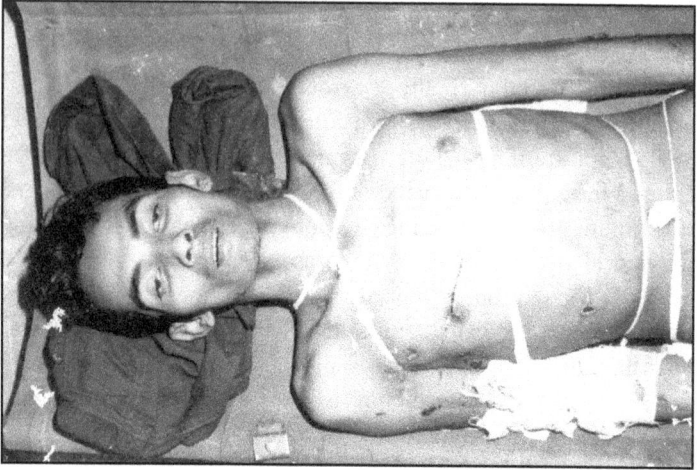

Photograph 4.6: Postmortem photograph of tortured prisoner at S-21 *(Courtesy of Documentation Center of Cambodia Archives)*

blindfold the prisoner and tie his or her hands. The prisoner would then be escorted to a prearranged room for torture. A variety of implements would already be on display, such as a knife, clamp, or electrocution wires. These were not always used, but their display was to induce both fear and compliance. The actual interrogation of prisoners became increasingly systematic over time, reflecting an iterative process with substantial input from staff interrogators, Duch, Hor, and members of the Standing Committee, notably Nuon Chea and Son Sen. In general, Duch trained his subordinates to begin with soft questioning. This was referred to as "doing politics." Prisoners would be questioned on their past activities and asked to admit their crimes. When these cool methods proved ineffective, hot methods would be introduced.[71] On one occasion, for example, Duch was ordered by Nuon Chea (through Son Sen) to inform one prisoner, Mil Kavin (alias Kdat), that if he confessed, he would be released. Interrogators were to explain to the detainee that other prisoners, having already confessed, had been sent home.

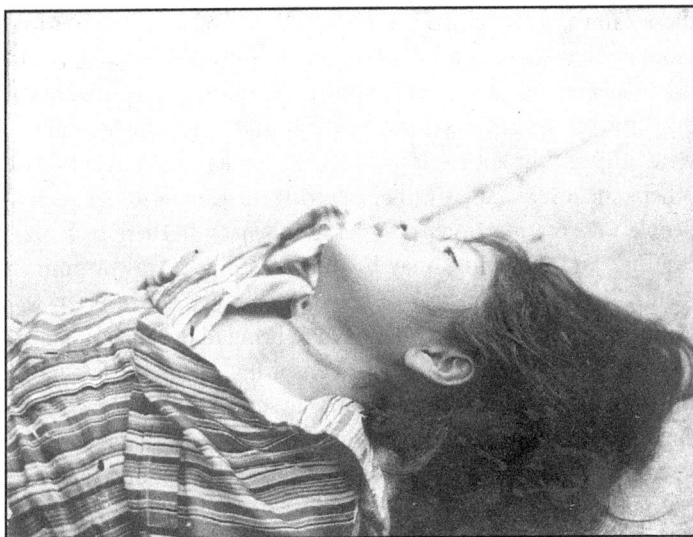

Photograph 4.7: Postmortem photograph of possible suicide victim at S-21 *(Courtesy of the Documentation Center of Cambodia Archives)*

When this deception proved ineffective, however, Nuon Chea ordered Duch to physically torture the prisoner.[72]

Much speculation surrounds the use of torture at S-21. In his historical account of S-21, Chandler finds no precedent, whether in precolonial or colonial Cambodia. He does identify superficial linkages with penal systems in Communist China, Vietnam, and the Soviet Union, but cannot unequivocally say that any of these systems provided a model for S-21. My sense is that torture, as an interrogative technique, evolved on an ad hoc basis. During the civil war years, for example, the Khmer Rouge captured enemy soldiers and suspected spies. These individuals would be detained, usually in makeshift camps, and potentially subjected to torture. These acts of violence were in part utilized to extract information on enemy activities; one cannot discount this violence as a form of retribution. After the victory of April 1975, an unknown number of these camps, such as M-13, were converted and transformed into more permanent structures while new security centers were established as the need arose. When men and women were arrested at branch-level security centers, physical and psychological abuses were utilized, but not necessarily for the same reasons as at S-21 or other zone-level security centers. During the Khmer Rouge period, people were often arrested for theft or idleness. In these instances, beatings and whippings may be understood as forms of punishment. The systematic use of torture as practiced at S-21 was different. It was pragmatic, designed to bring to light the supposed strings of traitors who were conspiring against the Party. Bureaucrats, such as Duch and Hor, who staffed the various security apparatuses, were responsible for uncovering these networks. If detainees would not divulge their criminal activities or name their traitorous associates, then additional forms of physical and psychological coercion were deemed necessary.

The endpoint of interrogative procedures and torture was the production of a confession. In practice, these were working documents, in the sense that confessions were written and rewritten many times, depending on the prisoner in question. Thus, when a detainee finally capitulated to providing a confession, he or she would be provided with pen and paper. If the prisoner was illiterate, confessions were tape-recorded and staff working in the Documentation Unit would transcribe these to paper. There was initially no standardized form. Prisoners were compelled to provide a chronology of their traitorous activities.[73] Chandler explains, however, that by the end of 1976, most confessions assumed a four-part format. First, prisoners would provide life stories, including information on relatives, friends, and other social contacts; information was also provided on where the prisoner was stationed. A second component of the confession would entail a history of traitorous activities and other incriminating evidence. Third, prisoners were required to confess to ongoing plans—criminal activities that they had not yet carried out, but were preparing. Fourth, a list of accomplices was enumerated. These lists could include upward of one hundred people or more.[74]

As working documents, confessions would be read, analyzed, and annotated by Duch, who would then send the marked-up confession to Nuon Chea and Son Sen for their assessment. A draft confession of Khek Bin (alias Sou), for example, indicates that "Brother Nuon" had already received a copy and "two copies of the [name] list were submitted to Sou, under secretary of sector." Additional annotations specify that the confession "involves Comrades Khleng, Ren, Ku, Muon and Comrade Pring." Other specific comments are directed at individuals listed in the confession. Thus, for example, comments indicate that "Bunthan had been arrested" and subsequently committed suicide, but his wife was "still alive"; that Ing Kim Seng had "already been arrested"; and that Heng Heu had "already been captured. He had pictures [and] letters relating to his CIA activities."[75] Here, it is possible to gain a sense of evaluative procedures that accompanied the interrogation and torture of prisoners, and how confessions in particular were analyzed in an attempt to establish the presence of conspiratorial networks. Through this process the manifestation of power was materialized. Written confessions, articulated as official documents, established a connection between text and facts. Paper, in the form of filed confessions, afforded criminality a material form that became inseparable from the subject in question. Following Robertson, we see that the information contained in the written confession constitutes an administrative identity—that of being a traitor, for example—and acquires in the process a functional presence that has been authenticated by the sovereign authority.[76]

Firsthand accounts of torture are exceptionally rare. This stems from the fact that only seven prisoners are known to have survived their imprisonment.[77] Chum Mey was arrested on October 28, 1978. His torture began almost immediately. He writes:

They began to beat me, and they kept on beating me for 12 days and 12 nights. Every morning at 7 o'clock I was brought out of my cell to the interrogation room and I was returned to my cell at 11am. Then from 1pm to 5pm, I was interrogated some more, and again at night from 7pm to 11pm. . . . They beat me, and sometimes they stopped and asked me questions and then beat me again.[78]

Throughout his interrogation, Chum Mey was asked repeatedly about his contacts with the CIA and about any conspiratorial networks with which he was involved. At one point, an interrogator named Seng informed Chum Mey that he would pull out his toenail if he did not confess. Chum Mey recalls:

At first he had a hard time getting the nail out. He got a pair of pliers and he stepped on my foot and tugged on the nail, but it wouldn't come off. So he twisted it back and forth. It took him a long time and I bit my lip to try to bear the pain. And then he gave a big tug using all his strength and yanked it out . . . I think he wanted to pull out the other big toenail too, but maybe because he saw so much blood on the floor he stopped.[79]

Chum Mey refused to confess, so other forms of torture were used. Eventually, the staff members at S-21 decided to use electrocution. Chum Mey explains that he could tolerate the pain from beatings, he could tolerate the pain from having his toenail ripped out, but the pain of electrocution was too much. He remembers:

They attached a wire to my left ear and it was like my head exploded. . . . My head felt like a machine and my eyes were on fire. I fell on the floor unconscious two times. When I woke up I started telling them what they wanted to hear. At that point, I couldn't tell what was right or wrong. I was so afraid they would electrocute me again, so I made up stories. . . .[80]

Duch was kept informed of the progression of torture. His subordinates would submit reports detailing, for example, the techniques used and the duration, frequency, and intensity of torture. Such reports might indicate the number of lashes a prisoner received, or whether a detainee was suffocated with a plastic bag. In turn, Duch would provide annotations on the report, specifying further courses of action. There was no set period of time allocated for interrogating prisoners; it all depended on the information provided in the confession. If, after two or three interrogation sessions, the upper echelon was satisfied with the evidence obtained, the prisoner would be scheduled to be executed. If further clarification was needed, additional interrogative sessions were ordered.[81]

The final administrative function was that of execution. Duch referred to the process as the activity line (not unlike kill chains) for it was the activity of the S-21 Committee to follow orders and make sure the process was smooth, that the prison would not become overcrowded, and that prisoners were executed at the appropriate time.[82] As indicated, for those prisoners considered unimportant and not worthy of interrogation, the process was relatively quick but no less brutal, ghastly, or deadly. These detainees were held for a few days or weeks until they were taken to be executed. During mass purges, prisoners were not even processed and detained, but taken straight to the killing site. Throughout December 1978, according to Duch, prisoners from the East Zone were never interrogated but taken away immediately to be smashed.[83] For those men and women who had been interrogated, it was important that their execution be confirmed by Duch and his superiors. Indeed, during his trial, Duch repeatedly mentioned a person who was smashed by Hor before the interrogation was complete.[84] Duch testified also that written records were not always kept when the committee reached a decision to execute a prisoner, nor were any minutes of the meetings recorded. Here, our record remains occluded, for in these instances, only verbal instructions were issued by Duch to his subordinates, usually Hor, regarding the execution. Duch clarified, though, that written orders may be issued if he needed to inform a staff member not serving on the committee.

Schedules of those to be executed were compiled, often by Hor or under his supervision. A prisoner list dated July 1, 1977, for example, includes the names of 63 women who were scheduled to be smashed that day. These were mostly women who were wives of male prisoners who had already been purged.[85] Another execution schedule, dated July 2, 1977, lists 85 sons and daughters of previously executed prisoners.[86] Lists would also be compiled of prisoners who had already been executed. On June 11, 1977, Hor signed a report indicating that 198 prisoners from Division 310 had been "smashed" the previous day.[87] One month later, Hor reported that 173 prisoners from the North Zone had been smashed on July 8. According to an annotation, Sao Khun (alias Kim) had not yet been removed, as this individual was "kept for doing documentation work."[88] Also killed that day were 18 female prisoners, smashed by Brother Huy Sre's section.[89] Later that month, Hor confirmed on July 23, 1977, that 178 people—of whom 160 were unnamed children—were also smashed.[90] Apart from these daily recordings, summary reports of prisoners smashed would be compiled. One document indicates that 162 prisoners died between March 2 and 30, 1976. Of these deaths, 153 had been smashed while nine died of sickness.[91]

Executions mostly took place away from the main facility at S-21, although Duch testified that some bodies, especially of children, were buried within the compound. Throughout 1975 and into 1976, however, most executions and burials were conducted at the Ta Khmau Psychiatric Hospital. Other killings were carried out in the vicinity of S-21, with bodies buried in the streets of Phnom Penh, notably along Street 613 near Wat Mohamon Trey.[92] Once in charge of S-21, Duch worried about the possible outbreak of epidemics resulting from the rapidly accumulating and deteriorating bodies. Hence, he decided that executions and burials would take place at Choeung Ek, a Chinese cemetery located 15 kilometers southwest of Phnom Penh. Duch confirmed that he did not solicit advice or seek permission from the Standing Committee to transfer the killings to Choeung Ek. Having made the decision, he merely informed his superiors.[93]

Upward of nine thousand skeletal remains have been exhumed at Choeung Ek, although it is unknown exactly how many men, women, and children were executed there. As indicated earlier, although the staff at S-21 kept meticulous records, and many surviving execution schedules have been archived, records are incomplete. Moreover, it is known that during the last months of the purges, many prisoners went unrecorded. It is quite possible that hundreds, if not thousands, of men, women, and children were transported directly to Choeung Ek, having never set foot inside S-21. The temporal pattern of executions—that is, the hour-by-hour and day-by-day systematic process of killing—is also only marginally understood. On any given day, upward of twenty to more than one hundred people were executed. During his trial, Duch surmised that it might take six days for the guards to smash one hundred prisoners.

The transportation of prisoners to the killing fields usually occurred at night, normally between 7:00 and 9:00 p.m. Prior to being transported to Choeung Ek, prisoners were blindfolded and handcuffed. Deception was often used to keep the condemned prisoners unaware of their ultimate fate. Guards, for example, would inform the prisoners that they were being processed for release or that they were being transferred to another security center.[94] Staff members at S-21 would then cross-check the execution lists, concerned more so that no detainee was to be executed prematurely. From S-21 prisoners were transported by truck. It is unclear how many prisoners were taken at any time, nor how many trips were made on any given night.

Prisoner lists were again checked upon arrival at Choeung Ek, a procedure implemented to safeguard against the escape or the unauthorized release of prisoners. Following this final administrative act, prisoners were then detained in a wooden hut until taken for execution. As indicated in Chapter 3, execution was brutal but efficient. One by one, prisoners were marched, blindfolded and handcuffed, to predug burial pits, whereupon they were ordered to kneel down and face the grave. A member of the Special Guard Unit would then apply a blow to the back of the head or neck using a wagon axle or other blunt instrument. It was also common practice to slash the prisoner's neck with a knife to ensure death. Blindfolds, handcuffs, and often any remaining clothes were then removed.[95]

Procedures for executing important prisoners, such as high-ranking Party members, were slightly different. Members of the Standing Committee generally required additional confirmation that these men and women were in fact executed. Thus, Koy Thuon, Vorn Vet, Hu Nim, and other key officials were taken during the daytime, somewhere in the vicinity of Mao Tse Tong Boulevard, to be executed. Postmortem photographs were taken of the corpses and sent to the Standing Committee as verification.[96] It was also not uncommon for corpses to be exhumed to provide visual evidence of their execution. As a case in point, Duch testified that the body of Ly Phel, who had been dead for three days, was exhumed so that a postmortem photograph could be taken.[97]

The killing of children was different. When asked about the protocols for executing children during his trial, Duch answered bluntly, "Let me conclude it in one word: they were killed." Duch affirmed that very young children were separated from their parents immediately upon arrival at S-21 and that the longest any child would remain in detention was one day. Some were killed at Choeung Ek, while others were probably murdered in and around Phnom Penh. According to Duch, "They were thrown against the trees or something at Choeung Ek but in Phnom Penh probably they were killed quietly in the same way as the adult prisoners were killed." Duch could not confirm how many children were killed, most likely because they were simply not recorded.[98]

Empirical Analysis of Purges

Previous scholarship has considered mass executions from the standpoint of Khmer Rouge victims. Steve Heder, for example, has identified three targeted populations within Democratic Kampuchea: military personnel and civilian administrators of the Khmer Republic government; non-Party members, especially April 17 people, who were allegedly guilty of serious crimes against the revolution; and CPK cadre and Khmer Rouge soldiers.[99] It remains unclear if the CPK targeted groups based specifically on class, ethnicity, or religion.[100] Certainly Vietnamese nationals, derogatorily called Yuon, were smashed; such murders followed CPK members' long-standing mistrust of the Vietnamese. Also targeted were people alleged to be part of the so-called imperialist or capitalist class. And a strong case has been made that the Cham, a Muslim minority, were singled out for elimination.[101] However, as Heder explains, "according to the CPK's class-based analysis, certain class groups and ethnic and religious communities were associated with the opposition, and consequently individuals from these same groups were more likely to be targeted for execution."[102] Subsequent analyses, including those conducted under the auspices of the Extraordinary Chambers in the Courts of Cambodia, may establish that the CPK did in fact target specific groups.[103] At this point, what is documented is that "from the day of liberation until the last day of [Democratic Kampuchea], the security services, assisted by the *chhlop* and 'the people,' arrested, detained and executed wave after wave of alleged counter-revolutionaries and spies they identified in multiple population categories."[104]

In this penultimate section I provide a different, complementary analysis of Khmer Rouge purges associated with S-21.[105] Rather than focusing on the broader coordinates of the purges, that is, how these transpired over time, my concern lies with the more immediate period of administrative oversight between the date of arrest and the date of execution. My intention, therefore, is to evaluate the duration of detainment, for it is my contention that this variable provides insight into the bureaucratic functioning of S-21.

Before proceeding, it is necessary to express my concerns regarding any empirical analysis of arrests and executions associated with S-21. The aforementioned documentary procedures initiated and carried out at S-21 dehumanized countless men, women, and children. These people arrived at the compound blindfolded and bound, terrified and confused. Most were hurriedly processed, personal details recorded, mug-shot photographs taken, and shackled in either a communal or isolated cell. Many were subjected to horrific forms of torture and forced to confess to crimes they did not commit. All were subjected to deplorable conditions of starvation, disease, and abuse. Detainees were no longer viewed as people but as *neak tos*—those who are already convicted. Moreover, as David Hawk explains, literal translations of the prison archives reveal the deliberate dehumanization of the victims. Named individuals are frequently given the adjectives "contemptible" or "wicked." When the death of a prisoner is recorded, the word is translated as "croak," the Khmer word used for animal deaths as opposed to human deaths.[106] Consequently, I am sensitive to the appearance of reducing the lives of these men, women, and children to datum: to a postdeath objectification of flesh and blood to that of the same type of bureaucratic procedures that typified S-21. I do believe, however, that an evaluation of arrest and execution records provides insight into the bureaucratic structure and administrative processes that made widespread purges possible and, in some small way, gives voice to those who were denied.

The duration of detainment was highly dependent on both the individual detained and the time of arrest. On the one hand, more important prisoners, such as high-ranking CPK cadre, were forced to endure long and brutal periods of torture before their eventual execution. Less important prisoners, from the CPK's point of view, were often not interrogated and were frequently executed shortly following arrest. These people included spouses, children, and other relatives of people already detained. Also included were members of the lower echelons, such as rank-and-file combatants. On the other hand, the duration period was dependent upon the overall time of arrest. As the purges intensified throughout 1977 and 1978, S-21 functioned less as a bureaucratic facility responsible for the so-called documentation of crimes as it did a preparatory site for mass killings. Any semblance of legality steadily evaporated as the killings quickened in pace.

Archival data on arrests and executions are directly related to the overall documentation practices of S-21 staff. As indicated earlier, most, but not all, detainees sent to S-21 were registered and photographed upon arrival. Consequently, prisoner lists form the bulk of data on the timing of arrests. This information can also be corroborated with photographs. There are, however, significant limitations. Recall that spouses and children were often not recorded. Moreover, countless men, women, and children were never processed at S-21, although their arrests and executions were directly associated with decisions rendered by Nuon Chea, Son Sen, Duch, and Hor as part of the overall administrative functions of

S-21. Two other sources of information have been readily used. First, for those men and women who were interrogated, confessional records remain. Chandler's chronology of purges is based on confessions. Second, when prisoners were sent for execution, their names were registered on various execution schedules. These constitute another complementary record of information that may be used to corroborate dates of arrest and execution.

Caution must be taken, however, when examining prison records. First, there is the problem of double entries. Some records contain listings of identical names, and without cross-checking, it is not known if the same individual was recorded twice, or if in fact there were two (or more) people with the same name. Second, the prevalence of aliases compounds the problem, although at times these may help identify any given person. Third, a not insignificant number of records have incomplete information, for example, many prisoner entries provide a name, but no information on sex, age, or position. Also missing for many records are complete dates for arrest and/or execution. By way of illustration, compare the records of Buoy Sreng, Kim Thy, and Chhay Reasey. Records indicate that Buoy Sreng (alias Peng Sruoy), a forty-year-old man and former director of the *Khmer Salvation Newspaper*, was arrested in Region 25 on February 22, 1976, and executed on May 27, 1976. The record of Kim Thy, a thirty-two-year-old teacher arrested in Phnom Srok, is less complete. His date of arrest is listed only as "1976," but he was executed on May 23, 1976. Finally, Chhay Reasey was a twenty-six-year-old woman, with no information provided for her position, where or when she was arrested, or when she was executed.

During Duch's trial, researchers associated with the Extraordinary Chambers in the Courts of Cambodia compiled a master list of 12,273 men, women, and children who were detained at S-21 and this provides the basis of my analyses.[107] This list was gathered largely from arrest lists, execution lists, and prisoner confessions. Cross-examination of all sources enabled staff to (mostly) eliminate duplication and to verify records. The official ECCC lists consequently provide a partial but highly informative overview of the prisoners arrested, detained, and executed at S-21.

Of the total number of prisoners who can be verified and for whom sufficient information is available, we know the sex of 63 percent of all prisoners: 5,994 men and 1,698 women. Of those detainees for whom a position is indicated, 5,609 (46 percent) were members of the Khmer Rouge army; 4,371 (36 percent) were unspecified Khmer Rouge cadres; 876 (0.07 percent) were relatives or spouses of other detainees; and 155 (0.01 percent) were former S-21 staff members. Conversely, only 328 (0.03 percent) were soldiers of the former government; 279 (0.02 percent) were listed as teachers, professors, students, or some other professional position; and 266 (0.02 percent) were listed as Vietnamese soldiers or spies. This disaggregation is significant in that it accentuates the uniqueness of S-21 as a facility designed primarily to purge CPK Party members and Khmer Rouge cadres. Indeed, we may conclude that upward of 90 percent of all detainees were somehow affiliated with the Khmer Rouge. S-21 was therefore distinct from zone-level and other lower-level security centers in that it did not receive a substantial number of base or new people.

Subsequent analyses are based on the ECCC list. However, additional checking and revision was required.[108] For example, as discussed earlier, the record of Buoy Sreng contains a complete matching record whereas the entries for Kim Thy and Chhay Reasey do not. Given that the intention is to document the duration of detainment, incomplete records for dates of arrest and execution are not included in this analysis. This is in no way meant to disrespect those who died or to discount their lives simply because of incomplete records. It is also necessary to exclude from analysis those records with discernable inaccuracies. For example, forty-two records indicate execution dates as being prior to arrest. Likewise, analyses revealed noticeable errors, such as the record of Say Kim-Kheat. Listed as the "wife of Luon," Say Kim-Khet was, according to the official list, arrested on February 7, 1975, and executed on May 12, 1977, indicating that she was detained for 825 days. This is (most likely) incorrect and we know this for two reasons. First, as the wife of another prisoner, Say Kim-Kheat was probably not (in the eyes of the staff at S-21) an important prisoner. More pressing, however, is that her date of arrest is said to have occurred several months prior to the establishment of S-21. In fact, the date would indicate that she was arrested two months prior to the fall of Phnom Penh. Most likely, she was arrested February 7, 1977, but without additional corroborating information, this cannot be known with certainty.[109]

How long were prisoners detained between date of arrest and date of execution? It is noteworthy that during the tribunal, David Chandler was asked precisely this question. In his response, Chandler could not provide any definitive conclusion, but instead provided a range of "no time" (that is, immediately transferred for execution) to "several months." He concluded that "most of the people were there between two and three weeks."[110] My analysis reveals that for all prisoners for which a complete record is available, the mean duration of detention is 180 days. This average stay of internment, however, belies significant variability. Figure 4.1 illustrates the frequency of detention days, that is, how prevalent was it that a prisoner was detained for 1, 2, or more days? Of the 8,283 usable records, 206 people were arrested and executed on the same day, 312 were executed within 1 day of arrest, and 395 were executed within 2 days of arrest. Keep in mind that countless others were not recorded. These men, women, and children would obviously have been killed within a day or two of arrest.

It is also not known with any degree of certainty who was imprisoned at S-21 for the longest time. During his trial Duch noted that a prisoner named Phing Ton was detained for twenty months. Chandler, in his testimony, could neither corroborate nor refute this claim. Moreover, Chandler concluded that it seemed "quite strange" that someone would be imprisoned for such a long period. The official ECCC prisoner list records ninety-five entries of men and women detained longer than three hundred days. Even a cursory examination of this subset indicates numerous recording errors. Hem Ang Sin, for example, is identified as the "wife of Sok." Records indicate that she was arrested on April 26, 1977, and scheduled for execution on April 29, 1978. It is most probable that she was arrested and executed within three days, either in 1977 or 1978, as opposed to being detained for over one year. Without additional

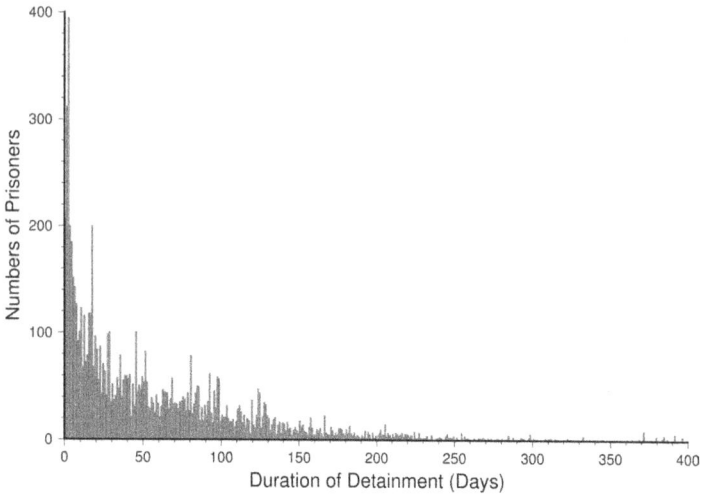

Figure 4.1: Duration of Detainment between Date of Arrest and Date of Execution (n=8,283)

supporting documents and cross-checking, however, the duration of Hem Ang Sin's detainment cannot be verified.[111]

Figure 4.2 illustrates the cumulative frequency of arrest and execution. Of those individuals for whom a paired date of arrest and execution is possible, 518 men, women, and children were executed within one day of arrest; 1,720 detainees were executed within one week, 3,707 were executed within one month, and 5,156 were executed within two months. In other words, over 80 percent of detainees were executed within two months of arrest. This overall pattern, though, does not hold constant throughout the existence of S-21 (Table 4.1). For the period 1976–78, the interval between arrest and execution shortened considerably. Of the 8,241 individuals for whom complete records are available, nearly 63 percent were executed within two months of arrest. However, disaggregation by year indicates that the duration of detainment decreased appreciably. Stated differently, over time the rapidity in which prisoners were executed increased significantly. This is empirical evidence of

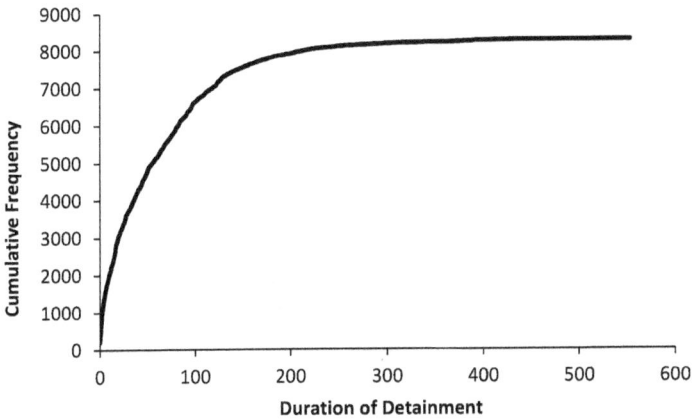

Figure 4.2: Cumulative Distribution of Duration between Date of Arrest and Date of Execution (n=8,283)

the transformation of S-21 as it moved from a facility purportedly investigating criminal activities to an institution geared almost exclusively to mass murder. By 1978, for example, two-thirds of all prisoners were executed within one month of arrest; over 90 percent were executed within two months. Figure 4.3, however, illustrates even greater complexity to this trend. In May 1975, for example, the mean length of detainment (for those men and women arrested in May) was twenty-five days; however, by October of that year, the length of detainment peaked at forty days. Afterwards, the mean period of detainment fluctuated, although the overall trend is one of shorter detainment prior to execution. Figure 4.3 is also notable in that it reflects three months of exceptionally short detainment periods: June 1976, June 1978, and December 1978. These months correspond to a series of intensive purges that took place. Consequently, most of these detainees would most likely not have been subjected to intensive interrogations.

Geographically, significant variation is also evident. Conclusions, however, must be tempered with a lack of detailed records.[112]

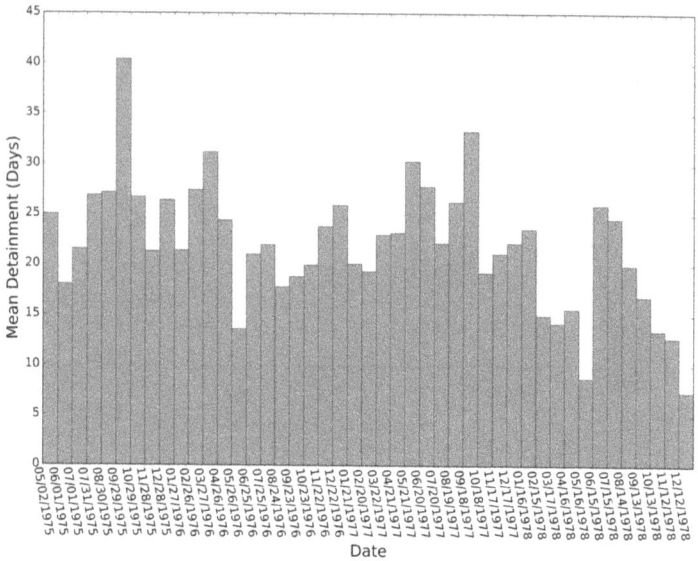

Figure 4.3: Mean Length of Detention by Month (n=8,289)

Although prisoner biographies often include information on place of arrest, this information is often incomplete or indeterminate. For example, many records indicate the place of arrest not according to administrative divisions (e.g., zone, sector, or district) but rather the unit to which the individual was assigned (e.g., motor-pool division or Division 505). For some records, cross-checking with the known location of specific units or division facilitates the identification of place of arrest. An additional complication results from the myriad paths to S-21 and the many ambiguities surrounding the actual recording of information. If a person was initially arrested at a district-level prison, for example, and subsequently transferred to a zone-level security center before being transported to S-21, it is not clear whether that prisoner would be entered (at S-21) as having been arrested at the district- or zone-level facility. With these qualifications in mind, however, a preliminary

YEAR	EXECUTED WITHIN		
	ONE WEEK	ONE MONTH	TWO MONTHS
1976 (n=1,422)	16%	35.3%	50%
1977 (n=4,434)	18.6%	36.5%	50.7%
1978 (n=2,385)	27.9%	66.5%	92.1%
Total (n=8,241)	20.9%	45%	62.6%

Table 4.1: Duration of Detainment Prior to Execution by Year

geographic accounting of detainment suggests that those men and women arrested from the East and Southwest zones were detained for shorter periods prior to execution than those people from other regions (Table 4.2). Sex differences by administrative zone are illustrated in tables 4.3 and 4.4. In general, for all zones, women were executed following shorter periods of imprisonment than their male counterparts. Of those arrested in the North Zone, for example, over 76 percent of female prisoners were executed within two weeks of arrest, compared to only 48 percent of male prisoners from this same zone. It is not surprising that Duch, during his trial, would state matter-of-factly that "the majority of the female prisoners . . . they were not important, so I did not pay much attention to the female prisoners entering S-21."[113]

In his analysis of prisoner confessions, Chandler calls attention to two broad periods of purges: September 1975 through September 1976, and November 1976 through January 1979.[114] He explains that prior to September 1976, the Khmer Rouge targeted mostly people associated with the previous military and civilian government, but that after this date, attention was directly primarily toward internal enemies. An analysis provided by Steve Heder confirms this general

ZONE	EXECUTED WITHIN		
	ONE WEEK	ONE MONTH	TWO MONTHS
Central (n=110)	0	16.4%	25.5%
East (n=881)	34.5%	69%	92.1%
North (n=699)	27.5%	50.6%	64.4%
Northeast (n=52)	9.6%	36.5%	65.4%
Northwest (n=1,214)	16%	40.8%	62.9%
Southwest (n=260)	38.8%	52.7%	65.4%
West (n=260)	0	16.3%	25.6%

Table 4.2: Duration of Detainment Prior to Execution by Zone

periodization, although Heder further divides the latter period into a purge initially of non-Party members of Democratic Kampuchea followed by a purge of CPK cadre.[115] According to these accounts, during the first major purge—that of former Lon Nol soldiers and civilian employees of the previous regime—most victims were summarily executed and detainment was less common. Conversely, during the second major purge, as the CPK began targeting senior Khmer Rouge cadre, many prisoners were detained for longer periods of time, as important prisoners were forced to undergo lengthy interrogation sessions.

Although informative, Chandler's two-phase chronology is limited. Indeed, as Figure 4.3 reveals, a chronology of detainment derived from arrest and execution dates indicates a series of peaks and valleys, thereby suggesting a greater complexity both to CPK

ZONE	EXECUTED WITHIN		
	ONE WEEK	ONE MONTH	TWO MONTHS
Central (n=26)	0%	3.8%	19.2%
East (n=50)	4%	30%	52%
North (n=99)	28.3%	47.5%	57.6%
Northeast (n=13)	0%	0%	30.8%
Northwest (n=248)	11.7%	23%	44.4%
Southwest (n=29)	3.4%	6.9%	17.2%
West (n=0)	n/a	n/a	n/a

Table 4.3: Duration of Detainment of Male Prisoners by Zone

ZONE	EXECUTED WITHIN		
	ONE WEEK	ONE MONTH	TWO MONTHS
Central (n=0)	n/a	n/a	n/a
East (n=134)	56.7%	87.3%	97.8%
North (n=64)	31.3%	76.6%	81.3%
Northeast (n=7)	28.6%	57.1%	85.7%
Northwest (n=7)	28.6%	57.1%	85.7%
Southwest (n=15)	40%	46.7%	53.3%
West (n=0)	n/a	n/a	n/a

Table 4.4: Duration of Detainment of Female Prisoners by Zone

practice and to S-21 functions. In testimony provided during Duch's trial, for example, Craig Etcheson calls attention to several purges of individual units or administrative groupings. Many of these purges would last for a period of a few months to over a year. A purge of Division 310 of the Revolutionary Army of Kampuchea, for example, began in earnest in December 1976 and continued throughout 1977.[116] Required, therefore, are more refined analyses of particular purges, with special attention directed to both the sequence of arrests and the variation in length of detainment. Here, I can only make some preliminary observations.

Figures 4.4 and 4.5 provide a chronology of daily records of arrests and executions, respectively. Notably, a clustering of arrests occurred between March 1977 and April 1978. Moreover, a few key days are remarkable for the intensity of activity. On October 28, 1976, for example, 107 people were arrested. Significantly, most of those arrested on this date were identified as "wives" of other detainees. Equally significant is that these women were generally executed within two days of arrest. Execution records show a similar waxing and waning and, most importantly, begin to illustrate a systematic approach to the periodic sweeping clean of S-21. Here, May 27, 1978, is especially prominent, in that 580 people are recorded as having been taken away for execution. Of the 564 prisoners for whom complete records exist, the mean length of detainment prior to execution on May 27, 1978, was just under forty-three days. Moreover, 306 (54 percent) of these prisoners were executed following a detainment of two months or less, while 156 (28 percent) were executed within one month of arrest. At least 352 of these victims were from Sector 23 of the East Zone.

Ben Kiernan categorizes May 1978 as the month in which East Zone purges reached a crescendo. And to Kiernan's point, May 1978 is notable.[117] However, it is also telling that May 27, 1978, appears as the last major gasp of recorded CPK purges—in so far as S-21 is concerned. Again, caution must be taken in interpreting these records. Numerous purges took place outside the administrative structure of S-21. Consequently, these records say nothing about the mass executions that occurred, for instance, at zone-level security

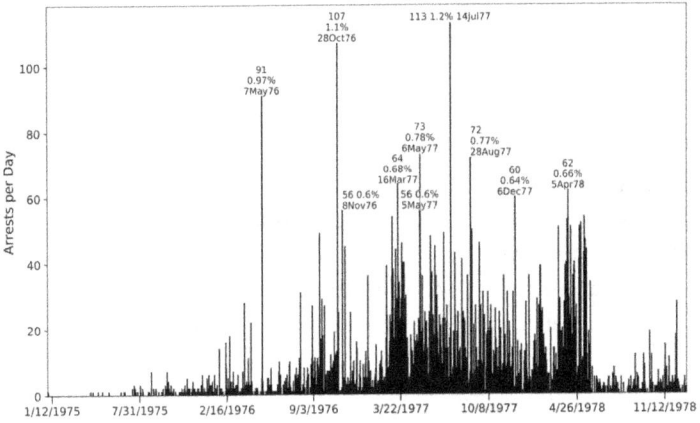

Figure 4.4: Arrests by Date (n=9,394)

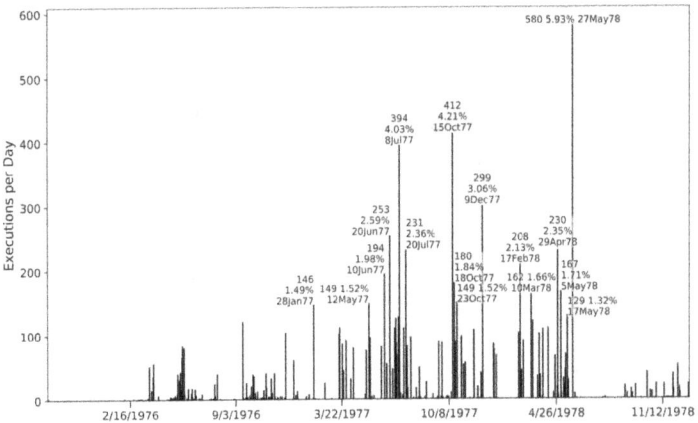

Figure 4.5: Executions by Date (n=9,778)

centers. Furthermore, as repeatedly stated, as the purges associated with S-21 continued, it became more and more the case that prisoners were taken straightaway for execution, hence untold numbers of men, women, and children were simply never documented.[118] That being said, documented evidence for the first five months of 1978 indicate that the scheduling of executions was more clustered than the arrest of individuals. Hence, the majority of executions occurred on just six days in 1978: February 17, March 10, April 29, May 5, May 17, and May 27. Moreover, beginning in March, these peak killings happened roughly every ten to twelve days.

Duch, as mentioned earlier, claimed that decisions were made to periodically empty S-21 so as not to overburden his staff. In other words, periodic purges of S-21 itself were conducted in response to overcrowding. Duch, however, was conspicuously vague with respect to this practice. To what extent is it possible to provide empirical evidence of these internal purges? In order to provide a more refined accounting of arrests and executions, Figure 4.6 shows the relationship between detainment (i.e., the length of time between arrest and execution) and entry date. For example, of those men and women who were arrested on, say, January 1, 1976, or on July 1, 1978, what was the length of detainment? By way of illustration, consider the aforementioned date of May 27, 1978, on which 580 prisoners were scheduled for execution. Prisoners who were executed on that day, but arrested on May 17, 1978, would have been held for ten days; prisoners arrested on May 16, 1978, would have been imprisoned for nine days; and so on. The resulting pattern is one of a series of ever-shortening periods of detention as the prison population increased. Results as indicated in Figure 4.6 show a clear regularity to patterns of detainment, providing empirical evidence of a systematic emptying of the prison.

At this point, results are preliminary and subsequent research is necessary to further disaggregate who was being killed and for how long they were detained. Crucial information not yet currently available relates to the actual assignment of prisoners to either solitary or communal cells. For example, if twenty prisoners from

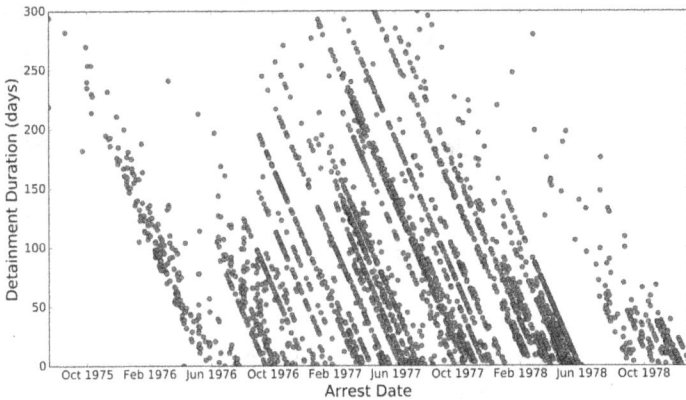

Figure 4.6: Length of Detainment Days by Date of Arrest (n=8,289)

Region 23 and fifteen prisoners from the State Warehouse were arrested and processed on the same day, would all thirty-five detainees be sent to one communal cell? Were those prisoners from Region 23 sent as a group to a specific communal prison cell and those from the State Warehouse to another? Alternatively, was an attempt made to separate prisoners from those in their unit? By extension, when the prison was swept clean, was it done on a cell-by-cell basis, or were prisoners selected individually from different cells? And, if the latter, how were these decisions made? At this point, the day-to-day procedures are unclear and the microgeographies of S-21 remain frustratingly partial. A general pattern, however, is emerging of the broader process. For any given purge, one or two key people are arrested and detained. These individuals, subjected to torture and interrogation, confess to innumerable confederates. These names are in turn compiled to form a list of traitors. These men and women are subsequently arrested, as are the spouses and family members of the original detainees. Given that these latter individuals are considered less important to the CPK, they are not held for interrogation but marked by Duch for execution. Hor and his staff consequently made arrangements to transport these prisoners to Choeung Ek for execution.

This process is illustrated by a purge of S-24 prisoners during the summer of 1976. Beginning in June 1976, various squad chiefs and commanders who were initially detained at S-24 were transferred to S-21. By and large, these individuals (mostly men) were detained for upward of three to four weeks. Throughout September 1976, an increasing number of men listed simply as combatant were arrested and, for the most part, were executed within two days. For example, twenty-one men were arrested on September 22, 1976, and scheduled for execution on September 23, 1976. Beginning in November 1976, the purge was extended to include the wives, sisters, and mothers of previous detainees. On November 8, 1976, thirty women were arrested from S-24 and all were scheduled for execution on November 9, 1976. With two exceptions, the position listed for these women was wife, daughter, mother, or sister, as in "Yun Sok Im, wife of Un Saravuth" or "Kuong Vann Than, sister of Kuong Vantha."[119]

The peaks and valleys of arrests and executions, but especially the clear sequencing of detainment in Figure 4.6, provide strong empirical evidence of how S-21 was managed. As strings of traitors were identified and arrested, and as key bureaucrats such as Nuon Chea, Son Sen, and Duch processed and evaluated the biopolitical data derived from personal biographies, confessions, and other reports, more and more people were arrested and detained. Subsequently, when any person was considered to have nothing else of importance to offer, he or she was literally written off as expendable. Thousands of others were never considered important enough to be interrogated, and were left to languish in overcrowded cells, starved of food, water, hygiene, and subject to constant physical and psychological abuse. They too would be written off, scheduled to be executed. Unfortunately, we do not yet know with any level of certainty how this final decision was made, or of how any given prisoner or prison cell was identified to be smashed on any given day.

Conclusions

Prisons are not simply institutions that correspond to crime, as Moran and her colleagues explains, but rather are places that reflect and mediate social, political, and cultural values.[120] Prisons are, in other words, institutions that provide legitimacy and validity; they provide the semblance of order within a context of disorder. At S-21, order was reflected in the bureaucratic banality of processing, cataloging, photographing, and interrogating those who were convicted to death. CPK officials' need to meticulously record those who were already condemned established the limits of participation within society.

The essence of sovereignty is not the monopoly to sanction but rather the monopoly to decide: to decide when, or where, or to whom the law is to apply.[121] Nowhere is this more salient than in the presumed sovereign right over life and death—and in the legal practice of capital punishment. Thus, during and in the immediate aftermath of civil war, the CPK established a system of security centers; these were deemed necessary in an effort to spatially centralize governance and to restore legal order to society. At S-21, we witness the sublimation of law-making violence into law-preserving violence.

Following Walter Benjamin, law-making violence is foundational; it is the performative violence of a new constitution or a declaration of independence.[122] For the Khmer Rouge, an original moment of direct violence was necessary in an attempt to solidify legitimacy in the aftermath of armed revolution. It is seen in the initial purge of former Khmer Republic soldiers and civilians of the previous regime. Consequently, documentary evidence was necessary, from the vantage point of the CPK, to not only justify and legitimate their ascension to power, but also to defend their newly installed regime. Significant here is Benjamin's observation that law-making violence is forward-looking. This form of legalized violence is anticipatory in its effect and captures the precrime policing procedures and preemptive killing established within the Khmer Rouge security apparatus.

Once established, law-making violence elides with practices of law-preserving violence, understood here as actions that are conservative and protective, designed to defend or fortify a preexisting legal order.[123] As a bureaucratic institution, S-21 emerged as a crucial pivot in this transformation. Laws were not legislated at S-21, but legal claims were asserted. Likewise, laws were physically enacted at S-21, as bureaucrats were tasked with the enforcement of traitorous crimes—crimes threatening to the emergent political order. Consequently, S-21 was both a means to an end as well as an end that justified its means. For the tremendous purchase of Benjamin's observation of violence is that law-making and law-preserving practices are not oppositional but dialectic. Law, in this way, is never fully constituted but always, continually rearticulated. For Benjamin, "in the exercise of violence over life and death more than in any other legal act, law reaffirms itself." Every investigation conducted, every prisoner registered, every biography compiled, every photograph taken, every interrogation performed, and every execution carried out reconstituted the political authority and legitimacy of the Standing Committee of the CPK. All of these were documented, as countless bureaucratic functionaries compiled prisoner dossiers, daily arrest logs, interrogation workloads, and execution schedules. The direct physical violence of torture and execution were thus complementary to the indirect bureaucratic violence of S-21. Both may be understood as the continuation of the foundation of law—a legal order that ultimately is embodied, individuated, revealed, and exposed.

CHAPTER 5

Conclusions

On October 5, 1977, Son Sen, deputy prime minister for defense, sent a brief letter to Duch, chairman of the S-21 security center. Son Sen writes: "Paper must be saved, however, more importantly attention must be paid to the content." The topic of the letter, it appears at first blush, is rather banal, expressing concern as it does for the conservation of paper. However, Son Sen continues, "The confessions must be thorough and responsible. Scribbling or guesswork cannot be accepted." Here, the true meaning becomes clear. Son Sen counseled Duch that his office needed to be more efficient in its duties. For high-ranking prisoners, or those deemed more important, Son Sen specified that confessions should be tape-recorded and transcribed. Experience showed that tape-recording the forced confessions took less time and were more accurate in the documentation of necessary information. For all other prisoners, Son Sen conceded that paper records may be sufficient.[1]

In his letter Son Sen expresses concern not for the lives of men, women, and children; he appears nonplussed with respect to widespread torture taking place at S-21. Rather, his anxiety centers on making the interrogative procedures more efficient and, in the process, less wasteful of office supplies. How are we to make sense of this letter? How exactly do Son Sen's worries inform our understanding of mass violence, not only within Democratic Kampuchea but beyond? For Son Sen's apparent callousness is not an aberration. Many thousands of kilometers away from Phnom Penh, in the town of Alkoven, Austria, sits Hartheim Castle. Between May 1940 and December 1944, the Nazi state used the castle as a killing center as part of its broader euthanasia program designed to eliminate mentally and physically challenged adults. Documents discovered after the end of the Second World War indicate that administrators at the castle had calculated that the disinfection—that is, murder—of 70,273 men and women resulted in a savings of over 245,955 Reichsmarks per day. These calculations, however, were computed not in currency but on the savings of food items. In other words, the murder of tens of thousands of people contributed to such savings as 239,067 kilograms of marmalade and 653,516 kilograms of meats and sausages.[2] In both instances, human lives were equated with material products: paper, jams, and frankfurters. In both instances, the management of human life was calculated according to bureaucratic procedures.

Michel Foucault postulates that knowledge is inseparable from power. He explains that power and knowledge directly imply one another; that there is no power relation without the correlative constitution of a field of knowledge, nor any knowledge that does not presuppose and constitute power relations at the same time.[3] For Foucault, power is exercised rather than possessed. Foucault elaborates: "Power must be analyzed as something which circulates, or rather as something which only functions in the form of a chain. It is never localized here or there, never in anybody's hands, never appropriated as a commodity or piece of wealth."[4]

Power circulates by means of the materiality of information. For this reason, geographers, historians, anthropologists, legal scholars, and other researchers working in the social sciences and humanities have turned their attention toward the *work* that paper and other objects perform.[5] As Katharine Meehan and colleagues explain, "objects enable, disable, and transform state power."[6] To this end, they argue that it is necessary to "move beyond the textual and symbolic realm, where objects are often containers or reflections of power, and toward an approach that situates objects as *generative* of power."[7]

Studies of genocide have long recognized the importance of state functions. Both Zygmunt Bauman and Irving Horowitz explore the statist character of genocide and the technological methods that transformed "nightmares into realities."[8] Recent work has pushed these earlier studies, calling for a more sustained engagement with the materiality of statecraft. Stewart Clegg and his coauthors, for example, call upon scholars to consider "the sociomateriality of genocide, that is, the way in which objects may help to create the contexts in which acts of genocide unfold."[9] An object-oriented approach provides insight into the salience of the seemingly routine day-to-day practices of governance beyond a statist framework.

An exclusive focus on grand-scale operations of power over-shadows our appreciation of the more ordinary instances of governmental intervention into matters of life and death.[10] In recognition of this, Joe Painter underscores the "prosaic manifestations of state processes" and "the ways in which everyday life is permeated by stateness in various guises." That is, it is important to address the myriad social relations that comprise the state. Thus, Painter highlights the "mundane practices through which something we label 'the state' becomes present in everyday life."[11] In so doing, however, we must not lose sight of the materiality of these everyday practices. As Meehan et al. explain, "human-centered accounts of state power are undeniably important, but they leave out the nonhuman trafficking of power."[12] To this end, analytic focus has gravitated toward the "small techniques of notation, of registration, of constituting files, of arranging facts in columns and tables."[13] In short, scholarship has taken seriously the claim that bureaucracies matter. This is all the more important when one considers, in the words of Bauman, that "Bureaucracy is intrinsically *capable* of genocidal action."[14]

It is necessary to "unpack the bureaucratic processes" and to "investigate how bureaucracies become socially embedded in particular places and, conversely, how they constitute places."[15] As Robertson explains, documents are located in bureaucratic institutions; the authority of documents is embedded and enacted in these institutions; and in reciprocal manner, the authority of institutions is constituted and enacted in documents.[16] Even something as ordinary as a letter assumes greater importance when situated within the circuits of bureaucratic power. For Jonathan Darling, letters become expressions of governmental practice in more than discursive ways. Calling for an engagement with the materiality of letters, with how they are produced, transported, and interpreted, Darling "approaches letters through their effects, through the relations they enact and the effects they produce."[17] The letter forwarded by Son Sen had material effects that extended well beyond its immediate receipt in the form of revised interrogative techniques and torture.

Files and folders, invoices and inventories, letters and ledgers: these constitute the material manifestation of authorial power, with authorial power assuming a dual function, implying both authorship and also authoritarianism. In other words, knowledge is produced through the act of authoring, broadly conceived, whether in the form of letters, telegrams, invoices, or any of the other innumerable means of transcription. Here, Jason Dittmer foregrounds "the role of materials in shaping political subjectivity and action."[18] He explains that "In focusing on people to the exclusion of things, materials and their relations, such a vision can eliminate from view the paper, wires, cables, gifts, and so on, that serve as the material infrastructure" of governance.[19]

The Khmer Rouge bureaucracy was not a singular entity but instead composed of myriad centers of calculation occupied and served by countless men and women, from the village level to the Standing Committee. They served as members of commune committees, security centers, and countless departments and ministries. Collectively, they produced volumes of information that was codified, classified, and ultimately made operational in the form of arrests, interrogations, and execution. In crafting *The Politics of Lists*, the ordinary list assumes prominence, for I see in the list a particular expression of power with immediate, tangible effects of everyday violence. Lists of men, women, and children to be arrested; lists of men, women, and children to be interrogated; lists of men, women, and children to be tortured; and lists of men, women, and children to be executed. Lists of foodstuffs to be exported, with the effect of men, women, and children enduring malnutrition and famine. Lists of medicines to be imported and yet denied to men, women, and children because they were considered bad elements, unworthy, or undeserving.

The spectacular violence that materialized in the form of beatings, torture, rape, starvation, and murder was made possible by the everyday actions of ordinary men and women—those individuals who comprised the Khmer Rouge bureaucracy. The inscription of a name on a list, the sending of a list via telegram, the safekeeping of a written biography in a filing cabinet—everyday mundane activities that facilitate the writing, the recording, the storing of information, which, in turn, is compiled, collated, and interpreted—in a word, it was materialized information made actionable.

As Bauman explains in the context of the Holocaust, "Bureaucracy started from what bureaucracies start with: the formulation of a precise definition of the object, then registering those who fitted the definition and opening a file for each."[20] In Democratic Kampuchea, it started with the collection and compilation of biopolitical information. The term *biopolitics* is widely, albeit inconsistently, used in many academic disciplines.[21] Here, I follow Thomas Lemke, whereby "the notion of biopolitics refers to the emergence of a specific political knowledge and new disciplines such as statistics, demography, epidemiology, and biology."[22] Lemke elaborates that these "disciplines make it possible to analyze processes of life on the level of populations and to 'govern' individuals and collectives by practices of correction, exclusion, normalization, disciplining, therapeutics, and optimization."[23] In short, an engagement with biopolitics directs attention to the myriad ways in which bodies and populations are governed. As Jeremy Crampton and Stuart Elden write, "Forms of organizing, conceptualizing and managing the population can be seen in technologies such as the census and representational discourses, statistics, planning and cartography, as well as political expressions such as geopolitics, government and colonial ordering."[24] These forms of organization, moreover, are complemented by pervasive information and communication technologies embedded within the fabric of everyday life: smart phones, computers, credit cards, e-tickets, and so on.[25] What is important is that these data increasingly are mined and analyzed by algorithms that identify patterns and possible deviations to inform security-related and business-related practices.[26]

Throughout Democratic Kampuchea, the Khmer Rouge utilized low-tech forms of biopolitical data collection, such as personal biographies, handwritten confessions, and forms of lateral surveillance. Nevertheless, Khmer Rouge cadres used these procedures to great effectiveness. Personal biographies, for example, were mined for apparent contradictions; networks of traitors were computed based on the analysis of confessions; and enemy activity was established through the pervasive surveillance of society. In short, the paper documents produced by countless men and women throughout all levels of the Khmer Rouge bureaucracy enabled the Party to *know* its citizens and to identify potential enemies. As Robertson explains, "Paper, in the form of files, documents, and certificates, gives identity a distinct official shape that allows it to circulate."[27] He continues that "identity becomes evidence that can be stored and moved because of the process of inscription: the people who mark paper, the techniques they use, and the administrative location where that information is inscribed on paper."[28]

"Forms help to enframe and categorize," Akhil Gupta writes, for "they are containers for standardization, replicability, anonymity, and portability. Applicants who have filled in forms can be more easily compared to each other, and the information contained therein can be more easily converted into statistics."[29] Consequently, the production and circulation of personal biographies, forced confessions, and even the mundane list of names compiled at a work site, facilitated the discursive construction of traitors, saboteurs, and enemies. By extension, everyday social relations were transfigured into the existence of subversive networks of traitors that required preemptive forms of violence.

That these documents were both written and archived by the Khmer Rouge is not inconsequential. The utilization and standardization of forms, for example, "allows writing to be stored and retrieved under appropriate conditions."[30] Not surprisingly, the compilation of biographies, confessions, and records of suspicious activities afforded a veneer of legitimacy and authority to the CPK, as these documents provided the material basis upon which a legal order was established. Archives, as Francis Blouin and William Rosenberg write, appear as repositories of truth and authenticity.[31] Thus, within Democratic Kampuchea, the collection of meeting minutes, telegrams, memos, and other material statements enabled Khmer Rouge cadres to make "evaluative, descriptive, prescriptive, or advisory decisions."[32] The bureaucratic procedures of classifying, listing, filing, and transmitting of knowledge established a structure of governance that determined greatly the resultant purges of so-called traitors and enemies of the state. Bureaucratic invocations of guilt brought security fears into existence and made possible preemptive intervention. It was through this process that the seemingly banal compilation of biopolitical data, of one's life history and network of friends, colleagues, and even distant acquaintances, mutated into a form of necropolitical bureaucracy.

Biometrics beyond Democratic Kampuchea

Necropolitical bureaucracies, or more simply necrobureaucracies, function through the knowing of political subjects, whereby the compilation of embodied knowledge serves the purpose of commanding death. A particular legal order comes into existence through the production and circulation of statements materialized, and governance is enacted through the mundane task of preparing lists, filing reports, and archiving documents. My overall thesis is that the bureaucratic practices of the Khmer Rouge were not unique. Indeed, the biopolitical production of knowledge and the subsequent necropolitical practice of mass arrest, detainment, and execution are ever-present conditions of sovereign rule. Accordingly, in this final section I resituate Cambodia's violent past as a particular moment of the state management of life and death and thus as a cautionary rejoinder in the deployment of biometric security practices.[33]

Well into the twenty-first century, a wide range of sophisticated biometric techniques have been developed and utilized by innumerable bureaucracies. To this end, "specific data about one's body are being used to distinguish one person from the next by matching up the corporeal body presented at a border checkpoint with the digital data of that body stored on a database or a credit card."[34] Widely used technologies include computer-based facial recognition programs, DNA analysis, and retinal identification systems.[35] Technologies need not be so advanced, however. Indeed, the long-standing practice of profiling remains a stalwart feature of the security apparatus. Simply put, profiling entails the compilation— the listing—of information on people based on observed physical or behavioral traits, and profiles are developed and stored in databases for further analysis. Crucially, "profiling enables the prediction of eventualities in order to prevent them."[36] Here, I want to explore further, in the abstract, the inherent danger of security discourses founded upon biopolitical governance.

Lists composed of suspected criminals or terrorists based on biopolitical profiles are problematic on at least two counts. Anya Bernstein effectively captures the problem. First, lists become all-inclusive, establishing a precedent whereby anyone ultimately may be viewed as a suspect. The point of a terrorist database, for example, is to prevent any potential threat from materializing. Inherent in any particular watch list or kill list is a preemptive component. Accuracy is important insofar as potential threats are identified, not that innocent people may inaccurately be placed on a list. For those bureaucrats who are responsible for the compilation of lists, the danger is that someone initially adjudged to be safe, i.e., not placed on the list, may at some point in the future commit a crime—an omission known as a false negative. Only by suspecting everyone is it possible (theoretically) to eliminate false negatives.[37]

As corollary, the ever-expanding list of suspects will necessarily include some indeterminate number of false positives, that is, innocent people who should not come under suspicion. As efforts to eliminate false negatives increase, there is a greater probability that the acceptance of false positives will also increase. The only way to afford complete security and to prevent all security breaches is to monitor everyone; in time, everyone becomes suspect. And once placed on a security list, guilt is presumed.[38] The political ontology of anticipatory security threats is such that civil liberties are too readily cast aside in the compilation of lists. Any right to due process is bypassed in an effort to prevent any and all future threats from occurring. Within Democratic Kampuchea, as with present-day security lists, anyone whose name appeared in a confession, with few exceptions, was prejudged as guilty and thus sentenced to death. Duch would later testify that he knew many men and women who were innocent, but in due course they were put to death. He rationalized at the time that it was better to adjudge everyone guilty rather than miss one.

Digital surveillance, as Stephen Graham and David Wood explain, makes information more amenable to storage, transmission, and computation; but more importantly, these modes of surveillance result "in the creation of subjects through databases that do not replicate or imitate the original subject, but create a multiplicity of selves that may be acted upon without the knowledge of the original."[39] To this end, Louise Amoore and Marieke de Goede write of data wars and of wars by other means; of the production of perceived threats, such as terrorists and terrorist networks, not from information derived from individual men and women but through associations of recorded behavior. More precisely, they call attention to the flourishing of surveillance practices, data-collection techniques, predictive analytics, and other computational innovations that are "intimately tied to the contemporary turn to pre-emptive security techniques."[40] As Mark Andrejevic and Kelly Gates explain, "what is significant about the big data moment is not simply that it has become possible to store quantities of data that are impossible for any individual to comprehend . . . but the fact that this data can be put to use in novel ways."[41]

At issue is the collection of big data, of the voracious appetite of the modern security apparatus, gobbling up ever more bits of data, which anonymous bureaucrats then process through sophisticated algorithms in search of spatial and temporal patterns. For our present purposes, this is significant in that the very notion of a surveillance target takes on a somewhat different meaning when surveillance relies on mining large-scale databases: the target becomes the "hidden pattern" revealed computationally in the data, rather than existing as any particular individual or event.[42] Big data surveillance therefore is not simply or even predominantly about understanding the data, nor is it typically about explaining or understanding the world captured by that data. Instead, it is about intervening in a world based on spatial and temporal patterns available to and made knowable by those with access to the data and the processing power.[43] Accordingly, the role of the bureaucrat assumes an even greater function in the overall security apparatus, contributing to a political system described by Irving Horowitz as "governance through data control."[44]

Within the context of the war on terror, we understand lists, but especially security lists, as crucial components of state-sanctioned counterterrorism practices. The blacklisting of individuals, the establishment of terrorist watch lists, the compilation of no-fly lists: these become essential political instruments that underscore a host of security-related practices, including the imposition of travel bans, the freezing of assets, and the targeted killing of suspected terrorists.[45] Arguably, nothing captures the concept of necrobureaucracies more than the compilation of kill lists.[46]

Conceptually, the motivation behind the kill list is not novel. Governments have long maintained lists of suspected enemies. Such kill lists are often, though not always, part of broader coordinated counterinsurgency programs, such as the United States–led Phoenix Program during the Vietnam War. Under the veneer of the war on terror, however, the kill list has expanded greatly in scale and scope and has elevated the practice of targeted killings to unprecedented levels. In 2012 investigative reports revealed that the administration of then U.S. President Barack Obama was utilizing a particular list known as the "disposition matrix."[47] Devised two years earlier by then CIA Director John Brennan, the disposition matrix merges diverse kill lists, including the Terrorist Identities Datamart Environment, managed by the National Counterterrorism

Center, and the Federal Bureau of Investigation's Terrorist Screening Database, in which between 680,000 and 875,000 people are registered.[48] Regardless of the agency involved, "bureaucrats—far removed from public scrutiny and oftentimes outside the reach of courts—are essential to the success of the program."[49] Indeed, the production of a target is, following Ian Shaw and Majed Akhter, an intensely bureaucratic process that is part and parcel of an even larger security apparatus.[50] To this point, they detail that as of 2010, an estimated 854,000 people worked on programs related to counterterrorism, intelligence, and homeland security in 10,000 locations across the United States. This does not include the untold thousands of personnel working around the globe.[51]

How does the disposition matrix become operationalized? Different procedures have been established for the various governmental agencies involved in targeted killings.[52] In general, however, there are four elements: identification, vetting, validation, and nomination. Identification entails the initial selection of men or women to be added to the respective kill list. In general, someone may be added if he or she falls into one of two categories: known membership in an organized armed group and/or by his or her effectiveness within an organization.[53] The latter may include, for example, a known bomb maker. Over time, however, the criteria for inclusion have steadily expanded. Not only are men and women suspected of engaging in violent acts, such as hostage taking, assassination, or bombings placed on the list; also included are those suspected of destroying government property, cyber-attacks and, increasingly, nonviolent political activities and any action that is deemed to challenge the dominant political order.[54]

Once identified, potential targets are vetted and validated, whereby intelligence agencies evaluate a range of concerns, including the likelihood of success, the costs and benefits of eliminating the individual, and the overall legality of the operation. Input from these sessions is subsequently placed in the growing dossier kept on all potential targets. Lastly, names must be nominated—that is, official approval for someone to be targeted—in a process not unlike that performed by the Standing Committee of the CPK. Under the

Obama administration, the president assumed a very active role in this process, whereby the president, key advisers, and upward of one hundred officials would hold classified meetings to pore over intelligence briefings derived from the various lists. Participants would vet potential targets, based on compiled dossiers that included photographs and biographical information. Deliberations could be contentious and decisions to include or exclude a specific name could take five or six meetings; on average, it took President Obama fifty-eight days to give the final go-ahead. Once approved, names would be forwarded to officials who would arrange for the subsequent mission to eliminate the target. Notably, if the target wasn't captured or killed within thirty days, the case would in principle be rereviewed.[55]

"Although law delimits the categories of persons who can be killed," McNeal explains, "in practice, developing kill lists looks far beyond law to questions about the identity of a particular target and the accuracy and currency of the supporting intelligence."[56] According to Weber, new data infrastructures and analytics are playing a crucial and increasing role in the politics of intelligence production and targeted killing in contemporary U.S. warfare.[57] Crucially, the production of biometric knowledge elides readily with the oxymoronic concept of paranoia within reason.[58]

Coined by George Marcus, the notion of paranoia by reason "implies that under certain socio-political conditions paranoia is not only irrational but actually the most rational response."[59] For example, the fear that security apparatuses may overlook a terrorist induces a paranoia based on the need to eliminate false negatives. Such reasoning holds that it is better to suspect everyone. Individual civil liberties are sacrificed in the name of national security. This in turn contributes to an ever-deepening paranoia whereby vast conspiratorial networks are presumed to exist—a presumption seemingly confirmed through the network analysis of biometric data.

Once incorporated into biopolitical or necropolitical practice, paranoia becomes a "structural condition of rule" that may permeate all of society, as it did in Democratic Kampuchea.[60]

Nicholas Holm, for example, observes that the perceived "infiltration of the US administration and entertainment industry by communist agents were not only regarded as within reason by those in power, but had real concrete effects on the day to day lives of thousands, if not millions, of American citizens during the nineteen fifties."[61] A similar paranoia and resultant infringement on civil liberties occurred during the Second World War, as American officials incarcerated upward of 120,000 Japanese and Japanese Americans under the pretext of national security. It is readily apparent that the current war on terror is informed by a comparable paranoia, as networks of terrorists are compiled through the analytics of big data management. Indeed, it is this intersectionality of surveillance practices and militarized responses that forms the basis of Katherine Kindervater's notion of lethal surveillance and the justification for targeted killings.[62]

Targeted killings are defined as the officially authorized and premediated killing by military or intelligence officials of named and identified individuals without the benefit of any judicial process.[63] Targeted killings are ostensibly conducted in self-defense and therefore are considered (by some officials) as legal state action, although the separation of assassination and targeted killings has generated an intense moral and legal debate.[64] As Michael Gross explains, the "conventions of war permit combatants to use lethal force against enemy soldiers with relatively few restrictions. Law enforcement, on the other hand, permits officers to employ lethal force against suspected criminals but remains highly circumscribed."[65] More precisely, "police officers may kill in self-defense in unusually threatening and dangerous circumstances, but they may not otherwise harm a criminal in the absence of due process."[66] At issue, therefore, is the preemptive bureaucratic classification of people as either combatant or noncombatant. If those individuals who are targeted are declared noncombatants, then the conventions of war and laws of armed conflict make targeted killings illegal.[67] Such decisions ultimately are shaped by predominant discourses, modes of understanding, and sociopolitical contexts.[68] In Democratic Kampuchea, the bureaucratic classification of people into categories of loyalty, e.g., as base or new people, facilitated the subsequent production of traitorous or enemy identities, thereby providing justification for targeted arrests and executions.

In the contemporary war on terror, targeted killings are carried out primarily, although not exclusively, through the deployment of unmanned drones.[69] This is made possible, however, only through the performance of a complex bureaucracy and the compilation and interpretation of volumes of documentation. For as Gregory McNeal writes, "When the United States government kills people on traditional and non-traditional battlefields . . . bureaucrats play a key role in the killings."[70] In the United States–led war on terror, for example, U.S. drone strikes conducted through the auspices of a "disposition matrix" entail two types of targets and strikes.[71] On the one hand, there are personality strikes directed at specific individuals who have been manually identified by government officials. On the other hand, there are signature strikes whereby targets are not specifically identified by name but exist as "digital profiles across a network of technologies, algorithmic calculations, and spreadsheets."[72] Other signature strikes are decidedly more vague, if not outright random, as when a drone passes over a suspected insurgent training camp, whereby it is presumed that any person present, especially if the person is young, male, and armed, is deemed a legitimate target.

The practice of surveillance and subterfuge, and state actors' collection of data, are not new. Nor are political assassinations that are conducted in the name of security. Indeed, the historiography of security practices under the Khmer Rouge calls attention to the myriad forms in which the practice of lethal surveillance is enacted. On this point, an interpretation of the Khmer Rouge security apparatus viewed through the prism of lethal surveillance raises many uncomfortable parallels with current legal and moral criticisms of the United States–led war on terror. Jeremy Waldron, for example, identifies a number of criticisms associated with the practice of targeted killings as specifically carried out by drones: some critics, for example, are concerned about the effect of targeted killings on civilians; the processes by which individuals are targeted; the targeting of American citizens; the use of drones as a new form of warfare; and the way drones and drone technology presage a new era of surveillance.[73] For Waldron these are appropriate concerns, but they miss a more fundamental concern. He explains that taken in isolation, each of these criticisms leads to the conclusion that if only we can be certain of identifying the right terrorist, or if we could ensure that only the right terrorist was killed with no collateral damage, then targeted killings are appropriate state actions conducted in the war on terror. The central issue, Waldron argues, "Is not whether [governments] are killing the right people but whether killings of this kind are appropriate at all. The issue is the sheer existence and use of such death-lists by our government, however scrupulously and transparently they are maintained."[74] And it is this key issue that finds resonance with our historical engagement of the Communist Party of Kampuchea and the widespread practice of purging suspected traitors and enemies of the state. The techniques of data gathering, network analysis, and preemptive action, coupled with systematic state-sanctioned murder, were rudimentary in comparison to those deployed in the current war on terror. A blow to the back of the head, the slit of a throat by machete: neither of these actions approximates the high-tech circuitry of unmanned aerial drones and the launching of heat-seeking missiles. But they were no less lethal.

Notes

PREFACE

1. Geoffrey C. Bowker and Susan Leigh Star, *Sorting Things out: Classification and Its Consequences* (Cambridge, MA: MIT Press, 2000), 137.
2. Michelle Caswell, "Hannah Arendt's World: Bureaucracy, Documentation, and Banal Evil," *Archivaria* 70 (Fall 2010): 1–25; at 10.
3. Office of the Co-Investigating Judges (OCIJ), *Closing Order, Case File No.: 002/19–09–2007-ECCC-OCIJ* (Phnom Penh: Extraordinary Chambers in the Courts of Cambodia, 2010).
4. Franziska C. Eckelmans, "The *Duch* Case: The ECCC Supreme Court Chamber's Review of Case 001," in *The Extraordinary Chambers in the Courts of Cambodia*, ed. Simon M. Meisenberg and Ignaz Stegmiller (Berlin: Springer, 2016), 159–79; at 161.
5. Donald W. Beachler, "The Quest for Justice in Cambodia: Power, Politics, and the Khmer Rouge Tribunal," *Genocide Studies and Prevention* 8, no. 2 (2014): 67–80; at 71.
6. Ieng Thirith died on August 22, 2015. She never stood trial for her crimes committed during the Democratic Kampuchea period.
7. Russell Hopkins, "The Case 002/01 Trial Judgement: A Stepping Stone from Nuremberg to the Present?" in *The Extraordinary Chambers in the Courts of Cambodia*, ed. Simon M. Meisenberg and Ignaz Stegmiller (Berlin: Springer, 2016), 181–201; at 184.
8. See the website of the Extraordinary Chambers of the Courts of Cambodia (hereafter cited as ECCC), http://www.eccc.gov.kh.
9. Document No. E393.1, "The OCIJ S-21 Prisoner List and Explanation of the Applied Methodology," archived at the ECCC, Phnom Penh, http://www.eccc.gov.kh/en.
10. "Supreme Court Chamber Orders to Declassify over 1,700 Confidential Documents," Supreme Court Chamber of the ECCC, press release: September 6, 2012, http://www.eccc.gov.kh/en.

11. Kirsten Weld, *Paper Cadavers: The Archives of Dictatorship in Guatemala* (Durham, NC: Duke University Press, 2014).

12. Ibid., 6.

13. Ben Kiernan, "Bringing the Khmer Rouge to Justice," *Human Rights Review* 1, no. 3 (2000): 92–108; Michelle Caswell, "Khmer Rouge Archives: Accountability, Truth, and Memory in Cambodia," *Archival Science* 10, no. 1–2 (2010): 25–44; Michelle Caswell, "Using Classification to Convict the Khmer Rouge," *Journal of Documentation* 68, no. 2 (2012): 162–84.

14. Though see Caswell, "Hannah Arendt's World," 17–22; see also Stewart Clegg, Miguel Pina e Cunha, and Arménio Rego, "The Theory and Practice of Utopia in a Total Institution: The Pineapple Panopticon," *Organization Studies* 33, no. 12 (2012): 1735–57.

15. Weld, *Paper Cadavers*, 23.

16. Ibid., 13.

17. Ann Laura Stoler, *Along the Archival Grain: Epistemic Anxieties and Colonial Common Sense* (Princeton, NJ: Princeton University Press, 2009), 33.

18. William H. Starbuck, "Shouldn't Organization Theory Emerge from Adolescence?" *Organization* 10, no. 3 (2003): 439–52; at 439.

19. Ibid.

20. See, for example, Max Weber, *Economy and Society* (Berkeley: University of California Press, 1978); John O'Neill, "The Disciplinary Society: From Weber to Foucault," *The British Journal of Sociology* 37, no. 1 (1986): 42–60; Stewart Clegg, "Weber and Foucault: Social Theory for the Study of Organizations," *Organization* 1, no. 1 (1994): 149–78; Kenneth Dauber, "Bureaucratizing the Ethnographer's Magic," *Current Anthropology* 36, no. 1 (1995): 75–95; Matthew Kurtz, "Situating Practices: The Archive and the File Cabinet," *Historical Geography* 29 (2001): 26–37; Marie-Andrée Jacob, "Form-Made Persons: Consent Forms as Consent's Blind Spot," *PoLAR: Political and Legal Anthropology Review* 30, no. 2 (2007): 249–68; Matthew S. Hull, "Documents and Bureaucracy," *Annual Review of Anthropology* 41 (2012): 251–67; Martin Müller, "Opening the Black Box of the Organization: Socio-material Practices of Geopolitical Ordering," *Political Geography* 31, no. 6 (2012): 379–88; Merje Kuus, "Transnational Bureaucracies: How Do We Know What They Know?" *Progress in Human Geography* 39, no. 4 (2015): 432–48; Jason Dittmer, "Theorizing a More-Than-Human Diplomacy: Assembling the British Foreign Office, 1839–1874," *The Hague Journal of Diplomacy* 11, no. 1 (2016): 78–104.

21. Kuus, "Transnational Bureaucracies," 432.

22. Ben Kafka, "Paperwork: The State of the Discipline," *Book History* 12, no. 1 (2009): 340–53; at 341.

23. Hull, "Documents and Bureaucracy," 253.

24. Craig Robertson, "'You Lie!' Identity, Paper, and the Materiality of Information," *The Communication Review* 17, no. 2 (2014): 69–90; at 69.

25. Hull, "Documents and Bureaucracy," 257.

26. Katharine Meehan, Ian G. R. Shaw, and Sallie A. Marston, "Political Geographies of the Object," *Political Geography* 33 (March 2013): 1–10; at 2.

27. Hull, "Documents and Bureaucracy," 259.

28. Jacob, "Form-Made Persons," 251.

29. Hull, "Documents and Bureaucracy," 259.

30. Weber, *Economy and Society*, 225.

31. Madan Sarup, *An Introductory Guide to Post-structuralism and Postmodernism*, 2nd ed. (Athens: University of Georgia Press, 1993), 72.

32. Michel Foucault, *Discipline and Punish: The Birth of the Prison*, trans. A. Sheridan (New York: Vintage Books, 1979), 27.

33. Michel Foucault, "Two Lectures," in *Power/Knowledge: Selected Interviews and Other Writings, 1972–1977*, ed. Colin Gordon (New York: Pantheon Books, 1980), 98.

34. Hannah Arendt, *On Violence* (New York: Harvest Books, 1969), 51.

35. Ibid., 49.

36. Ibid., 38.

37. Claire Blencowe, "Foucault's and Arendt's 'Insider View' of Biopolitics: A Critique of Agamben," *History of the Human Sciences* 23, no. 5 (2010): 113–30; at 120. See also Claire Edwards, "Cutting Off the King's Head: The 'Social' in Hannah Arendt and Michel Foucault," *Studies in Social and Political Thought* 1, no. 1 (1999): 3–20.

38. Dauber, "Bureaucratizing the Ethnographer's Magic," 75.

39. Ibid., 76.

40. Steven Brint, *In an Age of Experts: The Changing Role of Professionals in Politics and Public Life* (Princeton: Princeton University Press, 1994); Tim Mitchell, *Rule of Experts: Egypt, Techno-Politics, Modernity* (Berkeley: University of California Press, 2002); Dominic Boyer, "Thinking Through the Anthropology of Experts," *Anthropology in Action* 15, no. 2 (2008): 38–46; William Davies, "Knowing the Unknowable: The Epistemological Authority of Innovation Policy Experts," *Social Epistemology* 25, no. 4 (2011): 401–21.

41. Boyer, "Thinking Through," 39.

42. Ibid.

43. Nicholas Holm, "Conspiracy Theorizing Surveillance: Considering Modalities of Paranoia and Conspiracy in Surveillance Studies,"

Surveillance & Society 7, no. 1 (2009): 36–48; at 36. See also Sarah Kendzior, "'Recognize the Spies': Transparency and Political Power in Uzbek Cyberspace," *Social Analysis* 59, no. 4 (2015): 50–65.

44. Holm, "Conspiracy Theorizing Surveillance," 37.

45. Alexander L. Hinton, *Why Did They Kill? Cambodia in the Shadow of Genocide* (Berkeley: University of California Press, 2005); James A. Tyner, *From Rice Fields to Killing Fields: Nature, Life, and Labor under the Khmer Rouge* (Syracuse, NY: Syracuse University Press, 2017).

46. Foucault, "Two Lectures," 101.

47. Bruno Latour, *Science in Action: How to Follow Scientists and Engineers Through Society* (Cambridge, MA: Harvard University Press, 1987), 215 passim.

48. Akhil Gupta, *Red Tape: Bureaucracy, Structural Violence, and Poverty in India* (Durham, NC: Duke University Press, 2012); Matthew S. Hull, *Government of Paper: The Materiality of Bureaucracy in Urban Pakistan* (Berkeley: University of California Press, 2012); Dean Spade, *Normal Life: Administrative Violence, Critical Transpolitics, and the Limits of Law* (Durham, NC: Duke University Press, 2015); Jason Dittmer, *Diplomatic Material: Affect, Assemblage, and Foreign Policy* (Durham, NC: Duke University Press, 2017).

49. Caswell, "Hannah Arendt's World," 5; see also Katherine Kindervater, "The Emergence of Lethal Surveillance: Watching and Killing in the History of Drone Technology," *Security Dialogue* 47, no. 3 (2016): 223–38.

CHAPTER 1: EMERGING FROM THE SHADOWS

1. Document No. D30882, "Long Live the 17th Anniversary of the Communist Party of Kampuchea," archived at the Documentation Center of Cambodia, Phnom Penh.

2. Hinton, *Why Did They Kill?*, 48.

3. Document No. D30882, "Long Live the 17th Anniversary of the Communist Party of Kampuchea," 9.

4. John Marston, "Democratic Kampuchea and the Idea of Modernity," in *Cambodia Emerges from the Past: Eight Essays*, ed. Judy Ledgerwood (DeKalb: Northern Illinois University Press, 2002), 38–59; at 56.

5. Ibid.

6. Steve Heder, *Cambodian Communism and the Vietnamese Model: Imitation and Independence, 1930–1975* (Bangkok: White Lotus Press, 2004), 46.

7. Document No. D30882, "Long Live the 17th Anniversary of the Communist Party of Kampuchea," 17.

8. Ibid., 11.

9. Ibid., 55.

10. Ibid.

11. Ibid., 57.

12. Ibid.

13. Quoted in David Ayers, *Anatomy of a Crisis: Education, Development, and the State in Cambodia, 1953–1998* (Chiang Mai, Thailand: Silkworm Press, 2003), 32.

14. Ibid., 32.

15. David Chandler, *A History of Cambodia*, 3rd ed. (Boulder, CO: Westview Press, 2000), 189.

16. Ibid., 189; see also Margaret Slocomb, *An Economic History of Cambodia in the Twentieth Century* (Singapore: National University of Singapore Press, 2010), 76.

17. Slocomb, *An Economic History*, 77.

18. Heder, *Cambodian Communism*, 49.

19. Margaret Slocomb, *The People's Republic of Kampuchea, 1979–1989: The Revolution after Pol Pot* (Chiang Mai, Thailand: Silkworm Books, 2003), 10; Heder, *Cambodian Communism*, 93.

20. Heder, *Cambodian Communism*, 93.

21. It is probable that Sihanouk agreed to this arrangement in the hope that the Vietnamese would be able to restrain the Khmer Communists.

22. Slocomb, *The People's Republic of Kampuchea*, 10.

23. Heder, *Cambodian Communism*, 95.

24. Slocomb, *The People's Republic of Kampuchea*, 11.

25. David Chandler, *Brother Number One: A Political Biography of Pol Pot*, rev. ed. (Chiang Mai, Thailand: Silkworm Books, 1999), 72–73.

26. Kenton Clymer, *Troubled Relations: The United States and Cambodia since 1870* (DeKalb: Northern Illinois University Press, 2007), 99–100, 137.

27. Ibid., 99.

28. Ibid.

29. Operation Menu comprised a series of six bombing campaigns, known as Breakfast, Lunch, Snack, Dinner, Supper, and Dessert. Each campaign targeted a specific base area located in eastern Cambodia. See Ben Kiernan, "The American Bombardment of Kampuchea, 1969–1973," *Vietnam Generation* 1, no. 1 (1989): 4–41; William Shawcross, *Sideshow: Kissinger, Nixon, and the Destruction of Cambodia*, rev. ed. (New York: Cooper Square Press, 2002); Taylor Owen and Ben Kiernan, "Bombs over Cambodia," *Walrus Magazine* October (2006): 62–69; Ben Kiernan and Taylor Owen, "Making More Enemies Than We Kill? Calculating U.S. Bomb Tonnages Dropped on Laos and Cambodia, and Weighing Their Implications," *The Asia-Pacific Journal* 13, no. 16 (2015): 1–9.

30. Chandler, *A History of Cambodia*, 208; Shawcross, *Sideshow*, 122; Clymer, *Troubled Relations*, 102.

31. Initially, China attempted to align itself with the Lon Nol government, if three conditions were met: permission for the Chinese to continue to supply the Vietnamese Communists through Cambodian territory; authorization of Vietnamese Communists to maintain their bases inside Cambodia; and Khmer support of the Vietnamese Communists in government statements. In effect, the Chinese were willing to postpone the Cambodian revolution in order to help the Vietnamese revolution and to maintain a Chinese-Vietnamese front against the United States. The Lon Nol government, given its anti-Vietnamese and anti-Communist hard-line stance, predictably refused the Chinese overture. It is also likely that Lon Nol assumed that the United States would not abandon a loyal ally in its proxy war against the Communists.

32. Arnold Isaacs, *Without Honor: Defeat in Cambodia* (Baltimore: Johns Hopkins University Press, 1983), 199.

33. Donald M. Seekins, "Historical Setting," in *Cambodia: A Country Study*, ed. R. R. Ross (Washington, DC: U.S. Government Printing Office, 1990), 3–71; at 43–44. Khmer Rouge members of GRUNK claimed that it was not a government in exile because Khieu Samphan and other officials remained in Cambodia. Publicly, neither Pol Pot, Ieng Sary, nor Nuon Chea were identified as top leaders, although political and military authority was firmly in their hands.

34. Richard M. Nixon, "Address to the Nation on the Situation in Southeast Asia," April 30, 1970, www.nixonlibrary.org.

35. Ibid.

36. John Tully, *A Short History of Cambodia from Empire to Survival* (Crow's Nest, Australia: Allen & Unwin, 2005), 167.

37. Shawcross, *Sideshow*, 317.

38. Henry Kamm, *Report from a Stricken Land* (New York: Arcade Publishing, 1998), 116.

39. Kate G. Frieson, "Revolution and Rural Response in Cambodia: 1970–1975," in *Genocide and Democracy in Cambodia: The Khmer Rouge, the United Nations and the International Community*, ed. Ben Kiernan (New Haven, CT: Yale University Southeast Asia Studies, 1993).

40. Philip Short, *Pol Pot: Anatomy of a Nightmare* (New York: Henry Holt and Company, 2004), 218.

41. Quoted in Kiernan, "The American Bombardment," 8.

42. Anthony Barnett, "Democratic Kampuchea: A Highly Centralized Dictatorship," in*Revolution and Its Aftermath in Kampuchea: Eight Essays*, ed. David P. Chandler and Ben Kiernan (New Haven, CT: Yale University Southeast Asia Studies, 1983), 212–29; at 214.

43. Communist Party of Kampuchea (CPK), "Excerpted Report on the Leading Views of the Comrade Representing the Party Organization at a Zone Assembly," in *Pol Pot Plans the Future: Confidential Leadership Documents from Democratic Kampuchea, 1976–1977*, ed. David P. Chandler, Ben Kiernan, and Chanthou Boua (New Haven, CT: Yale University Southeast Asia Studies, Monograph Series 33, 1988), 13–25; at 24–25.

44. Ben Kiernan, *The Pol Pot Regime: Polices, Race and Genocide in Cambodia under the Khmer Rouge, 1975–1979* (New Haven, CT: Yale University Press, 1996); David P. Chandler, *Voices from S-21: Terror and History in Pol Pot's Secret Prison* (Berkeley: University of California Press, 1999); Hinton, *Why Did They Kill?*

45. Simon Locke, "Conspiracy Culture, Blame Culture, and Rationalisation," *The Sociological Review* 57, no. 4 (2009): 567–85; at 569.

46. Jovan Byford, *Conspiracy Theories: A Critical Introduction* (New York: Palgrave Macmillan, 2015), 21.

47. Ginna Husting and Martin Orr, "Dangerous Machinery: 'Conspiracy Theorist' as a Transpersonal Strategy of Exclusion," *Symbolic Interaction* 30, no. 2 (2007): 127–50; at 141.

48. Laura Jones, "The Commonplace Geopolitics of Conspiracy," *Geography Compass* 6, no. 1 (2012): 44–59; at 45.

49. Anne McClintock, "Paranoid Empire: Specters from Guantánamo and Abu Ghraib," *small axe* 13, no. 1 (2009): 50–74.

50. Jonathan Bach, "Power, Secrecy, Paranoia: Technologies of Governance and the Structure of Rule," *Cultural Politics* 6, no. 3 (2010): 287–302; at 290.

51. Ibid.

52. Ibid., 292.

53. McClintock, "Paranoid Empire," 53.

54. Ibid.

55. Byford, *Conspiracy Theories*, 4.

56. Roger Mac Ginty, "Social Network Analysis and Counterinsurgency: A Counterproductive Strategy?" *Critical Studies on Terrorism* 3, no. 2 (2010): 209–26; at 210.

57. Jutta Weber, "Keep Adding. On Kill Lists, Drone Warfare and the Politics of Databases," *Environment and Planning D: Society and Space* 34, no. 1 (2016): 107–25; at 111.

58. Marieke de Goede, "Fighting the Network: A Critique of the Network as a Security Technology," *Distinktion: Scandinavian Journal of Social Theory* 13, no. 3 (2012): 215–32; at 221.

59. Mac Ginty, "Social Network Analysis," 211.

60. Louise Amoore, "Lines of Sight: On the Visualization of Unknown Futures," *Citizenship Studies* 13, no. 1 (2009): 17–30; Marieke de Goede

and Gavin Sullivan, "The Politics of Security Lists," *Environment and Planning D: Society and Space* 34, no. 1 (2016): 67–88; Anna Leander, "The Politics of Whitelisting: Regulatory Work and Topologies in Commercial Security," *Environment and Planning D: Society and Space* 34, no. 1 (2016): 48–66; Urs Stäheli, "Indexing—the Politics of Invisibility," *Environment and Planning D: Society and Space* 34, no. 1 (2016): 14–29.

61. Cornelia Vismann, *Files: Law and Media Technology*, trans. Geoffrey Winthrop-Young (Stanford, CA: Stanford University Press, 2008), 6.

62. Stäheli, "Indexing," 14.

63. Ibid.

64. de Goede and Sullivan, "The Politics of Security Lists," 72.

65. Ibid., 70.

66. Ibid., 69.

67. Ibid. See also Daniel J. Steinbock, "Designating the Dangerous: From Blacklists to Watch Lists," *Seattle University Law Review* 30 (2006): 65–118; Anya Bernstein, "The Hidden Costs of Terrorist Watch Lists," *Buffalo Law Review* 61, no. 3 (2013): 461–535.

68. de Goede and Sullivan, "Politics of Security Lists," 72.

69. Weber, "Keep Adding," 111.

70. Mac Ginty, "Social Network Analysis," 220.

71. Leander, "Politics of Whitelisting," 52.

72. Weber, "Keep Adding," 112.

73. de Goede, "Fighting the Network," 221.

74. Ibid., 216.

75. Ibid., 217.

76. Marieke de Goede and Samuel Randalls, "Precaution, Preemption: Arts and Technologies of the Actionable Future," *Environment and Planning D: Society and Space* 27, no. 5 (2009): 859–78; at 861.

77. Bruce Braun, "Biopolitics and the Molecularization of Life," *cultural geographies* 14, no. 1 (2007): 6–28; at 19.

78. Christopher New, "Time and Punishment," *Analysis* 52, no. 1 (1992): 35–40; Saul Smilansky, "The Time to Punish," *Analysis* 54, no. 1 (1994): 50–53; Lucia Zedner, "Pre-crime and Post-criminology?" *Theoretical Criminology* 11, no. 2 (2007): 261–81; Lucia Zedner, "Pre-crime and Pre-punishment: A Health Warning," *Centre for Crime and Justice Studies* 81 (September 2010): 24–25; James Vlahos, "The Department of Pre-crime," *Scientific American* (January 2012): 62–67; Marieke de Goede, Stephanie Simon, and Marijn Hoijtink, "Performing Preemption," *Security Dialogue* 45, no. 5 (2014): 411–22.

79. Louise Amoore and Marieke de Goede, "Data and the War by Other Means," *Journal of Cultural Economy* 5, no. 1 (2012): 4.

80. Zedner, "Pre-crime and Post-criminology," 262.

81. Weber, "Keep Adding," 113.

82. Ibid.

83. Brian Massumi, "The Future Birth of the Affective Fact: The Political Ontology of Threat," in *Digital and Other Virtualities: Renegotiating the Image*, ed. Antony Bryant and Briselda Pollock (London: I. B. Tauris, 2010), 84.

84. Zedner, "Pre-crime and Pre-punishment," 24.

85. Massumi, "The Future Birth," 85.

86. Laurie Calhoun, "The Strange Case of Summary Execution by Predator Drone," *Peace Review* 15, no. 2 (2003): 209–14.

87. Ibid., 211.

88. Ibid.

89. Ibid., 212.

90. See also Stewart R. Clegg, Miguel Pina e Cunha, Arménio Rego, and Joana Dias, "Mundane Objects and the Banality of Evil: The Sociomateriality of a Death Camp," *Journal of Management Inquiry* 22, no. 3 (2013): 325–40.

91. Document No. E3/13 (00940336), "Minutes of the Meeting of Secretaries and Deputy Secretaries of Divisions and Independent Regiments," archived by the ECCC, http://www.eccc.gov.kh/en.

92. Michel Foucault, *"Society Must be Defended": Lectures at the Collège de France, 1977–1978*, trans. David Macey (New York: Picador, 2003), 240.

93. Ibid.

94. Foucault, *Discipline and Punish*, 26.

95. Paul Rabinow and Nikolas Rose, "Biopower Today," *BioSocieties* 1 (2006): 195–217.

96. Achille Mbembe, "Necropolitics," trans. Libby Meintjes, *Public Culture* 15, no. 1 (2003): 11–40; see also Melissa W. Wright, "Necropolitics, Narcopolitics, and Femicide: Gendered Violence on the Mexico-U.S. Border," *Signs* 36, no. 3 (2011): 707–31; John Round and Irina Kuznetsova, "Necropolitics and the Migrant as a Political Subject of Disgust: The Precarious Everyday of Russia's Labour Migrants," *Critical Sociology* 42, no. 7–8 (2016): 1017–34; Ian G. R. Shaw, "The Urbanization of Drone Warfare: Policing Surplus Populations in the Dronepolis," *Geographical Helvetica* 71, no. 1 (2016): 19–28.

97. Mbembe, "Necropolitics," 12.

98. Jamie Allinson, "The Necropolitics of Drones," *International Political Sociology* 9, no. 2 (2015): 113–27; at 118.

CHAPTER 2: A TALE OF TWO LISTS

1. Document No. E3/4123 (00322176), "Letter to Angkar," archived by the ECCC, http://www.eccc.gov.kh/en.

2. Document No. E3/1640 (00767226), "Respectfully Submitted to: The Embassy of the Socialist Federal Republic of Yugoslavia," archived by the ECCC, http://www.eccc.gov.kh/en.
3. Document No. E3/4123 (00322176), "Letter to Angkar." The letter indicates two other people suspected of committing crimes against Angkar.
4. Document No. E3/1640 (00767226), "Respectfully Submitted to: The Embassy of the Socialist Federal Republic of Yugoslavia."
5. Francis X. Blouin Jr. and William G. Rosenberg, *Processing the Past: Contesting Authority in History and the Archives* (Oxford: Oxford University Press, 2011), 26.
6. Gupta, *Red Tape*, 45.
7. Ibid.
8. Ibid., 47.
9. For a complementary perspective, see Andrew Mertha, *Brothers in Arms: Chinese Aid to the Khmer Rouge, 1975–1979* (Ithaca, NY: Cornell University Press, 2014), especially Chapter 2. See also Craig Etcheson, *The Rise and Demise of Democratic Kampuchea* (Boulder, CO: Westview Press, 1984).
10. Clark and Dear, *State Apparatus*, 45.
11. See, for example, Friedrich Engels, *The Origin of the Family, Private Property and the State* (New York: Penguin, 2010), 8.
12. Vladimir I. Lenin, *Essential Works of Lenin: 'What Is to Be Done?' and Other Writings*, ed. Henry M. Christman (New York: Dover Publications, 1987).
13. Ibid., 292; emphasis in original.
14. Karl Marx and Friedrich Engels, *The Communist Manifesto*, trans. Samuel Moore (Chicago: Charles H. Kerr, 1945).
15. Lenin, *Essential Works*, 274.
16. Ibid., 290.
17. Quoted in Slocomb, *The People's Republic of Kampuchea*, 21.
18. Lenin, *Essential Works*, 137.
19. Ibid., 143.
20. In Khmer, the word *angkar* is translated as *organization*. As Steve Heder explains, *angkar* was used as early as the 1940s within the Cambodian Communist movement. In time, it would obtain more sinister connotations. Heder, *Cambodian Communism and the Vietnamese Model.* See also Hinton, *Why Did They Kill?*
21. Document No. E3/12 (00182809), "Decision of the Central Committee Regarding a Number of Matters," archived by the ECCC, http://www. eccc.gov.kh/en.
22. Document No. E3/130 (00184022), "Communist Party of Kampuchea: Statute," archived by the ECCC, http://www.eccc.gov.kh/en.
23. Ibid.

24. Karl Marx and Friedrich Engels, *The German Ideology* (Amherst, NY: Prometheus Books, 1998), 36–37.

25. Communist Party of Kampuchea (CPK), "The Party's Four-Year Plan to Build Socialism in All Fields, 1977–1980," in Chandler, Kiernan, and Boua, *Pol Pot Plans the Future*, 51.

26. Marx and Engels, *The German Ideology*, 37.

27. Karl Marx, *A Contribution to the Critique of Political Economy* (New York: International Publishers, 1970), 20.

28. Ibid., 20–21.

29. Clark and Dear, *State Apparatus*, 36.

30. Charles Perrow, "The Analysis of Goals in Complex Organizations," *American Sociological Review* 26, no. 6 (1961): 854–66.

31. Ibid., 855.

32. Ibid.

33. Dittmer, "Theorizing a More-Than-Human Diplomacy," 86. See also Müller, "Opening the Black Box of the Organization."

34. Document No. E3/186 (00182663), "Minutes of Meeting of Standing Committee 3–5-76," archived by the ECCC, http://www.eccc.gov.kh/en.

35. Clark and Dear, *State Apparatus*, 48–54.

36. Mertha, *Brothers in Arms*, 2.

37. For a more extensive discussion, see Tyner, *From Rice Fields to Killing Fields*.

38. Document No. D30882, "Long Live the 17th Anniversary of the Communist Party of Kampuchea."

39. Document No, D55874, [no title], archived at the Documentation Center of Cambodia, Phnom Penh.

40. Ibid. It is noteworthy that Article 2 also specifies that "Articles for everyday use remain the personal property of the individual." This demonstrates that as of December 1975, when the text of the Constitution was being written, individual private property was not yet abolished.

41. Membership also fluctuated because of repeated purges. Usually, membership consisted of upward of thirty men and women. Apart from the Standing Committee members (who served on both committees), the Central Committee included Khieu Samphan, Koy Thuon, Ney Saran, and Ke Pok. The Central Committee also included a Specialist Military Committee that included Pol Pot, Nuon Chea, Son Sen, So Phim, and Ta Mok; Vorn Vet and Ke Pauk would later be added. See also Office of the Co-Investigating Judges, *Closing Order*, 18.

42. Ibid., 17.

43. Ibid., 21.

44. The third committee member may at times be simultaneously occupied by two or more people.

45. Mertha, *Brothers in Arms*, 30.
46. Boraden Nhem, *The Khmer Rouge: Ideology, Militarism, and the Revolution That Consumed a Generation* (Santa Barbara, CA: Praeger, 2013), 30.
47. The Northeast, for example, was designated 108. In practice, numeric codes at the zonal level were rarely utilized.
48. Michael Vickery, *Cambodia, 1975–1982* (Chiang Mai, Thailand: Silkworm Books, 1984), 71–73.
49. Office of the Co-Prosecutors, *Co-Prosecutors' Rule 66 Final Submission* (public redacted version), Case No.: 002/19/09/20007-ECCC/OCIJ, 53, ECCC, http://www.eccc.gov.kh.
50. Mertha, *Brothers in Arms*, 33.
51. Clark and Dear, *State Apparatus*, 50.
52. Ibid., 50–51.
53. Document No, D55874, [no title], archived at the Documentation Center of Cambodia, Phnom Penh.
54. Document No. D00674, "Communist Party of Kampuchea: Statute," archived at the Documentation Center of Cambodia, Phnom Penh. See also OCIJ, *Closing Order*, 16.
55. Ibid.
56. Ibid.
57. Ibid.
58. Ibid.
59. Ibid.
60. Ibid.
61. Ibid.; OCIJ, *Closing Order*, 17.
62. The People's Representative Assembly met once, during a meeting held on April 11–13, 1976.
63. Isaacs, *Without Honor*, 224. See also Noam Chomsky and Edward S. Herman, *After the Cataclysm: Postwar Indochina and the Reconstruction of Imperial Ideology* (Chicago: Haymarket Books, 2014).
64. For an extensive discussion of Khmer Rouge agricultural policies, see Tyner, *From Rice Fields to Killing Fields*, Chapter 4.
65. CPK, "The Party's Four-Year Plan," 51.
66. Ibid.
67. Ibid., 96.
68. Tyner, *From Rice Fields to Killing Fields*, Chapter 3.
69. Karl D. Jackson, "The Ideology of Total Revolution," in *Cambodia 1975–1978: Rendezvous with Death*, ed. Karl D. Jackson (Princeton, NJ: Princeton University Press, 1989), 37–78; at 45.
70. Charles H. Twining, "The Economy," in *Cambodia, 1975–1978: Rendezvous with Death*, ed. Karl D. Jackson (Princeton, NJ: Princeton University), 109–50; at 110.

71. Brian R. Tomlinson, "What Was the Third World?" *Journal of Contemporary History* 38, no. 2 (2003): 307–21; at 309.

72. Kristin S. Tassin, "'Lift Up Your Head, My Brother': Nationalism and the Genesis of the Non-Aligned Movement," *Journal of Third World Studies* 23, no. 1 (2006): 147–68; at 148.

73. Ibid.

74. Document No. D55874, [no title], archived at the Documentation Center of Cambodia, Phnom Penh.

75. Ibid.

76. Ibid.

77. Ibid.

78. Michael P. Todaro, *Economic Development in the Third World*, 4th ed. (New York: Longman, 1989), 428.

79. Document No. D00698, "Cooperation with the Ministry of Commerce," archived at the Documentation Center of Cambodia, Phnom Penh.

80. Ibid.

81. CPK, "The Party's Four-Year Plan," 46.

82. Communist Party of Kampuchea (CPK), "Excerpted Report of the Leading Views of the Comrade Representing the Party Organization at a Zone Assembly," 27.

83. CPK, "The Party's Four-Year Plan," 51.

84. Ibid., 131.

85. Ibid., 132.

86. Ibid., 89.

87. Ibid.

88. As the Khmer Rouge liberated areas from 1971 onward, peasants were relocated from the cities and into agricultural cooperatives. In 1973, for example, Khmer Rouge soldiers seized half of Kompong Cham City, taking fifteen thousand townspeople into the countryside with them. Later, in March 1974, just weeks before the fall of Phnom Penh, Khmer Rouge forces emptied the former capital of Oudong, dispersing more than twenty thousand former residents throughout the countryside. Initially, peasants were organized into mutual aid teams (*krom provas dai*). Under this system, effective control—but not ownership—of land, stock, and equipment remained in peasant hands, usury and rental payments were abolished, and taxation was relatively light. Later, but especially after April 1975, these were merged into larger low-level cooperatives (*sahakor kumrit teap*) and, finally, into high-level coopera-tives (*sahakor kumrit khpuos*). Similar to the practice of collectivization in the Soviet Union and the People's Republic of China, the CPK viewed cooperatives as a spatial practice that could, in theory, increase agricultural productivity and thereby garner greater surplus with which to spur industrialization. Following their victory of April 17, 1975, the

Communist Party of Kampuchea began forcibly evacuating Phnom Penh, the capital of Cambodia. Upward of three million people, more than half of whom were peasants who had fled the fighting during five years of civil war, were relocated to cooperatives and work camps in neighboring provinces. Many were forced to walk; others were transported by truck or train. It is now apparent that little planning went into the specific details of evacuation—there was scant coordination and the resultant death toll, while not accurately known, was substantial. For more detailed discussions on the forced evacuations, see Kiernan, *The Pol Pot Regime*; James A. Tyner, Samuel Henkin, Savina Sirik, and Sokvisal Kimsroy, "Phnom Penh during the Cambodian Genocide: A Case of Selective Urbicide," *Environment and Planning A* 46 (2014): 1873–91. For more on Soviet and Chinese communes, see Evsey D. Domar, "The Soviet Collective Farm as Producer Cooperative," *The American Economic Review* 56, no. 4 (1966): 734–57; Michael E. Bradley, "Incentives and Labour Supply on Soviet Collective Farms," *The Canadian Journal of Economics* 4, no. 3 (1971): 342–52; Tse Ka-Kui, "Agricultural Collectivization and Socialist Construction: The Soviet Union and China," *Dialectical Anthropology* 2, no. 3 (1977): 199–221; Xin Meng, Nancy Qian, and Pierre Yared, "The Institutional Causes of China's Great Famine, 1959–1961," paper presented at the Centre for Economic Policy Research's Development Economics Symposium, June 2–3, 2010, www.cepr.org/meets/wkcn/7/780/papers/Qianfinal.pdf.

89. Ministry of Culture and Fine Arts and the Documentation Center of Cambodia, *The Forced Transfer: The Second Evacuation of People during the Khmer Rouge Regime* (Phnom Penh: Documentation Center of Cambodia, 2014).

90. In total, thirteen appointments were made at this meeting: Pol Pot, military and the economy; Nuon Chea, Party affairs, social action, culture, propaganda, and education; Ieng Sary, foreign affairs, both Party and state; Khieu Samphan, front and the Royal Government, and commerce for accounting and pricing; Koy Thuon, domestic and international commerce; Son Sen, general staff and security; Vorn Vet, industry, railroads, and fisheries; Sua Vasi, chairman, political office of 870; Ieng Thirith, culture—social action and foreign affairs; Hu Nim, propaganda and reeducation, both internal and external; Chey, agriculture; Yem, Bureau 870; and Pang, government office. Document No. E3/1733 (00183393), "Meeting of the Standing Committee 9 October 75," archived by the ECCC, http://www.eccc.gov.kh/en.

91. Nhem, *The Khmer Rouge*, 48.

92. On April 14, 1976, for example, the Standing Committee, ostensibly working through the People's Representative Assembly, publicly

announced the governmental structure of Democratic Kampuchea: Pol Pot (prime minister), Ieng Sary (deputy prime minister responsible for foreign affairs), Vorn Vet (deputy prime minister responsible for economics), Son Sen (deputy prime minister for national defense), Hu Nim (minister responsible for information and propaganda), Chuon Choeun (minister of public health), Ieng Thirith (minister of social affairs), Touch Phoeun (minister of public works), and Yun Yat (ministry of culture, training, and education). In addition, six committees were established under the direction of the Ministry of Economy: agriculture, industry, commerce, rubber plantations, transportation, and energy. The respective ministers of these committees are: Chey Soun, Cheng An, Koy Thuon, Ek Sophon, Mei Brang, and Ta Che. It is unclear as to how active any of these committees truly were; preliminary archival evidence suggests that the Agriculture and Commerce Committees were most active. OCIJ, *Closing Order*, 23; Document No. E3/165 (00184048), "Document on Conference of Legislature of the People's Representative Assembly of Kampuchea 11–13 April 1976," archived by the ECCC, http://www.eccc.gov.kh/en; Document No. D21227, [no title], archived at the Documentation Center of Cambodia, Phnom Penh.

93. Mertha, *Brothers in Arms*, 48–49.
94. Twining, "The Economy."
95. Tyner et al., "Phnom Penh," 1884; Mertha, *Brothers in Arms*, 49.
96. Tyner et al., "Phnom Penh," 1882, 1886.
97. Mertha, *Brothers in Arms*, 53.
98. Document No. E3/494 (00142826), "Report by Craig Etcheson," archived by the ECCC, http://www.eccc.gov.kh/en.
99. Tyner et al., "Phnom Penh," 1886–87.
100. Mertha, *Brothers in Arms*, 50.
101. Ibid., 52.
102. Clark and Dear, *State Apparatus*, 52.
103. See, for example, James A. Tyner, "Genocide as Reconstruction: The Political Geography of Democratic Kampuchea," in *Reconstructing Conflict: Integrating War and Post-war Geographies*, ed. Scott Kirsch and Colin Flint (Aldershot, UK: Ashgate, 2011); James A. Tyner, "State Sovereignty, Bioethics, and Political Geographies: The Practice of Medicine under the Khmer Rouge," *Environment and Planning D: Society and Space* 30, no. 5 (2012): 842–60.
104. CPK, "Four-Year Plan," 113.
105. Thomas Clayton, "Building the New Cambodia: Educational Destruction and Construction under the Khmer Rouge, 1975–1979," *History of Education Quarterly* 38, no. 1 (1998): 1–16; at 5. See also Ayers, *Anatomy of a Crisis*; Thomas Clayton, "Re-orientations in Moral

Education in Cambodia since 1975," *Journal of Moral Education* 34, no. 4 (2005): 505–17.

106. Clayton, "Building the New Cambodia," 6.

107. Ibid.

108. Ibid., 8.

109. CPK, "Four-Year Plan," 113–14.

110. Ayers, *Anatomy of a Crisis*, 118–19. Three textbooks are known to have been produced by the CPK, including a math book and two geography texts. For a discussion of the second-grade political geography text produced by the CPK, see Tyner, "Genocide as Reconstruction," 60–63. See also James A. Tyner, Sokvisal Kimsroy, and Savina Sirik, "Nature, Poetry, and Public Pedagogy: The Poetic Geographies of the Khmer Rouge," *Annals of the Association of American Geographers* 105, no. 6 (2015): 1285–99; James A. Tyner, Sokvisal Kimsroy, and Savina Sirik, "Landscape Photography, Geographic Education, and Nation-Building in Democratic Kampuchea, 1975–1979," *The Geographical Review* 105, no. 4 (2015): 566–80; James A. Tyner, Mark Rhodes, and Sokvisal Kimsroy, "Music, Nature, Power, and Place: An Ecomusicology of Khmer Rouge Songs," *GeoHumanities* 2, no. 2 (2016): 395–412.

111. Document No. E3/216 (00850973), "Record of the Standing [Committee's] Visit to the Northwest Zone 20–24 August 1975," archived by the ECCC, http://www.eccc.gov.kh/en.

112. Document No. D00679, "Telegram Number 45," archived at the Documentation Center of Cambodia, Phnom Penh. I do not know if the request for medicines was ever addressed.

113. Document No. E3/232 (00182628), "Minutes of Meeting on Base Work 8 March 1976," archived by the ECCC, http://www.eccc.gov.kh/en.

114. Jan Ovesen and Ing-Britt Trankell, *Cambodians and Their Doctors: A Medical Anthropology of Colonial and Post-colonial Cambodia* (Copenhagen: Nordic Institute of Asian Studies, 2010), 9.

115. Sokhym Em, "Revolutionary Female Medical Staff in Tram Kak District I," *Searching for the Truth* 34 (October 2002): 24–27; at 25. See also Sokhym Em, "Female Patients," *Searching for the Truth* 33 (September 2002): 25–29; Sokhym Em, "Revolutionary Female Medical Staff in Tram Kak District II," *Searching for the Truth* 35 (November 2002): 17–19.

116. The motivation to volunteer varied; for some girls, it was an opportunity to escape oppressive conditions in their home village; for others it was a means of avoiding combat. See Em, "Revolutionary Female Medical Staff . . . District I," 25.

117. Ibid.

118. Ibid.; Em, "Revolutionary Female Medical Staff . . . District II."

119. Ovesen and Trankell, *Cambodians and Their Doctors*, 109.

120. Ibid., 107.
121. Sokhym Em, "Rabbit Dropping Medicine," *Searching for the Truth* 30 (June 2002): 22–23; at 22.
122. Mertha, *Brothers in Arms*, 42.
123. CPK, "Four-Year Plan," 114.
124. Document No. E3/749 (00182614), "Minutes—Meeting of the Standing Committee 9 January 1976," archived by the ECCC, http://www.eccc.gov.kh/en.
125. Document No. E3/231 (00183360), "Minutes of Meeting of Propaganda Work 8 March 1976," archived by the ECCC, http://www.eccc.gov.kh/en.
126. Ibid.
127. Following the arrest of Hu Nim in 1977, the Ministry of Propaganda and Information and was apparently merged with the Ministry of Education, with both falling under the supervision of Yun Yat, wife of Son Sen, the deputy prime minister of national defense.
128. Mertha, *Brothers in Arms*, 44–47.
129. Gupta, *Red Tape*, 188.
130. Ibid.

CHAPTER 3: INTO THE DARKNESS

1. Barnett, "Democratic Kampuchea," 215.
2. Document No. L0001022, "Minutes of the Standing Committee's Visit to the Southwest Zone," archived at the Documentation Center of Cambodia, Phnom Penh.
3. Ibid.
4. Ibid.
5. Lenin, *Essential Works*, 150.
6. Document No. L0001022, "Minutes of the Standing Committee's Visit to the Southwest Zone."
7. Ibid.
8. Ibid.
9. Ibid.
10. Kindervater, "The Emergence of Lethal Surveillance."
11. Gillian K. Hadfield and Barry R. Weingast, "What Is Law? A Coordination Model of the Characteristics of Legal Order," *Journal of Legal Analysis* 4, no. 2 (2012): 471–514; at 471.
12. Helen Fein, "Revolutionary and Antirevolutionary Genocides: A Comparison of State Murders in Democratic Kampuchea, 1975 to 1979, and in Indonesia, 1965 to 1966," *Comparative Studies in Society and History* 35, no. 4 (1993): 796–823; at 809.
13. Barnett, "Democratic Kampuchea," 216.

14. Hadfield and Weingast, "What Is Law," 472.
15. Ibid.
16. No document has yet surfaced that explains in detail the philosophical basis of the CPK's legal order. As a self-proclaimed Marxist-Leninist Party, it is safe to presume that CPK officials would have adhered to a variant of positive law as opposed to natural law. Furthermore, it is unclear to what extent leading members of the CPK were aware of, let alone adhered to, the various Marxist legal theories that were developed throughout the twentieth century.
17. Eugene Kamenka, "Law," in *A Dictionary of Marxist Thought*, 2nd ed., ed. Tom Bottomore (Malden, MA: Blackwell Publishing, 1991), 306–7.
18. Document No. E3/259 (00184833), "Constitution of Democratic Kampuchea," archived by the ECCC, http://www.eccc.gov.kh/en.
19. Ibid.
20. Ibid.
21. Ibid.
22. Justus M. van der Kroef, "Cambodia: From 'Democratic Kampuchea' to 'People's Republic,'" *Asian Survey* 19, no. 8 (1979): 731–50; at 737. See also Ian Harris, *Buddhism under Pol Pot* (Phnom Penh: Documentation Center of Cambodia, 2007).
23. Document No. E3/259 (00184833), "Constitution of Democratic Kampuchea," archived by the ECCC, http://www.eccc.gov.kh/en.
24. Ibid.
25. Ibid.
26. Ibid.
27. Gillian K. Hadfield, "The Problem of Social Order: What Should We Count as Law?" *Law & Social Inquiry* 42, no. 1 (2017): 16–27; at 18.
28. Document No. E3/130 (00184022), "Communist Party of Kampuchea—Statute," archived by the ECCC, http://www.eccc.gov.kh/en.
29. Ibid.
30. Ibid.
31. Hadfield and Weingast, "What Is Law," 473.
32. Document No. E3/130 (00184022), "Communist Party of Kampuchea—Statute."
33. Ibid.
34. Ibid.
35. Ibid.
36. See, for example, Tyner, *From Rice Fields to Killing Field*.
37. Herbert F. Schurmann, "Organizational Principles of the Chinese Communists," *The China Quarterly* 2 (April–June 1960): 47–58; at 52.
38. Tyner et al., "Phnom Penh."
39. Document No. E3/494 (00142826), "Report by Craig Etcheson."

40. Jonathan London, "Viet Nam and the Making of Market-Leninism," *The Pacific Review* 22, no. 3 (2009): 375–99; at 379.

41. Stephen C. Angle, "Decent Democratic Centralism," *Political Theory* 33, no. 4 (2005): 518–46; at 525–26.

42. Communist Party of Kampuchea (CPK), "Report of Activities of the Party Center According to the General Political Tasks of 1976," in Chandler, Kiernan, and Boua, *Pol Pot Plans the* Future, 202.

43. Ibid.

44. Ibid.

45. Ibid., 203.

46. Mertha, *Brothers in Arms*, 31–33.

47. Ibid., 33.

48. Document No. E3/12 (00182809, "Decision of the Central Committee Regarding a Number of Matters," archived by the ECCC, http://www.eccc.gov.kh/en.

49. Ibid.

50. Ibid.

51. Document No. E3/874 (00185060), "Telegram 50—Radio Band 948—Presented with Respect to Beloved and Missed Brother," archived by the ECCC, http://www.eccc.gov.kh/en. See also Document No. E3/494 (00142826), "Report by Craig Etcheson."

52. Document No. D02129, "To Angkar 870," archived at the Documentation Center of Cambodia, Phnom Penh. Ros Nhim would himself be arrested and sent to S-21 the following month.

53. Document No. E3/494 (00142826), "Report by Craig Etcheson."

54. Ibid.

55. James A. Tyner and Stian Rice, "Cambodia's Political Economy of Violence: Space, Time, and Genocide under the Khmer Rouge, 1975–79," *Genocide Studies International* 10, no. 1 (2016): 84–94; James A. Tyner and Stian Rice, "To Live and Let Die: Food, Famine, and Administrative Violence in Democratic Kampuchea, 1975–1979," *Political Geography* 52 (May 2016): 47–56; Tyner, *From Rice Fields to Killing Fields.*

56. See, for example, Craig Etcheson, *After the Killing Fields: Lessons from the Cambodian Genocide* (Lubbock: Texas Tech University Press, 2005), 107–28. See also Vickery, *Cambodia, 1975–1982*, 88–172.

57. Randle C. DeFalco, "Accounting for Famine at the Extraordinary Chambers in the Courts of Cambodia: The Crimes against Humanity of Extermination, Inhumane Acts and Persecution," *The International Journal of Transitional Justice* 5, no. 1 (2011): 142–58; at 141. See also Randle C. DeFalco, "Justice and Starvation in Cambodia: The Khmer Rouge Famine," *Cambodia Law and Policy Journal* 2 (2014): 45–84.

58. Randle DeFalco, "Voices of Genocide: Episodes of the Radio Program on Famine under the Khmer Rouge," *Searching for the Truth*, Second Quarter (2013): 26–32.

59. David Harper, "The Politics of Paranoia: Paranoid Positioning and Conspiratorial Narratives in the Surveillance Society," *Surveillance & Society* 5, no. 1 (2008): 1–32; Holm, "Conspiracy Theorizing Surveillance"; McClintock, "Paranoid Empire"; Bach, "Power, Secrecy, Paranoia," 287–302; Kendzior, "'Recognize the Spies'"; Sarah Nuttall and Achille Mbembe, "Secrecy's Softwares," *Current Anthropology* 56, no. 12 (2015): 317–24.

60. McClintock, "Paranoid Empire," 53.

61. Bach, "Power, Secrecy, Paranoia," 288.

62. Ibid., 290.

63. Document No. E3/798 (00183966), "Minutes of the Meeting of Secretaries and Deputy Secretaries of Divisions and Independent Regiments," archived by the ECCC, http://www.eccc.gov.kh/en.

64. Document No. E3/811 (00178149), "Minutes of Meeting with the Organization's Office, 703, and S-21," archived by the ECCC, http://www.eccc.gov.kh/en.

65. Document No. L01449_4p, "Minutes of Meeting of the Division Secretary, Division Deputy Secretary, and Independent Regiments," archived at the Documentation Center of Cambodia, Phnom Penh.

66. Document No. L01448_3p, "Minutes of Meeting of Comrade Tal, Division 290 and Division 170," archived at the Documentation Center of Cambodia, Phnom Penh. See also Document No. E3/810 (00195339), "Minutes of Meeting of Secretaries and Logistics of Divisions and Regiments," archived by the ECCC, http://www.eccc.gov. kh/en; Document No. E3/13 (00940336), "Minutes of the Meeting of Secretaries and Deputy Secretaries of Divisions and Independent Regiments"; Document No. E3/815 (00877015), "Minutes of Meeting of Secretaries and Deputy Secretaries of Divisions and Regiments," archived by the ECCC, http://www.eccc.gov.kh/en.

67. Document No. E1/112.1 (00841140), "Transcript of Trial Proceedings, Case File No. 002/19–09–2007-ECCC/TC, 22 August 2012, Trial Day 100," archived by the ECCC, http://www.eccc.gov.kh/en; Office of the Co-Investigating Judges, "Criminal Case File No. 002/14–08–2006," archived by the ECCC, http://www.eccc.gov.kh/en. During the course of the tribunal, Kim Vun learned that Chim Nary was arrested on May 1, 1978, and executed on May 27, 1978.

68. Bach, "Power, Secrecy, Paranoia," 290.

69. Ibid.

70. Haing Ngor (with R. Warner), *Survival in the Killing Fields* (New York: Carroll and Graf Publishers, 1987), 277.

71. Sreytouch Svay-Ryser, "New Year's Surprise," in *Children of Cambodia's Killing Fields: Memoirs by Survivors*, ed. Kim DePaul and comp. Dith Pran (New Haven, CT: Yale University Press, 1977), 38.

72. Roeun Sam, "Living in Darkness," in DePaul and Pran, *Children of Cambodia's Killing Fields*, 78.

73. Hannah Arendt, *The Origins of Totalitarianism* (New York: Harcourt, 1968), 431.

74. Ngor, *Survival in the Killing Fields*, 300.

75. Mark Andrejevic, "The Work of Watching One Another: Lateral Surveillance, Risk, and Governance," *Surveillance & Society* 2, no. 4 (2005): 479–97; at 488.

76. Mark Andrejevic, "The Discipline of Watching: Detection, Risk, and Lateral Surveillance," *Critical Studies in Media Communication* 23, no. 5 (2006): 391–407; at 396–97.

77. Michel Foucault, "Technologies of the Self," in *Technologies of the Self: A Seminar with Michel Foucault*, ed. Luther H. Martin, Huck Gutman, and Patrick H. Hutton (Amherst: University of Massachusetts Press, 1988), 16–49.

78. Ibid., 18.

79. Harper, "The Politics of Paranoia," 5; see also Maria Los, "The Technologies of Total Domination," *Surveillance & Society* 2, no. 1 (2004): 15–38.

80. Foucault, "Technologies of the Self," 27.

81. Ian Burkitt, "Technologies of the Self: Habitus and Capacities," *Journal for the Theory of Social Behaviour* 32, no. 2 (2002): 219–37; at 234–35.

82. Mbembe, "Necropolitics," 14.

83. Tyner and Rice, "To Live and Let Die," 55.

84. See, for example, Bach, "Power, Secrecy, Paranoia," 291–92; Timothy Melley, *Empire of Conspiracy: The Culture of Paranoia in Postwar America* (Ithaca, NY: Cornell University Press, 2000), 209.

85. Erving Goffman, *Asylums: Essays on the Social Situation of Mental Patients and Other Inmates* (Garden City, NY: Doubleday, 1961), 11.

86. Chandler, *Voices from S-21*; see also Clegg, Pina e Cunha, and Rego, "The Theory and Practice of Utopia in a Total Institution"; Miguel Pina e Cunha, Arménio Rego, and Stewart Clegg, "The Institutionalization of Genocidal Leadership: Pol Pot and a Cambodian Dystopia," *Journal of Leadership Studies* 9, no. 1 (2015): 6–18.

87. Chandler, *Voices from S-21*, 14.

88. Dominique Moran and Yvonne Jewkes, "Linking the Carceral and the Punitive State: A Review of Research on Prison Architecture, Design, Technology and the Lived Experience of Carceral Space," *Annales de Géographie* no. 702–703 (2015): 163–84; at 164 and 166.

89. Nick Gill, Deidre Conlon, Dominique Moran, and Andrew Burridge, "Carceral Circuitry: New Directions in Carceral Geography," *Progress in Human Geography* doi:10.1177/0309132516671823. See also Keith Farrington, "The Modern Prison as Total Institution? Public Perception Versus Objective Reality," *Crime & Delinquency* 38, no. 1 (1992): 6–26; Jenna Loyd, Andrew Burridge, and Matthew L. Mitchelson, "Thinking (and Moving) Beyond Walls and Cages: Bridging Immigrant Justice and Anti-prison Organizing in the United States," *Social Justice* 36, no. 2 (2016): 85–103; Dominique Moran, "Between Outside and Inside? Prison Visiting Rooms as Liminal Carceral Spaces," *Geoforum* 78, no. 2 (2013): 339–51; Jennifer Turner, *The Prison Boundary* (London: Palgrave Macmillan, 2016).

90. Farrington, "The Modern Prison," 6–7.

91. Turner, *The Prison Boundary*, 27.

92. Stephen Heder (with Brian D. Tittemore), *Seven Candidates for Prosecution: Accountability for the Crimes of the Khmer Rouge* (Phnom Penh: Documentation Center of Cambodia, 2004), 30.

93. There was not always a clear-cut distinction of security centers. The Koh Kyang security center, for example, reportedly operated as a detainment site for both Sector 37 and the West Zone. See OCIJ, *Closing Order*, Case File No.:002/19–09–2007-ECCC-OCIJ, 134.

94. Meng-Try Ea, *The Chain of Terror: The Khmer Rouge Southwest Zone Security System* (Phnom Penh: Documentation Center of Cambodia, 2005), 1.

95. The theft of food was often considered a minor offense; however, numerous accounts exist whereby men, women, and children were executed for such crimes.

96. Document No. E3/2423 (00322206), "Report—To Comrade Uncle Ann, for His Knowledge," archived by the ECCC, http://www.eccc.gov.kh/en.

97. Document No. E3/2423 (00322210), "Letter from San," archived by the ECCC, http://www.eccc.gov.kh/en.

98. Most evidence is derived from eyewitness accounts or through confessions obtained at larger security centers.

99. Document No. E3/494 (00142826), "Report by Craig Etcheson."

100. Ea, *The Chain of Terror*, 2.

101. Document No. E3/2423 (00322208), "To Respected Comrade Elder Brother," archived by the ECCC, http://www.eccc.gov.kh/en.

102. Document No. E3/2450 (00322163), "Report," archived by the ECCC, http://www.eccc.gov.kh/en.

103. Document No. E3/494 (00142826), "Report by Craig Etcheson."

104. Ibid.

105. Ibid.

106. OCIJ, *Closing Order*, 126. It was located in present-day Kus Subdistrict, Tram Kok District, Takeo Province.
107. Ibid., 130. Document No. E3/2109 (00276555), "Report," archived by the ECCC, http://www.eccc.gov.kh/en.
108. OCIJ, *Closing Order*, 127.
109. Ibid., 130.
110. Ibid.
111. Ibid., 132.
112. Ibid., 129.
113. Document No. E3/4166 (00694355), "Education Office of District 105—Report," archived by the ECCC, http://www.eccc.gov.kh/en.
114. OCIJ, *Closing Order*, 129.
115. Robertson, "'You Lie!'" 79.
116. OCIJ, *Closing Order*, 133.
117. Ibid., 122. It was located in present-day Trea Commune, Kandal Steung District, Kandal Province.
118. Ibid.
119. Ibid., 123.
120. Ibid., 124.
121. Ibid., 125.
122. Ea, *The Chain of Terror*, 98–99.
123. Document No. E3/874 (00185060), "Telegram 50—Presented with Respect to Beloved and Missed Brother," archived by the ECCC, http://www.eccc.gov.kh.en. See also Document No. E3/494 (00142826), "Report by Craig Etcheson."
124. Document No. E3/871 (00185241), "Telegram 21—Presented with Respect to Beloved and Missed Brother Pol," archived by the ECCC, http://www.eccc.gov.kh.en. See also Document No. E3/494 (00142826), "Report by Craig Etcheson."
125. Document No. E3/494 (00142826), "Report by Craig Etcheson."
126. OCIJ, *Closing Order*, 158–59.
127. Ibid., 160.
128. Ibid., 161.
129. Ea, *The Chain of Terror*, 98.
130. Ibid., 100–102.
131. Ibid., 100.
132. Document No. E3/798 (00183966), "Minutes of the Meeting of Secretaries and Deputy Secretaries of Divisions and Independent Regiments," archived by the ECCC, http://www.eccc.gov.kh/en.
133. Document No. E3/811 (00178149), "Minutes of Meeting with the Organization's Office, 703, and S-21," archived by the ECCC, http://www.eccc.gov.kh/en.
134. Quoted in Ea, *The Chain of Terror*, 100.

135. Locke, "Conspiracy Culture," 574.
136. Ian G. R. Shaw and Majed Akhter, "The Dronification of State Violence," *Critical Asian Studies* 46, no. 2 (2014): 211–34; at 229. See also Ian G. R. Shaw, *Predator Empire: Drone Warfare and Full Spectrum Dominance* (Minneapolis: University of Minnesota Press, 2016).
137. Kindervater, "Emergence of Lethal Surveillance," 224.
138. Louise Amoore and Marieke de Goede, "Transactions after 9/11: The Banal Face of the Preemptive Strike," *Transactions of the Institute of British Geographers* 33, no. 2 (2008): 173–85; at 176.

CHAPTER 4: MORTAL ACCOUNTINGS

1. The vast majority of prisoners executed on this date were all recorded as staff workers from Public Works.
2. Mao Hok, Ping Chun, Prakk Nat, and Seam Ho were all executed on July 20, 1977; Nuon Prang was executed on October 15, 1977.
3. Judy Ledgerwood, "The Cambodian Tuol Sleng Museum of Genocidal Crimes: National Narrative," *Museum Anthropology* 21, no. 1 (1997): 82–98; Paul Williams, "Witnessing Genocide: Vigilance and Remembrance at Tuol Sleng and Choeung Ek," *Holocaust and Genocide Studies* 18, no. 2 (2004): 234–54; Rachel Hughes, "Dutiful Tourism: Encountering the Cambodian Genocide," *Asia Pacific Viewpoint* 49, no. 3 (2008): 318–30; Bridgette Sion, "Conflicting Sites of Memory in Post-genocide Cambodia," *Humanity: An International Journal of Human Rights, Humanitarianism, and Development* 2, no. 1 (2011): 1–21; Stephanie Benzaquen, "Looking at the Tuol Sleng Museum of Genocidal Crimes, Cambodia, on Flickr and YouTube," *Media, Culture & Society* 36, no. 6 (2014): 790–809; James A. Tyner, "Violent Erasures and Erasing Violence: Contesting Cambodia's Landscape of Violence," in *Space and the Memories of Violence: Landscapes of Erasure, Disappearance and Exception*, ed. Estela Schindel and Pamela Colombo (New York: Palgrave Macmillan, 2014), 21–33; Caitlin Brown and Chris Millington, "The Memory of the Cambodian Genocide: The Tuol Sleng Genocide Museum," *History Compass* 13, no. 3 (2015): 31–39; James A. Tyner, *Landscape, Memory, and Post-violence in Cambodia* (New York: Rowman & Littlefield, 2017).
4. Lindsay French, "Exhibiting Terror," in *Truth Claims: Representation and Human Rights*, ed. M. P. Bradley and P. Petro (New Brunswick, NJ: Rutgers University Press, 2002), 131–55; Rachel Hughes, "The Abject Artefacts of Memory: Photographs from Cambodia's Genocide," *Media, Culture & Society* 25, no. 1 (2003): 23–44; Maria Elander, "Education and Photography at Tuol Sleng Genocide Museum," in *The*

Arts of Transitional Justice, ed. P. D. Rush and O. Simi (New York: Springer, 2014), 43–62.

5. Chandler, *Voices from S-21*. See also David Hawk, "Tuol Sleng Extermination Centre," *Index on Censorship* 1 (1986): 25–31; Clegg, e Cunha, Rego, "The Theory and Practice of Utopia in a Total Institution"; Clegg, e Cunha, Rego, and Dias, "Mundane Objects and the Banality of Evil"; Michelle Caswell, *Archiving the Unspeakable: Silence, Memory, and the Photographic Record in Cambodia* (Madison: University of Wisconsin Press, 2014); Terith Chy, *When the Criminal Laughs* (Phnom Penh: Documentation Center of Cambodia, 2014); Miguel Pina e Cunha, Stewart Clegg, and Arménio Rego, "The Ethical Speaking of Objects: Ethics and the 'Object-ive' World of Khmer Rouge Young Comrades," *Journal of Political Power* 7, no. 1 (2014): 35–61; Alexander L. Hinton, *Man or Monster? The Trial of a Khmer Rouge Torturer* (Durham, NC: Duke University Press, 2016).

6. Chandler, *Voices from S-21*, 15.

7. Document No. D390 (00744663), "Co-Prosecutors' Rule 66 Final Submission (Public Redacted Version)," archived by the ECCC, http://www.eccc.gov.kh/en, 118.

8. Ibid., 119.

9. Vannak Huy, "Prey Sar Prison," *Searching for the Truth* 29 (May 2002): 21–25; at 21.

10. Craig Etcheson describes the classification system as consisting of "light offence" prisoners, "serious-offence" prisoners, and an intermediate category whereby men and women were to be evaluated and subsequently classified as light or serious. Many who were classified as light-offense prisoners were eventually released—if they survived their detention. Those classed as serious were ultimately sent to S-21 and executed. See Document No. E1/21.1 (00328887), "Transcript of Trial Proceedings—Kaing Guek Eav 'Duch' Public, Case File No. 001/18–07–2007-ECCC/TC, 19 May 2009, Trial Day 17," archived by the ECCC, http://www.eccc.gov.kh/en.

11. OCIJ, *Closing Order*, 105–7.

12. Vannak Huy, "Prey Sar Prison," 21.

13. Document No. D390 (00744663), "Co-Prosecutors' Rule 66 Final Submission (Public Redacted Version)," 121.

14. Document No. E3/13 (00940336), "Minutes of the Meeting of Secretaries and Deputy Secretaries of Divisions and Independent Regiments."

15. Document No. D390 (00744663), "Co-Prosecutors' Rule 66 Final Submission (Public Redacted Version)," 279.

16. Ibid.

17. Ibid., 124.

18. Hawk, "Tuol Sleng Extermination Centre," 25; see also David Hawk, *Khmer Rouge Prison Documents from the S-21 (Tuol Sleng) Extermination Center in Phnom Penh* (Ithaca, NY: Cornell University Press, 1984).

19. Document No. D390 (00744663), "Co-Prosecutors' Rule 66 Final Submission (Public Redacted Version)," 121–22.

20. Chandler, *Voices from S-21*, 26; Document No. D390 (00744663), "Co-Prosecutors' Rule 66 Final Submission (Public Redacted Version)," 122.

21. Document No. E1/33.1 (00341955), "Transcript of Trial Proceedings—Kaing Guek Eav 'Duch' Public, Case File No. 001/18–07–2007-ECCC/TC, 16 June 2009, Trial Day 29," archived by the ECCC, http://www.eccc.gov.kh/en.

22. This should not be construed that Duch had any misgivings about female sexual abuse. Rather, Duch apparently expressed concern because he personally knew the abused woman. It should be noted, also, that Duch did not secure her release. Once the woman was no longer considered valuable from an investigative standpoint, she too was executed.

23. Document No. E1/33.1 (00341955), "Transcript of Trial Proceedings—Kaing Guek Eav 'Duch' Public, Case File No. 001/18–07–2007-ECCC/TC, 16 June 2009, Trial Day 29."

24. Chandler, *Voices from S-21*, 27.

25. Ibid.; Document No. D390 (00744663), "Co-Prosecutors' Rule 66 Final Submission (Public Redacted Version)," 123.

26. Document No. D390 (00744663), "Co-Prosecutors' Rule 66 Final Submission (Public Redacted Version)," 123–24.

27. Caswell, *Archiving the Unspeakable*, 52; see also Caswell, "Hannah Arendt's World."

28. Caswell, *Archiving the Unspeakable*, 53.

29. See Hinton, *Man or Monster?*; see also Document No. E1/32.1 (00341683), "Transcript of Trial Proceedings—Kaing Guek Eav 'Duch' Public, Case File No. 001/18–07–2007-ECCC/TC, 15 June 2009, Trial Day 28," archived by the ECCC, http://www.eccc.gov.kh/en; Document No. E1/33.1 (00341955), "Transcript of Trial Proceedings—Kaing Guek Eav 'Duch' Public, Case File No. 001/18–07–2007-ECCC/TC, 16 June 2009, Trial Day 29"; Document No. E1/34.1 (00342829), "Transcript of Trial Proceedings—Kaing Guek Eav 'Duch' Public, Case File No. 001/18–07–2007-ECCC/TC, 17 June 2009, Trial Day 30," archived by the ECCC, http://www.eccc.gov.kh/en.

30. Caswell, *Archiving the Unspeakable*, 55.

31. Document No. E3/1044 (00875624), "Request for the Removal of Bad Elements, Which Were Divided into Three Categories," archived by the ECCC, http://www.eccc.gov.kh/en.
32. Document No. E2/80/4.2 (00347466), "Brief Biography," archived by the ECCC, http://www.eccc.gov.kh/en.
33. Document No. E3/1043 (00224319), "Dear Beloved Brother Duch," archived by the ECCC, http://www.eccc.gov.kh/en.
34. Document No. E1/32.1 (00341683), "Transcript of Trial Proceedings—Kaing Guek Eav 'Duch' Public, Case File No. 001/18–07–2007-ECCC/TC, 15 June 2009, Trial Day 28."
35. Document No. E3/13 (00940336), "Minutes of the Meeting of Secretaries and Deputy Secretaries of Divisions and Independent Regiments."
36. Document No. E1/32.1 (00341683), "Transcript of Trial Proceedings—Kaing Guek Eav 'Duch' Public, Case File No. 001/18–07–2007-ECCC/TC, 15 June 2009, Trial Day 28."
37. Document No. D390 (00744663), "Co-Prosecutors' Rule 66 Final Submission (Public Redacted Version)."
38. Ibid.
39. Ibid.
40. Ibid.
41. Document No. E3/822 (00937114), "Minutes of the Meeting Comrade Tal of Division 290 and Division 170," archived by the ECCC, http://www.eccc.gov.kh/en.
42. Document No. E1/32.1 (00341683), "Transcript of Trial Proceedings—Kaing Guek Eav 'Duch' Public, Case File No. 001/18–07–2007-ECCC/TC, 15 June 2009, Trial Day 28."
43. Ibid.
44. Document No. E3/1645 (00809627), "Names of Prisoners Who Entered on 23 November 1977," archived by the ECCC, http://www.eccc.gov.kh/en.
45. During massive purges, when scores (if not hundreds) of prisoners were arrested simultaneously, registration was largely nonexistent.
46. Document No. E1/32.1 (00341683), "Transcript of Trial Proceedings—Kaing Guek Eav 'Duch' Public, Case File No. 001/18–07–2007-ECCC/TC, 15 June 2009, Trial Day 28."
47. Document No. E3/4145 (00762839), "Names of Prisoners Smashed on 31 May 1978," archived by the ECCC, http://www.eccc.gov.kh/en.
48. Document No. E1/32.1 (00341683), "Transcript of Trial Proceedings—Kaing Guek Eav 'Duch' Public, Case File No. 001/18–07–2007-ECCC/TC, 15 June 2009, Trial Day 28." Medical experimentation did take place at S-21. Medics undergoing training would practice drawing blood on prisoners; blood was also collected for use at nearby hospitals.

Evidence also indicates that surgery was conducted on prisoners in order for medical trainees to learn anatomy.

49. Ibid.

50. Document No. E3/1671 (00181789), "List of Female Prisoners— Unofficial Partial Translation by Bunsou Sour, OCP 14 March 2008," archived by the ECCC, http://www.eccc.gov.kh/en.

51. Document No. E1/34.1 (00342829), "Transcript of Trial Proceedings— Kaing Guek Eav 'Duch' Public, Case File No. 001/18–07–2007-ECCC/ TC, 17 June 2009, Trial Day 30."

52. Document No. E3/1533 (00242035), "Biography of Prisoner in Detention," archived by the ECCC, http://www.eccc.gov.kh/en.

53. Document No. E3/171 (00226076), "Prisoner's Biography," archived by the ECCC, http://www.eccc.gov.kh/en. According to the official ECCC list of S-21 prisoners, Lim Kimary was arrested in Battambang Province and entered S-21 on February 13, 1976; he was reported executed on May 27, 1976.

54. Document No. E3/1672 (00233690), "Names of Prisoners Interrogated on 27.4.78," archived by the ECCC, http://www.eccc.gov.kh/en. See also Document No. D57 (00767728), "List of Prisoners Interrogated on 7–5-1978," archived by the ECCC, http://www.eccc.gov.kh/en.

55. Document No. E3/1666 (00224659), "Name List of Enemies to be Interrogated," archived by the ECCC, http://www.eccc.gov.kh/en.

56. Document No. E3/1674 (00802404), "Names of Prisoners Interrogated on 11 April 1978," archived by the ECCC, http://www.eccc.gov.kh/en.

57. "Daily Report on Prisoners, April 25, 1977," compiled in Hawk, *Khmer Rouge Prison Documents from the S-21.*

58. Document No. E3/1541 (00233891), "Name List of Prisoners Put on Hold in January 1977," archived by the ECCC, http://www.eccc.gov.kh/ en.

59. Document No. E3/2231 (00785257), "Name List of Prisoners 'Kept,'" archived by the ECCC, http://www.eccc.gov.kh/en.

60. Caswell, *Archiving the Unspeakable*, 55.

61. Document No. E1/33.1 (00341955), "Transcript of Trial Proceedings— Kaing Guek Eav 'Duch' Public, Case File No. 001/18–07–2007-ECCC/ TC, 16 June 2009, Trial Day 29."

62. Document No. E3/13 (00940336), "Minutes of the Meeting of Secretaries and Deputy Secretaries of Divisions and Independent Regiments."

63. Hinton, *Man or Monster*, 148.

64. Ibid.

65. Ibid., 80.

66. Ibid., 145.

67. Document No. E1/33.1 (00341955), "Transcript of Trial Proceedings—Kaing Guek Eav 'Duch' Public, Case File No. 001/18–07–2007-ECCC/TC, 16 June 2009, Trial Day 29." Cadres were obliged to take notes during these sessions; examples of notebooks compiled by S-21 staff are archived at the Documentation Center of Cambodia.

68. Document No. E1/33.1 (00341955), "Transcript of Trial Proceedings—Kaing Guek Eav 'Duch' Public, Case File No. 001/18–07–2007-ECCC/TC, 16 June 2009, Trial Day 29."

69. Ibid.

70. Document No. E1/34.1 (00342829), "Transcript of Trial Proceedings—Kaing Guek Eav 'Duch' Public, Case File No. 001/18–07–2007-ECCC/TC, 17 June 2009, Trial Day 30."

71. Document No. E1/33.1 (00341955), "Transcript of Trial Proceedings—Kaing Guek Eav 'Duch' Public, Case File No. 001/18–07–2007-ECCC/TC, 16 June 2009, Trial Day 29."

72. Document No. D390 (00744663), "Co-Prosecutors' Rule 66 Final Submission (Public Redacted Version)."

73. Document No. E1/33.1 (00341955), "Transcript of Trial Proceedings—Kaing Guek Eav 'Duch' Public, Case File No. 001/18–07–2007-ECCC/TC, 16 June 2009, Trial Day 29."

74. Chandler, *Voices from S-21*, 89. Examples of various documents are reproduced in Chy, *When the Criminal Laughs.*

75. Document No. E3/1706 (00224632), "Color Copy Excerpt of Confession of Khek Bin alias Sou, Translation of Annotations Only," archived by the ECCC, http://www.eccc.gov.kh/en.

76. Robertson, "'You Lie!'" 71.

77. The Documentation Center of Cambodia has identified 179 people who possibly were released from S-21. If this finding is correct, however, these individuals were most likely released in the early months of S-21's existence, probably under the supervision of Nat. Apart from these survivors, there is no evidence—certainly during the command of Duch—that any prisoner was released. Dacil Q. Keo and Nean Yin, *Fact Sheet: Pol Pot and His Prisoners at Secret Prison S-21* (Phnom Penh: Documentation Center of Cambodia, 2011); Document No. E1/21.1 (00328887), "Transcript of Trial Proceedings—Kaing Guek Eav 'Duch' Public, Case File No. 001/18–07–2007-ECCC/TC, 19 May 2009, Trial Day 17," archived by the ECCC, http://www.eccc.gov.kh/en.

78. Chum Mey, *Survivor: The Triumph of an Ordinary Man in the Khmer Rouge Genocide* (Phnom Penh: Documentation Center of Cambodia, 2012), 34.

79. Ibid., 35.

80. Ibid.

81. Document No. E1/33.1 (00341955), "Transcript of Trial Proceedings—Kaing Guek Eav 'Duch' Public, Case File No. 001/18–07–2007-ECCC/TC, 16 June 2009, Trial Day 29."

82. Document No. E1/34.1 (00342829), "Transcript of Trial Proceedings—Kaing Guek Eav 'Duch' Public, Case File No. 001/18–07–2007-ECCC/TC, 17 June 2009, Trial Day 30."

83. Ibid.

84. Ibid.

85. "Execution Schedule for July 1, 1977," compiled in Hawk, *Khmer Rouge Prison Documents from the S-21.*

86. Execution Schedule for July 2, 1977, "compiled in ibid.

87. Document No. E3/2131 (00182876), "List of Prisoners from Military Division, Smashed on 10–6-1977 Division 310," archived by the ECCC, http://www.eccc.gov.kh/en.

88. E3/3861 (00657714), "List of Prisoners 'Smashed' on 8–7-77, North Zone," archived by the ECCC, http://www.eccc.gov.kh/en.

89. Document No. E3/3861 (00657725), "List of Prisoners 'Smashed' in the Section of Brother Huy Sre," archived by the ECCC, http://www.eccc.gov.kh/en.

90. Document No. E3/2133 (00242285), "Prisoners' Names Smashed by Brother Huy Sre," archived by the ECCC, http://www.eccc.gov.kh/en.

91. Document No. E3/1540 (00182892), "Names of Prisoners Who Died at Office S-21 C," archived by the ECCC, http://www.eccc.gov.kh/en.

92. Document No. E1/34.1 (00342829), "Transcript of Trial Proceedings—Kaing Guek Eav 'Duch' Public, Case File No. 001/18–07–2007-ECCC/TC, 17 June 2009, Trial Day 30."

93. Ibid.

94. Ibid.

95. Ibid.

96. Ibid.

97. Ibid.

98. Ibid.

99. Heder, *Seven Candidates*, 27–45.

100. One cannot discount the salience of networked logics underpinning the purges. In this case, it was not necessarily the group that was targeted, but rather the networks resultant from shared identities. By way of illustration, I am presently a faculty member in the Department of Geography and, as such, most of my closest associates are in the department. Beyond these proximate connections, my contacts with other departments across the university is uneven, a consequence of personal interests, past committee involvement, and so on. If I were to be arrested and forced to confess, a predominance of geographers would be listed. When subsequent scholars evaluate those groups

targeted, they may find an inordinate number of geographers. Can we say that geographers were targeted *because they were geographers*? Or is it because I, and not, say, a historian, was initially suspected?

101. Kiernan, *The Pol Pot Regime*; Ysa Osman, *Oukoubah: Justice for the Cham Muslims under the Democratic Kampuchea Regime* (Phnom Penh: Documentation Center of Cambodia, 2002); Ysa Osman, "The Cham Prisoners in the Khmer Rouge's Secret Prison," *Jebat: Malaysian Journal of History, Politics and Strategic Studies* 32 (2005): 100–133; Ysa Osman, *The Cham Rebellion: Survivors' Stories from the Villages* (Phnom Penh: Documentation Center of Cambodia, 2006); Farina So, *The Hijab of Cambodia: Memories of Cham Muslim Women after the Khmer Rouge* (Phnom Penh: Documentation Center of Cambodia, 2011); Philipp Bruckmayr, "Cambodian Muslims, Transnational NGOs, and International Justice," *Peace Review* 27, no. 3 (2015): 337–45.

102. Heder, *Seven Candidates*, 35.

103. Ryan Park, "Proving Genocidal Intent: International Precedent and ECCC Case 002," *Rutgers Law Review* 63, no. 1 (2011): 129–91; Andrew T. Cayley, "Prosecuting Mass Atrocities at the Extraordinary Chambers in the Courts of Cambodia (ECCC)," *Washington University Global Studies Law Review* 11, no. 2 (2012): 445–58; Mélanie Vianney-Liaud, "Legal Constraints in the Interpretation of Genocide," in *The Extraordinary Chambers in the Courts of Cambodia*, ed. Simon Meisenberg and Ignaz Stegmiller (The Hague: TMC Asser, 2016).

104. Heder, *Seven Candidates*, 37. At the time of writing, Case 002/02 was still underway at the ECCC. This case was to establish, in part, whether the Cham population was specifically targeted by the CPK. If proven, this would classify Khmer Rouge atrocities—as applied to this group—as genocide.

105. See James A. Tyner, Xinyue Ye, Sokvisal Kimsroy, Zheye Wang, and Chenjian Fu, "Emerging Data Sources and the Study of Genocide: A Preliminary Analysis of Prison Data from S-21 Security-Center, Cambodia," *GeoJournal* 81, no. 6 (2016): 907–18; James A. Tyner, Sokvisal Kimsroy, Chenjian Fu, Zheye Wang, and Xinyue Ye, "An Empirical Analysis of Arrests and Executions at S-21 Security-Center during the Cambodian Genocide," *Genocide Studies International* 10, no. 2 (2016): 268–86.

106. Hawk, "Tuol Sleng Extermination Centre," 26.

107. The official figure of 12,273 is a revised figure, down from an earlier number of 12,380 forwarded by the ECCC. Throughout the tribunal, it became clear that approximately one hundred individuals had been double-counted, hence the downward revision. However, given that many detainees, especially women and children, went unrecorded, the figure of 12,273 must remain an approximation. Indeed, as this

manuscript was being prepared, the Office of the Co-Investigating Judges twice revised the prisoner list. The most recent accounting places the total number of prisoners detained at S-21 at 15,101.

108. I am especially grateful for the collaborative work I conducted with Sokvisal Kimsroy, Chenjian Fu, Zheye Wang, and Xinyue Ye. Considerable insight was also provided through a series of email exchanges with Craig Etcheson.

109. Another possible but unlikely scenario is that Say Kim-Kheat was initially detained at M-13 and subsequently transferred to S-21.

110. Document No. E1/59.1 (00361336), "Transcript of Trial Proceedings—Kaing Guek Eav 'Duch' Public, Case File No. 001/18–07–2007-ECCC/TC, 6 August 2009, Trial Day 55," archived by the ECCC, http://www.eccc.gov.kh/en, 78–79.

111. For Chandler's testimony, see ibid., 78–80.

112. Indeed, it is currently not possible to disaggregate patterns simultaneously by space and over time.

113. Document No. E1/33.1 (00341955), "Transcript of Trial Proceedings—Kaing Guek Eav 'Duch' Public, Case File No. 001/18–07–2007-ECCC/TC, 16 June 2009, Trial Day 29."

114. Chandler, *Voices from S-21*, 43–45.

115. Heder, *Seven Candidates*, 32–45.

116. Document No. E1/21.1 (00328887), "Transcript of Trial Proceedings—Kaing Guek Eav 'Duch' Public, Case File No. 001/18–07–2007-ECCC/TC, 19 May 2009, Trial Day 17," archived by the ECCC, http://www.eccc.gov.kh/en.

117. Ben Kiernan, "Conflict in Cambodia, 1945–2002," *Critical Asian Studies* 34, no. 4 (2002): 483–96; at 487.

118. Craig Etcheson, personal communication.

119. Of these two exceptions, one woman was listed as "woman combatant" while another was described as "ordinary people."

120. Dominique Moran, Judith Pallot, and Laure Piacentini, "Lipstick, Lace & Longing: Constructions of Femininity inside a Russian Prison," *Environment and Planning D: Society and Space*, 27, no. 4 (2009): 700–720; at 701.

121. Giorgio Agamben, *Homo Sacer: Sovereign Power and Bare Life* (Stanford, CA: Stanford University Press, 1998), 16.

122. Walter Benjamin, "Critique of Violence," in *Reflections: Essays, Aphorisms, Autobiographical Writings*, ed. P. Demetz (New York: Schocken Books, 1978), 277–300. See also Mathew Abbott, "The Creature Before the Law: Notes on Walter Benjamin's Critique of Violence," *Colloqui: Text, Theory, Critique* 16 (2008): 80–96; at 82.

123. Abbott, "The Creature Before," 83.

CHAPTER 5: CONCLUSIONS

1. Document No. E3/1047 (00548892), "To Beloved Comrade Duch," archived by the ECCC, http://www.eccc.gov.kh/en. As discussed in Chapter 4, this letter continues that interrogators must exercise caution when dealing with "less important" prisoners, in that they would implicate anything or anyone. It is noteworthy that Son Sen was concerned both with the conservation of paper and of senior leaders of the CPK being implicated unjustly.

2. Robert N. Proctor, *Racial Hygiene: Medicine under the Nazis* (Cambridge, MA: Harvard University Press, 1988), 184.

3. Foucault, *Discipline and Punish*, 27.

4. Foucault, "Two Lectures," 98.

5. Jacques Derrida, *Archive Fever: A Freudian Impression*, trans. Eric Prenowitz (Chicago: University of Chicago Press, 1996); Kurtz, "Situating Practices," 26–37; Carolyn Steedman, *Dust: The Archive and Cultural History* (New Brunswick, NJ: Rutgers University Press, 2002); Ben Kafka, "The Demon of Writing: Paperwork, Public Safety, and the Reign of Terror," *Representations* 98, no. 1 (2007): 1–24; Vismann, *Files: Law and Media Technology*; Kafka, "Paperwork," 340–53; Gupta, *Red Tape*; Hull, *Government of Paper*; Meehan, Shaw, and Marston, "Political Geographies of the Object"; Robertson, "'You Lie!'"; Dittmer, "Theorizing a More-Than-Human Diplomacy"; Dittmer, *Diplomatic Material*.

6. Meehan et al., "Political Geographies," 2.

7. Ibid., 8.

8. Irving Louis Horowitz, *Taking Lives: Genocide and State Power* (New Brunswick, NJ: Transaction Books, 1980), 2; see also Zygmunt Bauman, *Modernity and the Holocaust* (Ithaca, NY: Cornell University Press, 1991).

9. Clegg, e Cunha, Rego, and Dias, "Mundane Objects and the Banality of Evil," 327.

10. James A. Tyner, *Genocide and the Geographical Imagination: Life and Death in Germany, China, and Cambodia* (Lanham, MD: Rowman & Littlefield, 2012), 15.

11. Joe Painter, "Prosaic Geographies of Stateness," *Political Geography* 25, no. 7 (2006): 752–74; at 753.

12. Meehan et al., "Political Geographies," 2.

13. Foucault, *Discipline and Punish*, 190.

14. Bauman, *Modernity and the Holocaust*, 106; emphasis in original.

15. Merje Kuus, "Bureaucracy and Place: Expertise in the European Quarter," *Global Networks* 11, no. 4 (2011): 421–39; at 422.

16. Robertson, "'You Lie!'" 86.

17. Jonathan Darling, "Another Letter from the Home Office: Reading the Material Politics of Asylum," *Environment and Planning D: Society and Space* 32, no. 3 (2014): 484–500; at 485.

18. Dittmer, "Theorizing a More-Than-Human Diplomacy," 83.

19. Ibid., 103.

20. Bauman, *Modernity and the Holocaust*, 105.

21. See, for example, Michel Foucault, *The History of Sexuality: An Introduction* (New York: Vintage Books, 1990); Agamben, *Homo Sacer*; Foucault, *Society Must Be Defended*; Mbembe, "Necropolitics," 11–40; Rabinow and Rose, "Biopower Today"; Stephen Legg, "Foucault's Population Geographies: Classifications, Biopolitics, and Governmental Spaces," *Population, Space and Place* 11, no. 3 (2005): 137–56; Roberto Esposito, *Bíos: Biopolitics and Philosophy* (Minneapolis: University of Minnesota Press, 2008); Matthew Coleman and K. Grove, "Biopolitics, Biopower, and the Return of Sovereignty," *Environment and Planning D: Society and Space* 27, no. 3 (2009): 489–507; Thomas Lemke, *Biopolitics: An Advanced Introduction* (New York: New York University Press, 2011); Elke Schwarz, "Prescription Drones: On the Techno-Biopolitical Regimes of Contemporary 'Ethical Killing'," *Security Dialogue* 47, no. 1 (2016): 59–75.

22. Lemke, *Biopolitics*, 5.

23. Ibid.

24. Jeremy W. Crampton and Stuart Elden, "Space, Politics, Calculation: An Introduction," 7, no. 5 (2006): 681–85; at 682.

25. Holger Pötzsch, "The Emergence of iBorder: Bordering Bodies, Networks, and Machines," *Environment and Planning D: Society and Space* 33, no. 1 (2015): 101–18; at 106.

26. Ibid., 106–7.

27. Robertson, "'You Lie!'" 71.

28. Ibid.

29. Gupta, *Red Tape*, 188.

30. Ibid.

31. Blouin Jr. and Rosenberg, *Processing the Past*.

32. Ibid., 19.

33. Mark Maguire, "The Birth of Biometric Security," *Anthropology Today* 25, no. 2 (2009): 9–14.

34. Peter Adey, "Facing Airport Security: Affect, Biopolitics, and the Preemptive Securitisation of the Mobile Body," *Environment and Planning D: Society and Space* 27, no. 2 (2009): 277.

35. Peter Adey, "Secured and Sorted Mobilities: Examples from the Airport," *Surveillance & Society* 1, no. 4 (2004): 500–519; Shoshana A. Magnet, *When Biometrics Fail: Gender, Race, and the Technology of Identity* (Durham, NC: Duke University Press, 2011); Mark Maguire,

"Biopower, Racialization and New Security Technology," *Social Identities* 18, no. 5 (2012): 593–607.

36. Adey, "Secured and Sorted Mobilities," 505; Adey, "Facing Airport Security," 279.

37. Bernstein, "The Hidden Costs of Terrorist Watch Lists," 472.

38. Ibid., 474.

39. Stephen Graham and David Wood, "Digitizing Surveillance: Categorization, Space, Inequality," *Critical Social Policy* 23, no. 2 (2003): 227–48; at 230–31.

40. Amoore and de Goede, "Data and the War by Other Means," 4.

41. Mark Andrejevic and Kelly Gates, "Big Data Surveillance: Introduction," *Surveillance & Society* 12, no. 2 (2014): 185–96; at 186.

42. Ibid., 190.

43. Ibid.

44. Horowitz, *Taking Lives*, 127.

45. Herbert Kalthoff, "Un/Doing Calculation: On Knowledge Practices of Risk Management," *Distinktion: Scandinavian Journal of Social Theory* 12, no. 1 (2011): 3–21; Margaret Hu, "Big Data Blacklisting," *Florida Law Review* 67 (2015): 1735–811.

46. Jeremy Waldron, "Death Squads and Death Lists: Targeted Killing and the Character of the State," *Constellations* 23, no. 2 (2016): 292–307. See also Richard Murphy and Afsheen John Radsan, "Notice and an Opportunity to Be Heard Before the President Kills You," *Wake Forest Law Review* 48 (2013): 829–85.

47. Shaw, "Predator Empire," 540; Weber, "Keep Adding."

48. Weber, "Keep Adding," 110. Also included are lists managed by the CIA, the Pentagon, and the Joint Special Operations Command.

49. Gregory S. McNeal, "Targeted Killing and Accountability," *Georgetown Law Journal* 102 (2013): 681–794; at 684.

50. Shaw and Akhter, "The Dronification of State Violence," 226.

51. Ibid.

52. Cf. McNeal, "Targeted Killing," 702–12.

53. The definition of "organized armed group" is itself a contested exercise.

54. Weber, "Keep Adding," 110.

55. Shaw and Akhter, "Dronification of State Violence," 226; Weber, "Keep Adding," 109; Murphy and Radsan, "Notice and an Opportunity," 845.

56. McNeal, "Targeted Killing," 707.

57. Weber, "Keep Adding," 108.

58. George Marcus, "The Paranoid Style Now," in *Paranoia within Reason*, ed. George Marcus (Chicago: University of Chicago Press, 1999), 1–12.

59. Holm, "Conspiracy Theorizing Surveillance," 39.

60. Bach, "Power, Secrecy, Paranoia."

61. Holm, "Conspiracy Theorizing Surveillance," 39.

62. Kindervater, "The Emergence of Lethal Surveillance."

63. Waldron, "Death Squads," 292.

64. See, for example, Amos N. Guiora, "Targeted Killing as Active Self-Defense," *Case Western Reserve Journal of International Law* 36 (2004): 319–34; Daniel Byman, "Do Targeted Killings Work?" *Foreign Affairs* 85, no. 2 (2006): 95–111; Michael L. Gross, "Assassination and Targeted Killing: Law Enforcement, Execution or Self-Defense?" *Journal of Applied Philosophy* 23, no. 3 (2006): 323–35; John Morrissey, "Liberal Lawfare and Biopolitics: US Juridical Warfare in the War on Terror," *Geopolitics* 16, no. 2 (2011): 280–305; Kyle Grayson, "The Ambivalence of Assassination: Biopolitics, Culture and Political Violence," *Security Dialogue* 43, no. 1 (2012): 25–41.

65. Gross, "Assassination and Targeted Killing," 323.

66. Ibid.

67. This is a key conceptual argument, given that perceived traitors within Democratic Kampuchea were frequently classified as enemy combatants.

68. Grayson, "The Ambivalence of Assassination," 25.

69. Shaw, *Predator Empire.*

70. McNeal, "Targeted Killing," 684.

71. Pötzsch, "The Emergence of iBorder," 109.

72. Ian G. R. Shaw, "Predator Empire: The Geopolitics of US Drone Warfare," *Geopolitics* 18, no. 3 (2013): 536–59; at 540. See also Pötzsch, "The Emergence of iBorder," 109.

73. Waldron, "Death Squads," 292–93.

74. Ibid., 293.

Bibliography

Abbott, Mathew. "The Creature Before the Law: Notes on Walter Benjamin's Critique of Violence." *Colloqui: Text, Theory, Critique* 16 (2008): 80–96.

Adey, Peter. "Facing Airport Security: Affect, Biopolitics, and the Preemptive Securitisation of the Mobile Body." *Environment and Planning D: Society and Space* 27, no. 2 (2009): 274–95.

———. "Secured and Sorted Mobilities: Examples from the Airport." *Surveillance & Society* 1, no. 4 (2004): 500–519.

Agamben, Giorgio. *Homo Sacer: Sovereign Power and Bare Life.* Stanford, CA: Stanford University Press, 1998.Allinson, Jamie. "The Necropolitics of Drones." *International Political Sociology* 9, no. 2 (2015): 113–27.

Amoore, Louise. "Lines of Sight: On the Visualization of Unknown Futures." *Citizenship Studies* 13, no. 1 (2009): 17–30.

Amoore, Louise, and Marieke de Goede. "Data and the War by Other Means." *Journal of Cultural Economy* 5, no. 1 (2012): 3–8.

———. "Transactions after 9/11: The Banal Face of the Preemptive Strike." *Transactions of the Institute of British Geographers* 33, no. 2 (2008): 173–76.

Andrejevic, Mark. "The Discipline of Watching: Detection, Risk, and Lateral Surveillance." *Critical Studies in Media Communication* 23, no. 5 (2006): 391–407.

———. "The Work of Watching One Another: Lateral Surveillance, Risk, and Governance." *Surveillance & Society* 2, no. 4 (2005): 479–97.

Andrejevic, Mark, and Kelly Gates. "Big Data Surveillance: Introduction." *Surveillance & Society* 12, no. 2 (2014): 185–96.

Angle, Stephen C. "Decent Democratic Centralism." *Political Theory* 33, no. 4 (2005): 518–46.

Arendt, Hannah. *On Violence.* New York: Harvest Books, 1969.

———. *The Origins of Totalitarianism.* New York: Harcourt, 1968.

Ayers, David. *Anatomy of a Crisis: Education, Development, and the State in Cambodia, 1953–1998.* Chiang Mai, Thailand: Silkworm Press, 2003.

Bach, Jonathan. "Power, Secrecy, Paranoia: Technologies of Governance and the Structure of Rule." *Cultural Politics* 6, no. 3 (2010): 287–302.

Barnett, Anthony. "Democratic Kampuchea: A Highly Centralized Dictatorship." In *Revolution and Its Aftermath in Kampuchea: Eight Essays*, edited by David P. Chandler and Ben Kiernan, 212–29. New Haven, CT: Yale University Southeast Asia Studies, 1983.

Bauman, Zygmunt. *Modernity and the Holocaust.* Ithaca, NY: Cornell University Press, 1991.

Beachler, Donald W. "The Quest for Justice in Cambodia: Power, Politics, and the Khmer Rouge Tribunal." *Genocide Studies and Prevention* 8, no. 2 (2014): 67–80.

Benjamin, Walter. "Critique of Violence." In *Reflections: Essays, Aphorisms, Autobiographical Writings*, edited by P. Demetz, 277–300. New York: Schocken Books, 1978.

Benzaquen, Stephanie. "Looking at the Tuol Sleng Museum of Genocidal Crimes, Cambodia, on Flickr and YouTube." *Media, Culture & Society* 36, no. 6 (2014): 790–809.

Bernstein, Anya. "The Hidden Costs of Terrorist Watch Lists." *Buffalo Law Review* 61, no. 3 (2013): 461–535.

Blencowe, Claire. "Foucault's and Arendt's 'Insider View' of Biopolitics: A Critique of Agamben." *History of the Human Sciences* 23, no. 5 (2010): 113–30.

Blouin, Francis X, Jr., and William G. Rosenberg. *Processing the Past: Contesting Authority in History and the Archives.* Oxford: Oxford University Press, 2011.

Bowker, Geoffrey C., and Susan Leigh Star. *Sorting Things Out: Classification and Its Consequences.* Cambridge, MA: MIT Press, 2000.

Boyer, Dominic. "Thinking Through the Anthropology of Experts." *Anthropology in Action* 15, no. 2 (2008): 38–46.

Bradley, Michael E. "Incentives and Labour Supply on Soviet Collective Farms." *The Canadian Journal of Economics* 4, no. 3 (1971): 342–52.

Braun, Bruce. "Biopolitics and the Molecularization of Life." *cultural geographies* 14, no. 1 (2007): 6–28.

Brint, Steven. *In an Age of Experts: The Changing Role of Professionals in Politics and Public Life.* Princeton, NJ: Princeton University Press, 1994.

Brown, Caitlin, and Chris Millington. "The Memory of the Cambodian Genocide: The Tuol Sleng Genocide Museum." *History Compass* 13, no. 3 (205): 31–39.

Bruckmayr, Philipp. "Cambodian Muslims, Transnational NGOs, and International Justice." *Peace Review* 27, no. 3 (2015): 337–45.

Burkitt, Ian. "Technologies of the Self: Habitus and Capacities." *Journal for the Theory of Social Behavior* 32, no. 2 (2002): 219–37.

Byford, Jovan. *Conspiracy Theories: A Critical Introduction.* New York: Palgrave Macmillan, 2015.

Byman, Daniel. "Do Targeted Killings Work?" *Foreign Affairs* 85, no. 2 (2006): 95–111.

Calhoun, Laurie. "The Strange Case of Summary Execution by Predator Done." *Peace Review* 15, no. 2 (2003): 209–14.

Caswell, Michelle. *Archiving the Unspeakable: Silence, Memory, and the Photographic Record in Cambodia.* Madison: University of Wisconsin Press, 2014.

———. "Hannah Arendt's World: Bureaucracy, Documentation, and Banal Evil." *Archivaria* 70 (Fall 2010): 1–25.

———. "Khmer Rouge Archives: Accountability, Truth, and Memory in Cambodia." *Archival Science* 10, no. 1–2 (2010): 25–44.

———. "Using Classification to Convict the Khmer Rouge." *Journal of Documentation* 68, no. 2 (2012): 162–84.

Cayley, Andrew T. "Prosecuting Mass Atrocities at the Extraordinary Chambers in the Courts of Cambodia (ECCC)." *Washington University Global Studies Law Review* 11, no. 2 (2013): 445–58.

Chandler, David. *Brother Number One: A Political Biography of Pol Pot.* Rev. ed. Chiang Mai, Thailand: Silkworm Books, 1999.

———. *A History of Cambodia.* 3rd ed. Boulder, CO: Westview Press, 2000.

———. *Voices from S-21: Terror and History in Pol Pot's Secret Prison.* Berkeley: University of California Press, 1999.

Chandler, David P., Ben Kiernan, and Chanthou Boua, eds. *Pol Pot Plans the Future: Confidential Leadership Documents from Democratic Kampuchea, 1976–1977.* Monograph Series 33, Yale University Southeast Asia Studies. New Haven, CT: Yale Center for International and Area Studies, 1988.

Chomsky, Noam, and Edward S. Herman. *After the Cataclysm: Postwar Indochina and the Reconstruction of Imperial Ideology.* Chicago: Haymarket Books, 2014.

Chy, Terith. *When the Criminal Laughs.* Phnom Penh: Documentation Center of Cambodia, 2014.

Clark, Gordon L., and Michael Dear. *State Apparatus: Structures and Language of Legitimacy.* Boston: Allen & Unwin, 1984.

Clayton, Thomas. "Building the New Cambodia: Educational Destruction and Construction under the Khmer Rouge, 1975–1979." *History of Education Quarterly* 38, no. 1 (1998): 1–16.

———. "Re-orientations in Moral Education in Cambodia since 1975." *Journal of Moral Education* 34, no. 4 (2005): 505–17.

Clegg, Stewart. "Weber and Foucault: Social Theory for the Study of Organizations." *Organizations* 1, no. 1 (1994): 149–78.

Clegg, Stewart, Miguel Pina e Cunha, and Arménio Rego, "The Theory and Practice of Utopia in a Total Institution: The Pineapple Panopticon." *Organization Studies* 33, no. 12 (2012): 1735–57.

Clegg, Stewart, Miguel Pina e Cunha, Arménio Rego, and Joana Dias. "Mundane Objects and the Banality of Evil: The Sociomateriality of a Death Camp." *Journal of Management Inquiry* 22, no. 3 (2013): 325–40.

Clymer, Kenton. *Troubled Relations: The United States and Cambodia since 1870.* DeKalb: Northern Illinois University Press, 2007.

Coleman, Matthew, and K. Grove. "Biopolitics, Biopower, and the Return of Sovereignty." *Environment and Planning D: Society and Space* 27, no. 3 (2009): 489–507.

Communist Party of Kampuchea (CPK). "Excerpted Report on the Leading Views of the Comrade Representing the Party Organization at a Zone Assembly." In Chandler, Kiernan, and Boua, *Pol Pot Plans the Future*, 13–35.

———. "The Party's Four-Year Plan to Build Socialism in All Fields, 1977–1980." In Chandler, Kiernan, and Boua, *Pol Pot Plans the Future*, 36–119.

———. "Report of Activities of the Party Center According to the General Political Tasks of 1976." In Chandler, Kiernan, and Boua, *Pol Pot Plans the Future*, 182–212.

Crampton, Jeremy W., and Stuart Elden. "Space, Politics, Calculation: An Introduction." *Social & Cultural Geography* 7, no. 5 (2006): 681–85.

Darling, Jonathan. "Another Letter from the Home Office: Reading the Material Politics of Asylum." *Environment and Planning D: Society and Space* 32, no. 3 (2014): 484–500.

Dauber, Kenneth. "Bureaucratizing the Ethnographer's Magic." *Current Anthropology* 36, no. 1 (1995): 75–95.

Davies, William. "Knowing the Unknowable: The Epistemological Authority of Innovation Policy Experts." *Social Epistemology* 25, no. 4 (2011): 401–21.

DeFalco, Randle C. "Accounting for Famine at the Extraordinary Chambers in the Courts of Cambodia: The Crimes against Humanity of Extermination, Inhumane Acts and Persecution." *The International Journal of Transitional Justice* 5, no. 1 (2011): 142–58.

———. "Justice and Starvation in Cambodia: The Khmer Rouge Famine." *Cambodia Law and Policy Journal* 2 (2014): 45–84.

———. "Voices of Genocide: Episodes of the Radio Program on Famine under the Khmer Rouge." *Searching for the Truth* Second Quarter (2013): 26–32.

DePaul, Kim, ed., and Dith Pran, comp. *Children of Cambodia's Killing Fields: Memoirs by Survivors.* New Haven, CT: Yale University Press, 1977.

Derrida, Jacques. *Archive Fever: A Freudian Impression.* Translated by Eric Prenowitz. Chicago: University of Chicago Press, 1996.

Dittmer, Jason. *Diplomatic Material: Affect, Assemblage, and Foreign Policy.* Durham, NC: Duke University Press, 2017.

———. "Theorizing a More-Than-Human Diplomacy: Assembling the British Foreign Office, 1839–1874." *The Hague Journal of Diplomacy* 11, no. 1 (2016): 78–104.

Documentation Center of Cambodia, Phnom Penh. www.DCCAM.org.

Domar, Evsey D. "The Soviet Collective Farm as Producer Cooperative." *The American Economic Review* 56, no. 4 (1966): 734–57.

Ea, Meng-Try. *The Chain of Terror: The Khmer Rouge Southwest Zone Security System.* Phnom Penh: Documentation Center of Cambodia, 2005.

Eckelmans, Franziska. "The *Duch* Case: The ECCC Supreme Court Chamber's Review of Case 001." In Meisenberg and Stegmiller, *The Extraordinary Chambers in the Courts of Cambodia*, 159–79.

e Cunha, Miguel Pina, Stewart Clegg, and Arménio Rego. "The Ethical Speaking of Objects: Ethics and the 'Object-ive' World of Khmer

Rouge Young Comrades." *Journal of Political Power* 7, no. 1 (2014): 35–61.

e Cunha, Miguel Pina, Arménio Rego, and Stewart Clegg. "The Institutionalization of Genocidal Leadership: Pol Pot and a Cambodian Dystopia." *Journal of Leadership Studies* 9, no. 1 (2015): 6–18.

Edwards, Claire, "Cutting Off the King's Head: The 'Social' in Hannah Arendt and Michel Foucault." *Studies in Social and Political Thought* 1, no. 1 (1999): 3–20.

Elander, Maria. "Education and Photography at Tuol Sleng Genocide Museum." In *The Arts of Transitional Justice*, edited by P. D. Rush and O. Simi , 43–62. New York: Springer, 2014.

Em, Sokhym. "Female Patients." *Searching for the Truth* 33 (September 2002): 25–29.

———. "Rabbit Dropping Medicine." *Searching for the Truth* 30 (June 2002): 22–23.

———. "Revolutionary Female Medical Staff in Tram Kak District I." *Searching for the Truth* 34 (October 2002): 24–27.

———. "Revolutionary Female Medical Staff in Tram Kak District II." *Searching for the Truth* 35 (November 2002): 17–19.

Engels, Friedrich. *The Origin of the Family, Private Property and the State*. New York: Penguin, 2010.

Esposito, Roberto. *Bíos: Biopolitics and Philosophy*. Minneapolis: University of Minnesota Press, 2008.

Etcheson, Craig. *After the Killing Fields: Lessons from the Cambodian Genocide*. Lubbock: Texas Tech University Press, 2005.

———. *The Rise and Demise of Democratic Kampuchea*. Boulder, CO: Westview Press, 1984.

Extraordinary Chambers of the Courts of Cambodia (ECCC). http://www.eccc.gov.kh.

Farrington, Keith. "The Modern Prison as Total Institution? Public Perception Versus Objective Reality." *Crime & Delinquency* 38, no. 1 (1992): 6–26.

Fein, Helen. "Revolutionary and Antirevolutionary Genocides: A Comparison of State Murders in Democratic Kampuchea, 1975 to 1979, and in Indonesia, 1965 to 1966." *Comparative Studies in Society and History* 35, no. 4 (1993): 796–823.

Foucault, Michel. *Discipline and Punish: The Birth of the Prison.* Translated by A. Sheridan. New York: Vintage Books, 1979.

———. *The History of Sexuality: An Introduction.* New York: Vintage Books, 1990.

———. *"Society Must Be Defended": Lectures at the Collège de France, 1977–1978.* Translated by David Macey. New York: Picador, 2003.

———. "Technologies of the Self." In *Technologies of the Self: A Seminar with Michel Foucault,* edited by Luther H. Marin, Huck Gutman, and Patrick H. Hutton, 16–49. Amherst: University of Massachusetts Press, 1988.

———. "Two Lectures." In *Power/Knowledge: Selected Interviews and Other Writings, 1972–1977,* edited by Colin Gordon, 78–108. New York: Pantheon Books, 1980.

French, Lindsay. "Exhibiting Terror." In *Truth Claims: Representation and Human Rights,* edited by M. P. Bradley and P. Petro, 131–55. New Brunswick, NJ: Rutgers University Press, 2002.

Frieson, Kate G. "Revolution and Rural Response in Cambodia, 1970–1975." In *Genocide and Democracy in Cambodia: The Khmer Rouge, the United Nations and the International Community,* edited by Ben Kiernan, 33–50. New Haven, CT: Yale University Southeast Asian Studies, 1993.

Gill, Nick, Deidre Conlon, Dominique Moran, and Andrew Burridge. "Carceral Circuitry: New Directions in Carceral Geography." *Progress in Human Geography.* doi:10.1177/0309132516671823.

Goede, Marieke de. "Fighting the Network: A Critique of the Network as a Security Technology." *Distinktion: Scandinavian Journal of Social Theory* 13, no. 3 (2012): 215–32.

Goede, Marieke de, and Samuel Randalls. "Precaution, Preemption: Arts and Technologies of the Actionable Future." *Environment and Planning D: Society and Space* 27, no. 5 (2009): 859–78.

Goede, Marieke de, Stephanie Simon, and Marijn Hoijtink. "Performing Preemption." *Security Dialogue* 45, no. 5 (2014): 411–22.

Goede, Marieke de, and Gavin Sullivan. "The Politics of Security Lists." *Environment and Planning D: Society and Space* 34, no. 1 (2016): 67–88.

Goffman, Erving. *Asylums: Essays on the Social Situation of Mental Patients and Other Inmates.* Garden City, NY: Doubleday, 1961.

Graham, Stephen, and David Wood. "Digitizing Surveillance; Categorization, Space, Inequality." *Critical Social Policy* 23, no. 2 (2003): 227–48.

Grayson, Kyle. "The Ambivalence of Assassination: Biopolitics, Culture and Political Violence." *Security Dialogue* 43, no. 1 (2012): 25–41.

Gross, Michael L. "Assassination and Targeted Killing: Law Enforcement, Execution or Self-Defense?" *Journal of Applied Philosophy* 23, no. 3 (2006): 323–35.

Guiora, Amos N. "Targeted Killing as Active Self-Defense." *Case Western Reserve Journal of International Law* 36 (2004): 319–34.

Gupta, Akhil. *Red Tape: Bureaucracy, Structural Violence, and Poverty in India*. Durham, NC: Duke University Press, 2012.

Hadfield, Gillian K. "The Problem of Social Order: What Should We Count as Law?" *Law & Social Inquiry* 42, no. 1 (2017): 16–27.

Hadfield, Gillian K., and Barry R. Weingast. "What Is Law? A Coordination Model of the Characteristics of Legal Order." *Journal of Legal Analysis* 4, no. 2 (2012): 471–514.

Harper, David. "The Politics of Paranoia: Paranoid Positioning and Conspiratorial Narratives in the Surveillance Society." *Surveillance & Society* 5, no. 1 (2008): 1–32.

Harris, Ian. *Buddhism under Pol Pot*. Phnom Penh: Documentation Center of Cambodia, 2007.

Hawk, David. *Khmer Rouge Prison Documents from the S-21 (Tuol Sleng) Extermination Center in Phnom Penh*. Ithaca, NY: Cornell University Press, 1984.

———. "Tuol Sleng Extermination Centre." *Index on Censorship* 1 (1986): 25–31.

Heder, Steve. *Cambodian Communism and the Vietnamese Model: Imitation and Independence, 1930–1975*. Bangkok: White Lotus Press, 2004.

Heder, Stephen (with Brian D. Tittemore). *Seven Candidates for Prosecution: Accountability for the Crimes of the Khmer Rouge*. Phnom Penh: Documentation Center of Cambodia, 2004.

Hinton, Alexander L. *Man or Monster? The Trial of a Khmer Rouge Torturer*. Durham, NC: Duke University Press, 2016.

———. *Why Did They Kill? Cambodia in the Shadow of Genocide*. Berkeley: University of California Press, 2005.

Holm, Nicholas. "Conspiracy Theorizing Surveillance: Considering Modalities of Paranoia and Conspiracy in Surveillance Studies." *Surveillance & Society* 7, no. 1 (2009): 36–48.

Hopkins, Russell. "The Case 002/01 Trial Judgement: A Stepping Stone from Nuremberg to the Present?" In Meisenberg and Stegmiller, *The Extraordinary Chambers in the Courts of Cambodia*, 181–201.

Horowitz, Irving Louis. *Taking Lives: Genocide and State Power*. New Brunswick, NJ: Transaction Books, 1980.

Hu, Margaret. "Big Data Blacklisting." *Florida Law Review* 67 (2015): 1735–811.

Hughes, Rachel. "The Abject Artefacts of Memory: Photographs from Cambodia's Genocide." *Media, Culture & Society* 25, no. 1 (2003): 23–44.

———. "Dutiful Tourism: Encountering the Cambodian Genocide." *Asia Pacific Viewpoint* 49, no. 3 (2008): 318–30.

Hull, Matthew S. "Documents and Bureaucracy." *Annual Review of Anthropology* 41 (2012): 251–67.

———. *Government of Paper: The Materiality of Bureaucracy in Urban Pakistan*. Berkeley: University of California Press, 2012.

Husting, Ginna, and Martin Orr. "Dangerous Machinery: 'Conspiracy Theorist' as a Transpersonal Strategy of Exclusion." *Symbolic Interaction* 30, no. 2 (2007): 127–50.

Huy, Vannak. "Prey Sar Prison." *Searching for the Truth* 29 (May 2002): 21–25.

Isaacs, Arnold. *Without Honor: Defeat in Cambodia*. Baltimore: Johns Hopkins University Press, 1983.

Jackson, Karl D., ed. *Cambodia 1975–1978: Rendezvous with Death*. Princeton, NJ: Princeton University Press, 1989.

———. "The Ideology of Total Revolution." In Jackson, *Cambodia 1975–1978*, 37–78.

Jacob, Marie-Andrée. "Form-Made Persons: Consent Forms as Consent's Blind Spot." *PoLAR: Political and Legal Anthropology Review* 30, no. 2 (2007): 249–68.

Jones, Laura. "The Commonplace Geopolitics of Conspiracy." *Geography Compass* 6, no. 1 (2012): 44–59.

Kafka, Ben. "The Demon of Writing: Paperwork, Public Safety, and the Reign of Terror." *Representations* 98, no. 1 (2007): 1–24.

———. "Paperwork: The State of the Discipline." *Book History* 12, no. 1 (2009): 340–53.

Ka-Kui, Tse. "Agricultural Collectivization and Socialist Construction: The Soviet Union and China." *Dialectical Anthropology* 2, no. 3 (1977): 199–221.

Kalthoff, Herbert. "Un/Doing Calculation: On Knowledge Practices of Risk Management." *Distinktion: Scandinavian Journal of Social Theory* 12, no. 1 (2011): 3–21.

Kamenka, Eugene. "Law." In *A Dictionary of Marxist Thought*, 2nd ed., edited by Tom Bottomore, 306–7. Malden, MA: Blackwell Publishing, 1991.

Kamm, Henry. *Report from a Stricken Land*. New York: Arcade Publishing, 1998.

Kendzior, Sarah. "'Recognize the Spies': Transparency and Political Power in Uzbek Cyberspace." *Social Analysis* 59, no. 4 (2015): 50–65.

Keo, Dacil Q., and Nean Yin. *Fact Sheet: Pol Pot and His Prisoners at Secret Prison S-21*. Phnom Penh: Documentation Center of Cambodia, 2011.

Kiernan, Ben. "The American Bombardment of Kampuchea, 1969–1973." *Vietnam Generation* 1, no. 1 (1989): 4–41.

———. "Bringing the Khmer Rouge to Justice." *Human Rights Review* 1, no. 3 (2000): 92–108.

———. "Conflict in Cambodia, 1945–2002." *Critical Asian Studies* 34, no. 4 (2002): 483–96.

———. *The Pol Pot Regime: Policies, Race and Genocide in Cambodia under the Khmer Rouge, 1975–1979*. New Haven, CT: Yale University Press, 1996.

Kiernan, Ben, and Taylor Owen. "Making More Enemies Than We Kill? Calculating U.S. Bomb Tonnages Dropped on Laos and Cambodia, and Weighing Their Implications." *The Asia-Pacific Journal* 13, no. 16 (2015): 1–9.

Kindervater, Katherine. "The Emergence of Lethal Surveillance: Watching and Killing in the History of Drone Technology." *Security Dialogue* 47, no. 3 (2016): 223–38.

Kurtz, Matthew. "Situating Practices: The Archive and the File Cabinet." *Historical Geography* 29 (2001): 26–37.

Kuus, Merje. "Bureaucracy and Place: Expertise in the European Quarter." *Global Networks* 11, no. 4 (2011): 421–39.

———. "Transnational Bureaucracies: How Do We Know What They Know?" *Progress in Human Geography* 39, no. 4 (2015): 432–48.

Latour, Bruno. *Science in Action: How to Follow Scientists and Engineers Through Society.* Cambridge, MA: Harvard University Press, 1987.

Leander, Anna. "The Politics of Whitelisting: Regulatory Work and Topologies in Commercial Security." *Environment and Planning D: Society and Space* 34, no. 1 (2016): 48–66.

Ledgerwood, Judy. "The Cambodian Tuol Sleng Museum of Genocidal Crimes: National Narrative." *Museum Anthropology* 21, no. 1 (1997): 82–98.

Legg, Stephen. "Foucault's Population Geographies: Classifications, Biopolitics, and Governmental Spaces." *Population, Space and Place* 11, no. 3 (2005): 137–56.

Lemke, Thomas. *Biopolitics: An Advanced Introduction.* New York: New York University Press, 2011.

Lenin, Vladimir I. *Essential Works of Lenin: "What Is to Be Done?" and Other Writings.* Edited by Henry M. Christman. New York: Dover Publications, 1987.

Locke, Simon. "Conspiracy Culture, Blame Culture, and Rationalisation." *The Sociological Review* 57, no. 4 (2009): 567–85.

London, Jonathan. "Viet Nam and the Making of Market-Leninism." *The Pacific Review* 22, no. 3 (2009): 375–99.

Los, Maria. "The Technologies of Total Domination." *Surveillance & Society* 2, no. 1 (2004): 15–38.

Loyd, Jenna, Andrew Burridge, and Matthew L. Mitchelson. "Thinking (and Moving) Beyond Walls and Cages: Bridging Immigrant Justice and Anti-prison Organizing in the United States." *Social Justice* 36, no. 2 (2016): 85–103.

Mac Ginty, Roger. "Social Network Analysis and Counterinsurgency: A Counterproductive Strategy?" *Critical Studies in Terrorism*, 3, no. 2 (2010): 209–26.

Magnet, Shoshana A. *When Biometrics Fail: Gender, Race, and the Technology of Identity.* Durham, NC: Duke University Press, 2011.

Maguire, Mark, "Biopower, Racialization and New Security Technology," *Social Identities* 18, no. 5 (2012): 593–607.

———. "The Birth of Biometric Security." *Anthropology Today* 25, no. 2 (2009): 9–14.

Marcus, George. "The Paranoid Style Now." In *Paranoia within Reason*, edited by George Marcus, 1–12. Chicago: University of Chicago Press, 1999.

Marston, John. "Democratic Kampuchea and the Idea of Modernity." In *Cambodia Emerges from the Past: Eight Essays*, edited by Judy Ledgerwood, 38–59. DeKalb: Northern Illinois University Press, 2002.

Marx, Karl. *A Contribution to the Critique of Political Economy*. New York: International Publishers, 1970.

Marx, Karl, and Friedrich Engels. *The Communist Manifesto*. Translated by Samuel Moore. Chicago: Charles H. Kerr, 1945.

———. *The German Ideology*. Amherst, NY: Prometheus Books, 1988.

Massumi, Brian. "The Future Birth of the Affective Fact: The Political Ontology of Threat." In *Digital and Other Virtualities: Renegotiating the Image*, edited by Antony Bryant and Briselda Pollock, 52–70. London: I. B. Tauris, 2010.

Mbembe, Achille. "Necropolitics." Translated by Libby Meintjes. *Public Culture* 15, no. 1 (2003): 11–40.

McClintock, Anne. "Paranoid Empire: Specters from Guantánamo and Abu Ghraib." *small axe* 13, no. 1 (2009): 50–74.

McNeal, Gregory S. "Targeted Killing and Accountability." *Georgetown Law Journal* 102 (2013): 681–794.

Meehan, Katharine, Ian G. R. Shaw, and Sallie A. Marston. "Political Geographies of the Object." *Political Geography* 33 (2013): 1–10.

Meisenberg, Simon, and Ignaz Stegmiller, eds. *The Extraordinary Chambers in the Courts of Cambodia*. The Hague: TMC Asser, 2016.

Melley, Timothy. *Empire of Conspiracy: The Culture of Paranoia in Postwar America*. Ithaca, NY: Cornell University Press, 2000.

Meng, Xin, Nancy Qian, and Pierre Yared. "The Institutional Causes of China's Great Famine, 1959–1961." Paper presented at the Centre for Economic Policy Research's Development Economics Symposium, June 2–3, 2010. www.cepr.org/meets/wkcn/7/780/papers/Qianfinal.pdf.

Mertha, Andrew. *Brothers in Arms: Chinese Aid to the Khmer Rouge, 1975–1979*. Ithaca, NY: Cornell University Press, 2014.

Mey, Chum. *Survivor: The Triumph of an Ordinary Man in the Khmer Rouge Genocide*. Phnom Penh: Documentation Center of Cambodia, 2012.

Ministry of Culture and Fine Arts and the Documentation Center of Cambodia. *The Forced Transfer: The Second Evacuation of People During the Khmer Rouge Regime.* Phnom Penh: Documentation Center of Cambodia, 2014.

Mitchell, Tim. *Rule of Experts: Egypt, Techno-Politics, Modernity.* Berkeley: University of California Press, 2002.

Moran, Dominique. "Between Outside and Inside? Prison Visiting Rooms as Liminal Carceral Spaces." *Geoforum* 78, no. 2 (2013): 339–51.

Moran, Dominique, and Yvonne Jewkes. "Linking the Carceral and the Punitive State: A Review of Research on Prison Architecture, Design, Technology and the Lived Experience of Carceral Space." *Annales de Géographie* 2/3, no. 702–703 (2015): 163–84.

Moran, Dominique, Judith Pallot, and Laure Piacentini. "Lipstick, Lace & Longing: Constructions of Femininity inside a Russian Prison." *Environment and Planning D: Society and Space* 27, no. 4 (2009): 700–720.

Morrissey, John. "Liberal Lawfare and Biopolitics: US Juridical Warfare in the War on Terror." *Geopolitics* 16, no. 2 (2011): 280–305.

Müller, Martin. "Opening the Black Box of the Organization: Socio-material Practices of Geopolitical Ordering." *Political Geography* 31, no. 6 (2012): 379–88.

Murphy, Richard, and Afsheen John Radsan. "Notice and an Opportunity to Be Heard Before the President Kills You." *Wake Forest Law Review* 48 (2013): 829–85.

New, Christopher. "Time and Punishment." *Analysis* 52, no. 1 (1992): 35–40.

Ngor, Haing (with R. Warner). *Survival in the Killing Fields.* New York: Carroll and Graf Publishers, 1987.

Nhem, Boraden. *The Khmer Rouge: Ideology, Militarism, and the Revolution That Consumed a Generation.* Santa Barbara, CA: Praeger, 2013.

Nixon, Richard M. "Address to the Nation on the Situation in Southeast Asia." April 30, 1970. www.nixonlibrary.org.

Nuttall, Sarah, and Achille Mbembe. "Secrecy's Softwares." *Current Anthropology* 56, no. 12 (2015): 317–24.

Office of the Co-Investigating Judges (OCIJ). *Closing Order, Case File No.: 002/19–09–2007-ECCC-OCIJ.* Phnom Penh: Extraordinary Chambers in the Courts of Cambodia, 2010.

O'Neill, John. "The Disciplinary Society: From Weber to Foucault." *The British Journal of Sociology* 37, no. 1 (1986): 42–60.

Osman, Ysa. "The Cham Prisoners in the Khmer Rouge's Secret Prison." *Jebat: Malaysian Journal of History, Politics and Strategic Studies* 32 (2005): 100–133.

———. *The Cham Rebellion: Survivors' Stories from the Villages.* Phnom Penh: Documentation Center of Cambodia, 2006.

———. *Oukoubah: Justice for the Cham Muslims under the Democratic Kampuchea Regime.* Phnom Penh: Documentation Center of Cambodia, 2002.

Ovesen, Jan, and Ing-Britt Trankell. *Cambodians and Their Doctors: A Medical Anthropology of Colonial and Post-colonial Cambodia.* Copenhagen: Nordic Institute of Asian Studies, 2010.

Owen, Taylor, and Ben Kiernan. "Bombs over Cambodia." *Walrus Magazine* (October 2006): 62–69.

Painter, Joe. "Prosaic Geographies of Stateness." *Political Geography* 25, no. 7 (2006): 752–74.

Park, Ryan. "Proving Genocidal Intent: International Precedent and ECCC Case 002." *Rutgers Law Review* 63, no. 1 (2011): 129–91.

Perrow, Charles. "The Analysis of Goals in Complex Organizations." *American Sociological Review* 26, no. 6 (1961): 854–66.

Pötzsch, Holger. "The Emergence of iBorder: Bordering Bodies, Networks, and Machines." *Environment and Planning D: Society and Space* 33, no. 1 (2015): 101–18.

Proctor, Robert N. *Racial Hygiene: Medicine under the Nazis.* Cambridge, MA: Harvard University Press, 1988.

Rabinow, Paul, and Nikolas Rose. "Biopower Today." *BioSocieties* 1, no. 2 (2006): 195–217.

Robertson, Craig. "'You Lie!' Identity, Paper, and the Materiality of Information." *The Communication Review* 17, no. 2 (2014): 69–90.

Round, John, and Irina Kuznetsova. "Necropolitics and the Migrant as a Political Subject of Disgust: The Precarious Everyday of Russia's Labour Migrants." *Critical Sociology* 42, no. 7–8 (2016): 1017–34.

Sam, Roeun. "Living in Darkness." In DePaul and Pran, *Children of Cambodia's Killing Fields*, 73–81.

Sarup, Madan. *An Introductory Guide to Post-structuralism and Postmodernism.* 2nd ed. Athens: University of Georgia Press, 1993.

Schurmann, Herbert F. "Organizational Principles of the Chinese Communists." *The China Quarterly* 2 (April–June 1960): 47–58.

Schwarz, Elke. "Prescription Drones: On the Techno-Biopolitical Regimes of Contemporary 'Ethical Killing.'" *Security Dialogue* 47, no. 1 (2016): 59–75.

Seekins, Donald M. "Historical Setting." In *Cambodia: A Country Study*, edited by R. R. Ross, 3–71. Washington, DC: U.S. Government Printing Office, 1990.

Shaw, Ian G. R. *Predator Empire: Drone Warfare and Full Spectrum Dominance*. Minneapolis: University of Minnesota Press, 2016.

———. "Predator Empire: The Geopolitics of US Drone Warfare." *Geopolitics* 18, no. 3 (2013): 536–59.

———. "The Urbanization of Drone Warfare: Policing Surplus Populations in the Dronepolis." *Geographical Helvetica* 71, no. 1 (2016): 19–28.

Shaw, Ian G. R., and Majed Akhter. "The Dronification of State Violence." *Critical Asian Studies* 46, no. 2 (2014): 211–34.

Shawcross, William. *Sideshow: Kissinger, Nixon, and the Destruction of Cambodia*. Rev. ed. New York: Cooper Square Press, 2002.

Short, Philip. *Pol Pot: Anatomy of a Nightmare*. New York: Henry Holt and Company, 2004.

Sion, Bridgette. "Conflicting Sites of Memory in Post-genocide Cambodia." *Humanity: An International Journal of Human Rights, Humanitarianism, and Development* 2, no. 1 (2011): 1–21.

Slocomb, Margaret. *An Economic History of Cambodia in the Twentieth Century*. Singapore: National University of Singapore Press, 2010.

———. *The People's Republic of Kampuchea, 1979–1989: The Revolution after Pol Pot*. Chiang Mai, Thailand: Silkworm Books, 2003.

Smilansky, Saul. "The Time to Punish." *Analysis* 54, no. 1 (1994): 50–53.

So, Farina. *The Hijab of Cambodia: Memories of Cham Muslim Women after the Khmer Rouge*. Phnom Penh: Documentation Center of Cambodia, 2011.

Spade, Dean. *Normal Life: Administrative Violence, Critical Transpolitics, and the Limits of Law*. Durham, NC: Duke University Press, 2015.

Stäheli, Urs. "Indexing—The Politics of Invisibility." *Environment and Planning D: Society and Space* 34, no. 1 (2016): 14–29.

Starbuck, William H. "Shouldn't Organization Theory Emerge from Adolescence?" *Organization* 10, no. 3 (2003): 439–52.

Steedman, Carolyn. *Dust: The Archive and Cultural History.* New Brunswick, NJ: Rutgers University Press, 2002.

Steinbock, Daniel J. "Designating the Dangerous: From Blacklists to Watch Lists." *Seattle Law Review* 30 (2006): 65–118.

Stoler, Ann Laura. *Along the Archival Grain: Epistemic Anxieties and Colonial Common Sense.* Princeton, NJ: Princeton University Press, 2009.

Svay-Ryser, Sreytouch. "New Year's Surprise." In *Children of Cambodia's Killing Fields: Memoirs by Survivors,* edited by Kim DePaul and compiled by Dith Pran, 35–41. New Haven, CT: Yale University Press, 1977.

Tassin, Kristin. "'Lift up Your Head, My Brother': Nationalism and the Genesis of the Non-Aligned Movement." *Journal of Third World Studies* 23 (2006): 147–68.

Todaro, Michael P. *Economic Development in the Third World.* 4th ed. New York: Longman, 1989.

Tomlinson, Brian R. "What Was the Third World?" *Journal of Contemporary History* 38, no. 2 (2003): 307–21.

Tully, John. *A Short History of Cambodia: From Empire to Survival.* Crow's Nest, Australia: Allen & Unwin, 2005.

Turner, Jennifer. *The Prison Boundary.* London: Palgrave Macmillan, 2016.

Twining, Charles H. "The Economy." In Jackson, *Cambodia 1975–1978,* 109–50.

Tyner, James A. *From Rice Fields to Killing Fields: Nature, Life, and Labor under the Khmer Rouge.* Syracuse, NY: Syracuse University Press, 2017.

———. *Genocide and the Geographical Imagination: Life and Death in Germany, China, and Cambodia.* Lanham, MD: Rowman & Littlefield, 2012.

———. "Genocide as Reconstruction: The Political Geography of Democratic Kampuchea." In *Reconstructing Conflict: Integrating War and Post-war Geographies,* edited by Scott Kirsch and Colin Flint, 49–66. Aldershot, UK: Ashgate, 2011.

———. *Landscape, Memory, and Post-violence in Cambodia.* New York: Rowman & Littlefield, 2017.

————. "State Sovereignty, Bioethics, and Political Geographies: The Practice of Medicine under the Khmer Rouge." *Environment and Planning D: Society and Space* 30, no. 5 (2012): 842–60.

————. "Violent Erasures and Erasing Violence: Contesting Cambodia's Landscape of Violence." In *Space and Memories of Violence: Landscapes of Erasure, Disappearance and Exception*, edited by Estela Schindel and Pamela Colombo, 21–33. New York: Palgrave Macmillan, 2014.

Tyner, James A., Samuel Henkin, Savina Sirik, and Sokvisal Kimsroy. "Phnom Penh during the Cambodian Genocide: A Case of Selective Urbicide." *Environment and Planning A* 46, no. 8 (2014): 1873–91.

Tyner, James A., Sokvisal Kimsroy, Chenjian Fu, Zheye Wang, and Xinyue Ye. "An Empirical Analysis of Arrests and Executions at S-21 Security-Center during the Cambodian Genocide." *Genocide Studies International* 10, no. 2 (2016): 268–86.

Tyner, James A., Sokvisal Kimsroy, and Savina Sirik. "Landscape Photography, Geographic Education, and Nation-Building in Democratic Kampuchea, 1975–1979." *The Geographical Review* 105, no. 4 (2015): 566–80.

————. "Nature, Poetry, and Public Pedagogy: The Poetic Geographies of the Khmer Rouge." *Annals of the Association of American Geographers* 105, no. 6 (2015): 1285–99.

Tyner, James A., Mark Rhodes, and Sokvisal Kimsroy. "Music, Nature, Power, and Place: An Ecomusicology of Khmer Rouge Songs." *GeoHumanities* 2, no. 2 (2016): 395–412.

Tyner, James A., and Stian Rice. "Cambodia's Political Economy of Violence: Space, Time, and Genocide under the Khmer Rouge, 1975–79." *Genocide Studies International* 10, no. 1 (2016): 84–94.

————. "To Live and Let Die: Food, Famine, and Administrative Violence in Democratic Kampuchea, 1975–1979." *Political Geography* 52 (May 2016): 47–56.

Tyner, James A., Xinyue Ye, Sokvisal Kimsroy, Zheye Wang, and Chenjian Fu. "Emerging Data Sources and the Study of Genocide: A Preliminary Analysis of Prison Data from S-21 Security-Center, Cambodia." *GeoJournal* 81, no. 6 (2016): 907–18.

Van der Kroef, Justus M. "Cambodia: From 'Democratic Kampuchea' to 'People's Republic.'" *Asian Survey* 19, no. 8 (1979): 731–50.

Vianney-Liaud, Mélanie. "Legal Constraints in the Interpretation of Genocide." In Meisenberg and Stegmiller, *The Extraordinary Chambers in the Courts of Cambodia*, 255–90.

Vickery, Michael. *Cambodia 1975–1982*. Chiang Mai, Thailand: Silkworm Books, 1984.

Vismann, Cornelia. *Files: Law and Media Technology*. Translated by Geoffrey Winthrop-Young. Stanford, CA: Stanford University Press, 2008.

Vlahos, James. "The Department of Pre-crime." *Scientific American* 306, no. 1 (January 2012): 62–67.

Waldron, Jeremy. "Death Squads and Death Lists: Targeted Killing and the Character of the State." *Constellations* 23, no. 2 (2016): 292–307.

Weber, Jutta. "Keep Adding. On Kill Lists, Drone Warfare and the Politics of Databases." *Environment and Planning D: Society and Space* 34, no. 1 (2016): 107–25.

Weber, Max. *Economy and Society*. Berkeley: University of California Press, 1978.

Weld, Kirsten. *Paper Cadavers: The Archives of Dictatorship in Guatemala*. Durham, NC: Duke University Press, 2014.

Williams, Paul. "Witnessing Genocide: Vigilance and Remembrance at Tuol Sleng and Choeung Ek." *Holocaust and Genocide Studies* 18, no. 2 (2004): 234–54.

Wright, Melissa. "Necropolitics, Narcopolitics, and Femicide: Gendered Violence on the Mexico-U.S. Border." *Signs* 36, no. 3 (2011): 707–31.

Zedner, Lucia. "Pre-crime and Post-criminology?" *Theoretical Criminology* 11, no. 2 (2007): 261–81.

———. "Pre-crime and Pre-punishment: A Health Warning." *Centre for Crime and Justice Studies* 81, no. 1 (2010): 24–25.

Index

www.ingramcontent.com/pod-product-compliance
Lightning Source LLC
Chambersburg PA
CBHW050346270326
41926CB00016B/3624